# DIVINE TRANSFORMATIONS

*Unveiling the Power of God's Creation*

## DR LEBEDE NGARTERA

# CONTENTS

# UNVEILING THE POWER OF GOD'S CREATION
## DIVINE TRANSFORMATIONS

---

"Explore 'Divine Transformations' daily and discover the exquisite intricacies of creation—each a reflection of divine artistry—inspiring you to deepen your faith and commit anew to cherishing and safeguarding our shared world."

---

Dr Lebede Ngartera

"As a specialist deeply committed to environmental conservation and sustainability, I find 'Divine Transformations: Unveiling the Power of God's Creation' by Dr. Lebede Ngartera to be a profound and essential read.

Dr. Ngartera masterfully integrates theological insight with ecological awareness, offering a compelling argument for why stewardship of our planet is not only a necessity but a sacred duty. His unique perspective enriches our understanding of environmental issues through a spiritual lens, inspiring action and deepening our commitment to Earth's care.

This book is a beacon of hope and a call to action for all who cherish our planet and seek to integrate their faith with environmental stewardship."

**Mr. Semingar Ngaryamngar, Environmental Scientist and Policy Advisor**

"Divine Transformations: *Unveiling the Power of God's Creation*" by Dr. Lebede Ngartera is a compelling journey that bridges the realms of faith and science, exploring the biblical narrative of creation alongside modern scientific understanding. This book delves into how the intricacies of the universe and life on Earth reveal the meticulous artistry of the Creator, enriching our awe and underscoring our duty as stewards of this magnificent creation.

Dr. Ngartera, with his unique blend of academic insight and deep faith, invites readers to reflect on their role in the natural world, advocating for stewardship as a sacred responsibility. Through thoughtful analysis and practical applications, "Divine Transformations" inspires personal and communal action towards sustainable living and spiritual growth.

A call to rediscover the sanctity of the natural world, this book is an essential read for those seeking to integrate their faith with a commitment to care for the planet.

# A NOTE TO THE READER



As you journey through the pages of "Divine Transformations: Unveiling the Power of God's Creation," I hope you become immersed in a narrative that explores not only the grandeur of the world around us but also the depths of our personal faith. It is my sincere wish that this book serves as a beacon of light, guiding you through the intricacies of spiritual growth and the beauty of living in harmony with God's creation.

The journey we embark upon together in this book is one of discovery, challenge, and profound transformation. It stands as a testament to the power of faith in illuminating the darkest corners of our lives and the world we inhabit. As you continue to navigate the chapters, you may find solace in the stories shared, wisdom in the lessons learned, and strength in the spiritual practices espoused.

I encourage you not only to persevere in your reading but also to embrace the principles and insights offered within these pages. Let them be a source of encouragement and a catalyst for your own journey of faith. Remember, each day presents a new opportunity to live out the divine truths we uncover, to reflect God's love in our actions, and to deepen our connection with the Creator.

Furthermore, if this book has touched your heart or sparked a light within you, I humbly ask you to consider sharing its message with others. Witnessing to friends, family, or community members about the transformative power of "Divine Transformations" can extend the reach of its encouragement and hope. Encourage them to embark on this journey themselves by securing a copy, as every new reader becomes a fellow traveler on the path to spiritual enlightenment and stewardship of

God's creation.

Together, let us spread the light of faith, hope, and love that this book endeavors to capture. Your support in witnessing to others not only amplifies the impact of the message contained within these pages but also strengthens the fabric of our shared faith community.

Thank you for your companionship on this journey. May you continue to find renewal and inspiration in the divine rhythm of work and rest, and may your faith be ever strengthened as you walk in the light of God's enduring love.

With deepest gratitude and blessings,

*Dr Lebede Ngartera*

# PROLOGUE

Before the dawn of time, before the first star sparkled in the vast expanse of the cosmos, there was a divine intention—a blueprint for creation that would unfold across the ages, bringing into being a world of breathtaking beauty and intricate balance. This sacred narrative, chronicled in the ancient texts and echoed in the whispering winds and flowing waters, serves as the backdrop for our journey in "Divine Transformations: Unveiling the Power of God's Creation."

As we stand at the threshold of this exploration, it is essential to acknowledge that the journey ahead is not merely an academic endeavor. It is a pilgrimage of the heart and mind, seeking to uncover the layers of divine wisdom woven into the fabric of the universe. Through the pages of this book, we are invited to traverse the boundary between the seen and the unseen, the known and the mysterious, guided by the light of faith and the quest for understanding.

This journey is rooted in the narrative of creation—a story that transcends time and culture, inviting us to reflect on our origins, our purpose, and our place within the vast tapestry of life. It is a story that challenges us to consider our relationship with the Earth, not as dominators or exploiters, but as stewards entrusted with a sacred duty to care for and preserve the masterpiece of God's handiwork.

In "Divine Transformations," we embark on a voyage that bridges the realms of science and spirituality, probing the depths of biblical wisdom while engaging with contemporary environmental and ethical dilemmas. It is a journey that demands courage and openness, for it calls us to confront uncomfortable truths about the impact of our actions on the planet and to grapple with the complexities of living out our faith in a world marked by diversity, conflict, and change.

Yet, this journey is also one of hope and possibility. It reveals the potential for faith to inspire a profound transformation in our lives and in the world around us. It offers a vision of a future where humans live in harmony with creation, where science and spirituality enrich one another, and where the ancient call to stewardship is embraced as a guiding principle for action.

As you turn these pages, I invite you to journey with me—a fellow traveler on the path of discovery. Let us set aside preconceptions and embark with open hearts and minds, ready to be challenged, inspired, and transformed. Together, let us explore the divine narrative of creation, uncovering its relevance for our lives today and its implications for the future of our planet.

Welcome to "Divine Transformations." Welcome to a journey of awakening, action, and hope—a journey that begins with the very first act of creation and continues within each of us, as we seek to live out our calling in a world that is both ancient and ever-new.

WHY THIS BOOK?

In an era where the clamor of daily life often drowns out the whispers of the divine, and the relentless pursuit of progress threatens the sanctity of the natural world, "Divine Transformations: Unveiling the Power of God's Creation" emerges as a beacon of light. This book is born from a deep conviction that within the narrative of creation lies a blueprint for living—a map guiding us through the complexities of contemporary existence toward a life that is spiritually fulfilling and harmonious with the Earth.

At the heart of this exploration is the belief that ancient texts and traditions carry within them timeless wisdom profoundly relevant today. They offer insights into navigating the challenges of modernity, not by retreating into the past but by applying this eternal wisdom in innovative and responsive ways. "Divine Transformations" seeks to bridge the perceived chasm between faith and science, between ancient scripture and contemporary environmental concerns, arguing that at their core, they speak a common language—the language of stewardship, responsibility, and awe.

In an age where the environmental crisis looms large, casting a shadow over future generations, this book serves as a clarion call to action. It challenges us to see environmental stewardship not as a burden but as a sacred duty, an act of worship that honors the Creator by caring for His creation. Through a blend of theological insight, scientific exploration, and personal narrative, "Divine Transformations" inspires a spirituality that is actively engaged with the world—a faith that plants trees, protects waters, and cherishes every breath of air and speck of soil as divine gifts.

Moreover, this book recognizes the need for a faith that is vibrant and adaptable, capable of engaging with the diverse and pluralistic society that characterizes our world. It advocates for a faith that sees in every human being the image of the divine, calling for actions and policies that reflect compassion, equality, and justice. "Divine Transformations" invites us to engage in meaningful dialogue, to build bridges where walls have been erected, and to find in our shared stewardship of the planet a common ground for unity and action.

## DIVINE TRANSFORMATIONS FOR TODAY

"Divine Transformations" is not just an academic discourse; it is a call to experience the divine in the everyday, to see in the ordinary the fingerprints of the extraordinary. It is for anyone who has ever gazed at the night sky and felt a sense of wonder, for anyone who has walked through a forest and felt the sacredness of life, for anyone who believes that faith should inform how we live on this planet and how we treat one another.

In these pages, you will find a journey from the origins of the universe to the pressing environmental and social issues of our day. It invites reflection, inspires action, and calls for transformation. "Divine Transformations" is an invitation to rediscover the awe-inspiring beauty of God's creation, to deepen our understanding of our place within it, and to live out our faith in ways that bring healing to our broken world.

Why this book? Because now, more than ever, we need a vision for the future that is rooted in the wisdom of the past, informed by the knowledge of the present, and inspired by hope for the future. "Divine Transformations: Unveiling the Power of God's Creation" offers just that —a pathway to a faith that is alive, dynamic, and transformative.

# PART I
# THE DAWN OF CREATION

# ACTION STEPS TO LIVE THE POWER OF GOD'S WORD ON THE FIRST DAY

## INTRODUCTION: A NEW BEGINNING

### EMBARKING ON A JOURNEY OF FAITH: FROM CHAD TO PENNSYLVANIA

My move from Chad to Pennsylvania was not just a change of location; it marked the beginning of a profound journey of faith. This transition was a leap into the unknown, propelled by my belief in the transformative power of God's Word. Leaving behind everything familiar—the comfort of my home, the warmth of my community, and the rich tapestry of shared history—I ventured into a radically different world, fueled by a deep desire for new beginnings. This was a quest for a life that mirrored the vast possibilities promised by faith in God.

This decision to embark on a new path was filled with uncertainty. The comfort and support of my home and community were weighed against the promise of a hopeful yet daunting future. During this whirlwind of change, my faith served as a steadfast anchor. This period of intense personal reflection brought the stories of biblical beginnings closer to my heart than ever before. The narrative of creation, where order emerged from chaos, reflected my own aspirations for the future. The divine act of bringing light into darkness resonated with me, offering hope that my journey could also be a creative process—one that breathes life into new dreams and possibilities.

Upon arriving in Pennsylvania, its sprawling cities and towering skyscrapers stood in stark contrast to Chad's landscapes. Each street corner, bustling market, and unfamiliar face underscored the new life I had chosen. This life, driven by a pursuit of growth and knowledge, presented its own set of challenges. Adapting to a new culture, overcoming language barriers, and keeping pace with the relentless rhythm of urban life often made me feel isolated, a world away from the community I had left.

In moments of solitude and doubt, I found solace and direction in my faith. The first day of creation, where light was introduced to the void, became a metaphor for my own journey. Like the world formed from the void, I was carving out a new existence, seeking light amidst my personal uncertainties.

The journey of transformation was gradual, with each step taken as an act of faith. Learning English, adapting to a new culture, and navigating the American job market were daunting challenges. Yet, as I overcame each obstacle, my faith grew stronger. The light of God's Word, once a distant beacon in my moments of doubt, became a tangible guide, leading me towards a future I had once thought unreachable.

My transition from Chad to Pennsylvania stands as a testament to the power of new beginnings and the unwavering strength of faith in the face of uncertainty. It mirrors the biblical creation story, where chaos gives way to order and darkness to light, heralding a life full of vibrancy and promise. This journey has taught me that with faith, we should not fear the unknown. Instead, we should embrace it, for it is within the uncharted waters of life that we discover our true purpose and experience the fullness of God's transformative power.

## THE DAWN OF TRANSFORMATION: WELCOMING NEW BEGINNINGS THROUGH CREATION'S FIRST DAY

Within the vast journey of our lives, marked by countless beginnings and endings, lies a profound metaphor reflecting our innate ability for renewal and transformation. This metaphor is rooted in the biblical story of creation's first day, symbolizing not just the universe's literal dawn but also the promise of light, hope, and new beginnings in our existence.

Genesis opens with a universe empty and formless, shrouded in darkness. Into this abyss, God's commanding words, "Let there be light," pierce the veil of night, introducing light and initiating creation's first dawn. This divine act, calling light from the void, stands as a poignant emblem of the transformative potential within every new start.

Similarly, our lives encounter moments beckoning us from our own voids of uncertainty. These crossroads of decision and change possess the divine capacity to reshape our journey and brighten our future. Whether it's a new career path, the embrace of faith, or a move away from the comfort of the known towards the promise of new territories, each beginning is imbued with the potential for profound transformation.

The narrative of the first day serves as a reminder that change is a fundamental element woven into the cosmos's fabric. It assures us that from darkness comes light and from chaos, a new order and purpose can arise. This is especially meaningful for those on the cusp of change, navigating the unknown with both trepidation and hope. It reassures us that, just as the universe emerged from darkness, our lives too can flourish anew under the light of fresh starts.

By embodying the essence of creation's first day, we are encouraged to view each new chapter as a gateway to transformation. It beckons us to trust in the forthcoming light, even when our path is obscured. This is a clarion call, urging us to step into the unknown with faith, secure in the belief that with each forward step, we partake in the continuous act of creation that began with the cosmos.

Thus, the first day of creation transcends its biblical origins, evolving into a perpetual promise of strength and inspiration for anyone seeking renewal and transformation. It is a testament that, armed with faith, we can welcome new beginnings, assured by the promise of light and the boundless prospects awaiting us at the dawn of our personal transformations.

## THE FIRST LIGHT OF CREATION ILLUMINATION AND GUIDANCE THROUGH GOD'S WORD

At creation's dawn, before stars filled the sky or the Earth took form, a divine command pierced the primordial darkness: "Let there be light" (Genesis 1:1-5). This first act of creation transcends a mere historical or cosmological milestone; it carries deep spiritual symbolism, resonating with the essence of human experience. The emergence of light signifies the onset of life, order, and comprehension, serving as a metaphor for enlightenment in acquiring knowledge and spiritual awareness.

Before creation, the universe was an empty, formless void. Into this nothingness, light was summoned as the foundational element, delineating darkness from light, night from day, thus instituting existence's rhythm. This demarcation stands as a powerful symbol, representing the discernment between ignorance and enlightenment, the unseen and the seen. Light, herein, transcends mere physical illumination to embody wisdom and insight, marking the journey towards the universe's intricate beauty and complexity—a nod to the divine intelligence at work.

Incorporating God's Word into our lives reflects the inaugural light of creation. As the initial illumination brought clarity and order to the cosmos, so does Scripture light our way, steering us through the shadows of doubt, fear, or confusion. In moments of uncertainty, the Bible offers a beacon of light, cutting through our perplexities to provide direction and solace. This spiritual light fosters an in-depth understanding of our purpose and positioning in the world, shaping our decisions and deeds according to divine intention.

The metaphor of light embodies more than guidance; it signifies the transformative essence of God's Word. Just as light nurtures life, the wisdom and truth contained within the Scriptures fuel our spiritual growth, empowering us to flourish and realize our full potential. By engaging deeply and reflectively with God's Word, we welcome this transformative light into our hearts, chasing away the shadows of sin and doubt, igniting the virtues of faith, hope, and love.

Furthermore, by embracing the light of Scripture, we are empowered to become luminaries in a realm often dimmed by spiritual obscurity. Bearing this light, we are tasked with sharing it, lighting the way for those adrift in darkness. Our lives, reshaped and directed by Scripture, stand as testimonies to God's enduring luminosity, encouraging others to find solace and guidance in His Word.

In essence, the genesis of light is a profound emblem of beginnings, of harmony birthed from chaos, heralding the break of comprehension. As we ponder Genesis 1:1-5, let's welcome the enlightenment and direction provided by God's Word. Let us tread confidently in its light, allowing it to shape our paths, transform our hearts, and compel us to radiate divinely in a world thirsting for enlightenment.


## ILLUMINATION OF THE SOUL

In the vibrant mosaic of Pennsylvania, as I navigated the complexities of assimilating into a new culture and surmounting challenges, there emerged moments of profound stillness where scripture shone as a beacon of hope and clarity. Enveloped by the solitude of my modest apartment, the enormity of my hurdles once felt overwhelming. It was in these serene moments that I sought solace and guidance in scripture.

Psalm 119:105, "Your word is a lamp for my feet, a light on my path," instilled in me an immediate tranquility. This verse transcended mere text; it served as a divine affirmation that I was not meandering in darkness alone. It reassured me that each step I took was under the illumination of God's wisdom, guiding me through the maze of uncertainty. This scripture evolved into a foundational element of my daily life, imbuing me with the strength to greet each day with renewed optimism and resolve.

Equally transformative was my encounter with Philippians 4:13, "I can do all this through him who gives me strength." This verse directly addressed the essence of my trials, enlightening me that my potential was not constrained by my present circumstances. It was a pivotal realization that the same God who summoned light into being was actively empowering me to transcend the obstacles in my path. These scriptures became more than just written words; they were vital lifelines that rescued me from the precipice of despair, providing clarity and hope as I maneuvered through the intricacies of a new existence in unfamiliar territory.

To those wandering through their own shades of darkness, in search of a spark of light, I extend this invitation: immerse yourself in the scriptures, seeking verses that echo your personal adversities. Let God's Word cast light on the segments of your life veiled in uncertainty or fear. In these pursuits, you will discover the brilliance of God's wisdom, eager to chart your course, imbuing your journey with clarity and hope. Just as the inaugural day of creation dispersed light across a vacant cosmos, may God's Word illuminate your existence, transforming your trials into avenues for growth and your skepticism into steadfast faith.

## WALKING IN THE LIGHT

Walking in God's light is an odyssey of harmonizing our lives with His teachings, living out His love, and manifesting His truth in every deed. It entails steering through life's complexities with a heart moored in divine wisdom, making sure every decision, interaction, and contemplation radiates the warmth and luminosity of His presence. This journey transcends merely shunning darkness; it's about zealously seeking the light, opting for a life that shines with kindness, integrity, and intentionality.

Choosing this path means our every action is a reflection of the divine, guiding us to embody qualities that draw others to His light. It's a commitment to conduct our lives as beacons of hope and bastions of faith, showing the world the transformative power of walking in alignment with God's will. Through this, we not only find our own way but also light the path for others, sharing the beacon of God's love and truth in a world greatly in need of illumination.

## LIVING BY HIS TEACHINGS

Living according to His teachings is a profound journey that demands we root our lives deeply in the scripture, allowing it to shape our perspectives, guide our decisions, and light our paths as we navigate the world. This commitment means viewing life through lenses of empathy and understanding, recognizing the divine spark in every person we meet. This path invites us to foster patience, freely offer forgiveness, and confront life's ups and downs with steadfast faith, believing that even in the stormiest times, God's guiding light leads us to peace.

Embarking on this spiritual odyssey transforms us, as every verse we read and every prayer we whisper gradually aligns our hearts more closely with God's. It involves allowing His word to deeply penetrate our being, influencing not only our thoughts but also our deeds and responses. This path teaches us to see beyond outward appearances, to understand the struggles and beauty in others, and to meet them not with judgment, but with grace. Living this way is an active choice to bring light to dark places, to replace despair with hope, and to sow peace where there is discord.

By living in harmony with His word, we shine as beacons of God's love in a world desperately in need of it. We come to understand the impact of gentle words and acts of kindness, realizing these can be as powerful as the most passionate prayers. We learn that forgiveness is not a sign of weakness but a testament to strength, an attribute of the divine that liberates us from bitterness and paves the way for healing and reconciliation. Our walk with God reveals that patience is more than waiting; it's an act of faith in His timing and design.

In walking in the light of God, we are reminded that we are never alone. His presence is a constant source of comfort and strength, especially in moments of doubt or fear. This knowledge empowers us to face life's challenges with courage, secure in the belief that His guidance is unfailing and His love knows no bounds. We begin to view obstacles not as dead ends but as opportunities for growth and as a means to witness God's faithfulness in leading us through every circumstance.

To live by His teachings is to wholeheartedly embrace a life of service, using our unique gifts and talents to glorify God and enrich the lives of others. It's understanding that every interaction is a chance to exhibit God's grace, share the essence of His love, and positively impact those we encounter. It's about creating a legacy of faith that mirrors the light of Christ, inspiring others to seek Him.

Ultimately, to walk in God's light is to undergo a life-changing transformation that redefines our very existence. It challenges us to live purposefully, love unconditionally, and place our unwavering trust in God's supreme authority over our lives. Through this transformative journey, we not only draw nearer to God but also become His instruments in the world, living out His teachings and spreading His boundless love to everyone we meet.

## EMBODYING HIS LOVE AND TRUTH

Embodying God's love and truth signifies a deep commitment to live in the full expression of His teachings, profoundly influencing our character and every action. This lifestyle transforms our existence into vibrant echoes of the Gospel, ensuring that every choice, every word, and every deed aligns with the transformative light of God's presence. Such a life sharply contrasts a society often motivated by self-interest, making acts of kindness and altruism not merely noteworthy but luminous, attracting others to the warmth of God's love.

To live out God's love and truth is to move through life with a grace that is both serene and formidable. It signifies a change of heart so impactful that it reshapes our interaction with the world. Choosing forgiveness over retaliation, offering assistance without expectation of return, and loving unconditionally in a world rife with conditions illuminate our paths as beacons of hope, vivid demonstrations of God's transformative work within us.

Upholding what is right, living truth in love, and keeping our faith authentic, even against societal norms, demand bravery and determination. It involves a steadfast adherence to our beliefs and values, not for judgment or exclusion but as a manifestation of God's steadfast love and truth. This stance isn't about claiming moral superiority but about humbly embodying truth with compassion, integrity, and a fervent wish to mirror God's kingdom on earth.

To embody God's love and truth is also to be an advocate for the marginalized, a protector for the vulnerable, and a companion for the solitary. It means addressing injustices not with hostility or revenge but with a love that aspires to heal and reconcile. Our words and deeds become tools of God's peace, fostering unity and cultivating communities anchored in love and respect.

Authentic faith aligns our public and private selves, mirroring our devotion to God's teachings across all facets of life, affecting our work, leisure, and relationships. This genuine faith attracts others not towards us but through us to Jesus Christ, the wellspring of our hope and strength.

By living and exemplifying God's love and truth, we extend an invitation to others to discover the vastness of His love. Our lives serve as open invitations to witness the Gospel's life-changing strength, navigating life's complexities with hope that inspires, joy that endures, and a peace that surpasses all understanding.

In essence, to embody God's love and truth is to engage in a relentless pursuit of growth and surrender. It's a daily choice to let His light radiate through us, impacting the world in visible and invisible ways. Committing to His teachings not only deepens our faith but also fortifies the faith of those around us, leaving a legacy of love and truth that resonates through the ages.

**Practical Action Steps to live in God's Light**

1. **Start Each Day with Scripture:** Make it a habit to read a passage from the Bible every morning. Let God's Word be the first influence on your mind and the guiding force for your day's actions. Imagine it as the dawn's first rays, bringing clarity and direction to your thoughts and deeds.

2. **Actively Practice Kindness:** Set a goal to perform at least one deliberate act of kindness each day. It could be an encouraging word, assisting a neighbor, or merely sharing a smile. Consider each act of kindness as a beam of light you're casting into the world, brightening someone else's day.

3. **Reflect Integrity in All You Do:** Ensure your actions mirror the integrity of your faith. Whether it's in your

workplace, within your relationships, or through personal pursuits, aim for honesty and fairness. Remember, your actions are a direct reflection of God's truth and a testament to His teachings.

4. **Find Your Purpose in Service:** Discover activities that resonate with your spiritual gifts and passions. Whether it's volunteering, mentoring, or engaging in community service, these acts of service not only fulfill your purpose but also spread the illuminating light of God's love and wisdom.

5. **Evening Reflection:** Conclude each day with a period of reflection. Assess the moments when you were able to embody God's light and identify areas for improvement. This introspection encourages personal growth and helps maintain your focus on living in alignment with His teachings.

Incorporating these practices into our daily routines enhances our journey in God's light, transforming us into luminaries for those around us. This path is marked by ongoing growth, learning, and the sharing of the divine illumination that has touched our lives. As we embrace these practical steps, let's proceed with assurance, knowing our paths are lit by the perpetual light of God's love and guidance.

## EMBRACING GOD'S TRUTH

Embracing God's truth invites us on a transformative journey, one that demands deep and steadfast commitment to immerse ourselves in His Word. This isn't merely about reading; it's an active, deliberate engagement that allows Scripture to permeate every aspect of our lives. By dedicating ourselves to thorough study and thoughtful reflection on the Bible, we begin to discern God's will, understand His truths, and progressively align our lives with His divine intent. This immersion in Scripture transcends academic pursuit, evolving into a deep spiritual practice with the power to fundamentally reshape our essence.

As we delve into God's Word, it serves as a mirror, reflecting our deepest thoughts and intentions, and unveiling areas ripe for His grace and transformation. This introspection, while sometimes uncomfortable, is vital for our spiritual growth and maturation. With guidance from the Holy Spirit, Scripture shapes our decision-making, influences our thought processes, and directs our actions towards harmony with God's plans for us. It becomes the prism through which we view the world, endowing us with wisdom and insight that surpass mere human comprehension.

The journey of embracing God's truth is inherently transformative, effecting profound internal change that shines outwardly. Aligning our minds and hearts with God's Word arms us with strength and courage to tackle life's challenges. The truths we internalize anchor us amidst life's storms, offering stability and hope in times of uncertainty. They compel us to live with integrity, make decisions confidently, and navigate life boldly, secure in the knowledge of our alignment with the Creator's will.

Furthermore, this embrace of God's truth fosters a resilient faith within us. This resilience, rooted in the assurance of God's immutable Word, enables us to endure trials without faltering, empowered by a conviction in God's unwavering faithfulness and sovereignty over our lives. Our engagement with Scripture becomes a bastion of strength, illuminating not just our path but also serving as a beacon of hope and encouragement for others.

In accepting God's truth, we are also called to be vessels of His grace and love in the world. The truths we embrace and embody are meant to be shared, radiating through our actions and words. As God's Word transforms us, we become channels of His truth, casting light in the darkness and offering hope to those in despair. This mission further solidifies our faith as we observe the life-changing impact of God's Word on others.

Ultimately, embracing God's truth is an act of bold faith, necessitating perseverance, humility, and an open heart. It's a lifelong quest that molds us closer to Christ's likeness, empowering us to fulfill our divine calling with confidence and joy. As we dedicate ourselves to this path, let's do so with the conviction that God's Word is vibrant and potent, capable of transforming even the faintest of spirits into formidable champions for His kingdom.

## THE IMPORTANCE OF DILIGENT STUDY AND REFLECTION

The path to discerning God's will and truth is fundamentally anchored in the meticulous study and reflective meditation on Scripture. This disciplined engagement with God's Word transcends mere intellectual endeavor, unfolding as an invitation to forge a deeper, more profound connection with the Creator. By dedicating ourselves to consistent study and contemplation, we open our hearts wide to grasp God's character, to hold His promises dear, and to uncover His plans for our lives. Such dedication equips us with necessary guidance to traverse life's complexities, resilience to weather adversity, and the wisdom to make decisions that dignify our faith.

The Bible, with its intricate weave of narratives, teachings, and parables, acts as a dynamic compass, speaking directly to our life's situations and challenges. It provides clarity amidst confusion, solace during grief, and hope in despairing times. Immersing ourselves in Scripture lets God's truth infiltrate our essence, refining our thoughts, guiding our actions, and coloring our perspectives.

Engaging with the Word is hardly a solitary endeavor; it knits us into the fabric of a widespread community of faith that crosses temporal and cultural boundaries. The shared accounts of victories and trials within the scriptures offer us camaraderie, motivation, and reminders of God's unwavering loyalty. The lives of those who've tread the path of faith before us embolden us, their stories fueling our courage to face our battles, inspired by their faith-driven victories.

Regular interaction with Scripture fosters a discerning heart, enabling us to distinguish truth from deception and to choose paths that align with God's will. Often, it's in the quietude of study and reflection that we perceive God's voice most distinctly, guiding us tenderly toward righteousness and serenity. This ongoing dialogue with God through His Word fortifies our faith, enriches our comprehension, and empowers us to embody lives that mirror His love and veracity.

Furthermore, the habit of studying and reflecting on Scripture ingrains in us a resilience anchored in divine truth. In a world that frequently contests our faith, God's Word stands as an indomitable pillar, providing stability amid chaos and assurance against uncertainties. This firm foundation emboldens us to uphold our beliefs, assured by the conviction that we are navigated by an eternal, immutable truth.

The value of rigorous study and meditation on Scripture is immense. It acts as a spring of spiritual sustenance, a repository of heavenly wisdom, and a driving force for personal transformation. Committing to this practice not only deepens our understanding of God but also enhances our ability to act as His emissaries in the world. Equipped with the essence of His Word, we are prepared for the road ahead, fortified by the assurance that God is ever-present, guiding our steps and illuminating our journey.

Hence, our faith journey is immensely enriched and fortified by our dedication to studying and pondering Scripture. This discipline is crucial for cultivating a resilient, bold faith capable of confronting life's hurdles and triumphing. Let us then approach the study of God's Word with fervor and commitment, confident in its capability to direct, metamorphose, and rejuvenate our inner selves.

**Methods for Immersing in Scripture**

1. **Daily Reading Plans:** Systematically immersing yourself in Scripture can be effectively achieved through daily reading plans. These plans can guide you through the Bible in a year, focus your study on thematic areas, or delve into specific books over a designated period. This structured approach ensures a thorough engagement with God's Word, allowing its truths to gradually reveal themselves and enrich your understanding day by day.

2. **Meditation on Specific Verses:** Select a verse or passage to meditate on each week. Write it down, keep it with you, and ponder its meaning throughout your day. This practice deepens your internalization of God's Word, influencing your thoughts and actions in profound ways. Meditation creates a personal bond with Scripture, transforming it into a wellspring of strength, guidance, and solace.

3. **Scripture Journaling:** Maintain a journal dedicated to your scripture reflections. Note down passages that touch you,

your insights on their application, and prayers they inspire.
Journaling serves as a potent tool for digesting what you've
read, forging personal ties to the Scripture, and monitoring
your spiritual evolution over time.

4. **Participate in Bible Studies:** Engaging in Bible study
   groups enriches your comprehension of Scripture. The
   collective insights, varied interpretations, and mutual
   reflections contribute to a deeper understanding of God's
   Word. This collaborative form of study promotes fellowship
   and a sense of communal responsibility in your spiritual walk.

5. **Pray Through Scripture:** Employ Scripture as the
   groundwork for your prayers. Integrating verses or passages
   into your prayer routine can invigorate your dialogue with
   God, infusing your prayer life with dynamism and a
   foundation in Scripture. This approach aids in memorizing
   scripture and applying its lessons meaningfully to your daily
   life.

Through these practices, God's truth elevates Scripture beyond mere
text, animating it as a guiding force in our lives. Committing to these
methods not only illuminates our journey with the light of His truth but
also shapes our decisions with His wisdom and fills our existence with
His enduring love.

## SHINING GOD'S LIGHT IN A DARKENED WORLD

In a reality often veiled by shadows of despair and apathy, choosing to
radiate God's light through acts of kindness and compassion stands as a
powerful rebuttal. It's a clear demonstration of the significant change
even the slightest gestures of love can initiate in the hearts and lives of
those around us. As followers of Christ, we are summoned to be beacons
in the gloom, mirroring the brilliance of God's love and hope through
our deeds and engagements.

## THE TRANSFORMATIVE IMPACT OF REFLECTING GOD'S LIGHT

To reflect God's light in a dim world is to make a deliberate decision to live out His love and compassion every day. This manifestation can take countless forms, from merely lending a sympathetic ear to someone craving companionship, to more concrete gestures of kindness such as aiding those in distress, volunteering at local shelters, or sharing words of encouragement with a passerby. Each act becomes a ray of God's love, piercing through the darkness with hope and warmth.

The influence of these acts of kindness ripples far beyond the immediate, nurturing a sense of community, mutual understanding, and a shared sense of humanity. They remind us that each person has a story deserving of empathy and that in giving, we also receive blessings. It is through these connections and acts of generosity that God's light truly radiates, guiding us towards a more compassionate and unified world.

### Examples of the Power of Kindness

1. **A Simple Meal:** My initial days in Pennsylvania were shadowed by intense loneliness and uncertainty. During this period, a neighbor, who knew little of my struggles apart from my recent move, offered a home-cooked meal. This gesture was a lighthouse of welcome in my solitude, a reminder of compassion's universal dialect. It motivated me to propagate kindness in my interactions, no matter the scale.

2. **Volunteering at a Local Shelter:** The kindness I experienced inspired me to volunteer at a local shelter, where I witnessed the collective power of benevolence. Volunteers from varied backgrounds united to offer warmth, sustenance, and hope to the destitute. The gratitude visible in those we assisted highlighted the significant impact our united efforts could have in erasing the shadows of adversity.

3. **Encouragement to a Stranger:** On a public transport journey, I encountered a distressed individual fretting over job loss and financial woes. Engaging in a simple dialogue, offering encouragement, and sharing snippets of my own challenges, I

was able to leave a lasting impact. Weeks later, our paths crossed again, and he recounted how that conversation had been a pivotal moment of hope during a challenging period.

These examples, among many others, reveal the profound truth that our minimal acts of kindness can ignite substantial transformations. They show that by opting to spread God's light in our routine actions, we can brighten the darkest corners of our globe with the lasting brilliance of empathy, hope, and love. Let us persist in shining vividly, seizing every chance to embody God's love through our kindness, and witnessing the profound change it can bring to the world, one act at a time.

Standing Strong Against Spiritual Darkness

In life's voyage, we frequently face moments that challenge our faith and determination, urging us to maneuver through a labyrinth of temptations and counterpoints to our spiritual beliefs. The environment we inhabit occasionally appears to conflict with the righteous path we aim to follow, brimming with distractions and disheartenments that risk overshadowing our faith's luminescence. However, it's within these testing times that our fortitude and dedication to our spiritual values prove most vital. Standing firm against spiritual darkness isn't just an act of defiance; it's a profound affirmation of our faith and a bold declaration of our commitment to God's truth.

## Challenges of Resisting Temptation and Maintaining Faith

1. **Navigating a Culture of Contradictions:** In a society that often exalts material achievement, self-gratification, and instant fulfillment, steadfastly adhering to spiritual virtues such as altruism, patience, and an everlasting outlook can prove daunting. The influx of messages conflicting with scriptural teachings might sow confusion and weaken our spiritual focus, obscuring the path toward genuine contentment and peace.

2. **The Lure of Immediate Gratification:** The digital era tempts us with the illusion that desires can be instantly satisfied, continually challenging our discipline of patience

and the virtue of contentment. Yielding to the temptation for quick satisfaction over lasting rewards may lead us into spiritual apathy, distancing us from the profound, sustaining connections with God.

**Strategies for Strengthening Spiritual Resolve**

1. **Anchoring in Prayer:** Prayer connects us directly to divine strength and wisdom, offering refuge from the tempests of temptation and doubt. Engaging in prayer invites God's presence into our trials, imbuing our spirits with His peace and our decisions with His guidance. Consistent, heartfelt prayer bolsters our resolve, arming us with the spiritual armor necessary to withstand forces that attempt to divert us from our path.
2. **Cultivating Community Support:** Encircling ourselves with a community of faith provides essential encouragement and accountability for maintaining spiritual integrity. Fellowship with fellow believers yields inspiration and a supportive network, allowing us to share our challenges openly and celebrate triumphs with authentic joy. Participating in group prayer, Bible studies, and collective worship strengthens our spiritual base, reminding us of our shared journey in faith.
3. **Focusing on Scriptural Promises:** Scripture brims with assurances that bring hope, certainty, and vigor amidst temptation and spiritual gloom. Immersing ourselves in God's Word arms our minds with His truths, serving as a shield and sword against worldly deceptions and despondency. Reflecting on passages that herald God's steadfastness, His supportive might, and His triumph over sin can ignite our bravery and rejuvenate our commitment to align with His will.

Confronting the spiritual battlefield demands more than mere human resolve; it calls for a profound reliance on God's might, the backing of a spiritually vibrant community, and the illuminating guidance of His Word. By embracing these strategies, we can confidently face the world's trials, assured by the conviction that He who dwells within us is greater than he who is in the world.


## PROCLAIMING THE GOSPEL

The mission to proclaim the Gospel, to share the profound message of God's love and salvation available through Jesus Christ of Nazareth, is a core calling for all who follow Him. This hallowed responsibility, charged with the potential to reshape hearts and minds, urges us to move beyond the confines of our spiritual havens and venture into the broader expanse of the world. It calls us to be heralds of hope, to bear the radiance of God's truth across terrains often veiled in skepticism and despair. Drawing on the reservoir of my personal faith and the life-altering experiences encountered on my path from Chad to Pennsylvania, I've grasped the significant influence that disseminating the Gospel can wield—not solely on its recipients but profoundly on the bearer as well.

This endeavor to articulate the Gospel embodies more than merely conveying information; it's an act of sharing life, offering a glimpse into the transformative journey of faith that has redefined my existence. It's about extending an invitation to explore the depths of God's love, to understand the sacrifice of Christ, and to experience the liberation and hope it brings.

Engaging in this divine commission enriches our spiritual journey, deepening our understanding and appreciation of the Gospel as we witness its impact on others. It serves as a reminder of the vastness of God's grace and the universality of His call to redemption. As we bear witness to the power of the Gospel to illuminate the darkest of circumstances, our faith is fortified, and our resolve to continue this mission is invigorated.

To share the Gospel is to participate in the ongoing story of God's love for humanity, a narrative that spans ages and cultures, touching lives in ways we may never fully comprehend but will always cherish. It is a privilege and a profound responsibility, one that calls for humility, prayer, and a deep reliance on the Holy Spirit to guide our words and actions. In proclaiming the Gospel, we not only offer hope to a world in need but also embark on a transformative journey that continually shapes us into the likeness of Christ, making us more effective instruments of His grace.

**The Importance and Power of Sharing the Gospel**

1. **A Catalyst for Transformation:** My personal narrative stands as a vivid illustration of the Gospel's transformative capacity. It served as the guiding light amidst the chaos of acculturating to a new environment and bridging the gaps of language and geographical distance. Opening up about this faith journey to others has transcended mere vulnerability; it has unfolded as a significant chance to observe how God's truth universally resonates, bridging vastly different walks of life. Every discussion, every shared testimony, forges a link between human hearts and the divine, sparking curiosity or reviving a once-dimmed faith.

2. **The Ripple Effect of Faith Sharing:** Proclaiming the Gospel is comparable to casting stones into the vast ocean of human consciousness; the ripples it generates can reach far beyond what we see, affecting lives in profound ways that might elude our full comprehension. By vocalizing our faith, we contribute to God's grand narrative of redemption and restoration, marking our role in the expansive saga of His love for humanity.

Engaging in the act of sharing the Gospel not only nurtures the seeds of faith in others but also reinforces our own understanding and commitment to the path Jesus laid out. It's a reminder that the message of Christ's love and salvation, while deeply personal, is also universally needed and applicable, crossing cultural, linguistic, and geographical barriers to touch hearts and transform lives. This sharing becomes not just a duty but a privilege, offering a glimpse of the kingdom of God at work in the world today, and inviting others to join in the journey towards everlasting hope and redemption.

## Guidance on Witnessing to Others

1. **Balancing Boldness with Humility:** Witnessing effectively entails a delicate balance between boldness and humility—boldness to proclaim the Gospel's truths unwaveringly, and humility to acknowledge our role as mere conduits for a divine message. We must understand that our task is to plant seeds of faith; it is ultimately God who cultivates these seeds and fosters spiritual growth. This equilibrium is developed through prayer, introspection, and a continuous quest for divine direction on the timing and manner of sharing God's truths with others.

2. **Leading with Love:** At its core, the Gospel radiates love—the boundless love God has for us, epitomized by Christ's ultimate sacrifice. Therefore, our method of conveying this profound message should be deeply rooted in this same spirit of love, patience, and empathy. Our mission to bear witness should arise not from a standpoint of judgment or perceived superiority but from a sincere wish for others to experience the fulfillment and tranquility found in communion with God. Often, the most compelling testimony begins not with grand declarations, but through simple acts of kindness, empathy, and a genuine investment in the wellbeing of those around us.

Sharing the Gospel is both an honor and a duty, reflecting our faith in a way that can both test and greatly enhance our spiritual journey. As we venture forth to fulfill this calling, let us approach it with open hearts, attuned to the Holy Spirit's guidance, prepared to serve as vessels of God's boundless grace and messengers of His infinite love.

CONCLUSION: LIVING EACH DAY IN THE LIGHT

As this opening chapter draws to a close, we take a moment to reflect on the profound journey from the first flicker of light in the cosmos to the illumination it casts in our lives. This narrative, spun from the divine act of creation, personal tribulations, and moments of spiritual enlightenment, serves not only as evidence of God's Word's transformative capacity but also as a source of hope for everyone maneuvering through the complexities of life.

**Key Points of the Chapter:**

1. **The Transformative Power of God's Word:** Spanning from the universe's vastness to our heart's innermost recesses, God's Word emerges as a beacon of light and truth. It shines on our darkest trails, guiding us towards renewal and purpose. My voyage from Chad to Pennsylvania, laden with uncertainty and the challenge of adaptation, was underpinned by this enduring truth. It was by embracing God's Word's radiance that I discovered clarity, strength, and direction.

2. **Embracing and Reflecting God's Light:** To walk in God's Word's light is an active endeavor that goes beyond mere recognition. It entails a deep engagement with His teachings and embodying His love in our every deed. By embodying principles of kindness, integrity, and intentionality, we not only draw closer to God but also act as channels of His light to others. Sharing the Gospel and manifesting God's love through tangible acts of kindness are vital in reflecting His light in a realm often veiled in spiritual darkness.

3. **Resisting Spiritual Darkness:** In a world that frequently contests our faith and principles, it is critical to stand firm against temptation and spiritual obscurity. Through prayer, the support of our faith community, and clinging to the promises in Scripture, we can bolster our spiritual resilience and navigate life's hurdles with steadfast faith.

4. **The Ongoing Journey of Faith:** The path of embracing God's truth and living in His light is not a momentary act but a continual journey of growth and metamorphosis. It involves everyday decisions to delve into Scripture, radiate God's light through kindness, and share the Gospel's hope with those we encounter.

## ENCOURAGEMENT FOR THE JOURNEY AHEAD:

As we proceed, let's renew our dedication to living daily under God's Word's luminance. Let's wholeheartedly embrace the hope and transformation it brings, earnestly striving to comprehend and apply its truths in all life facets. This faith journey is replete with opportunities for personal development, learning, and forging a deeper bond with our Creator.

I urge you, dear reader, to take practical steps towards living in this divine illumination. Whether through daily Scripture engagement, acts of kindness, or sharing your faith narrative, each action is a stride towards embodying God's love and truth. Let us walk together, inspired by the light's promise and the potential for transformation each new day holds.

As we continue exploring creation, stewardship, and faith themes throughout this book, may we always be conscious of God's Word's incredible capacity to enlighten our paths, transform our hearts, and steer us towards a purposeful and fulfilling life. May we live every day in the light, embarking on the faith journey with courage, joy, and unwavering trust in the One who beckons us to follow His ways.

# PART II
# CLARITY AND DIVISION

# CHAPTER 2

# BEYOND THE DIVIDE: EMBRACING THE SKY OF CLARITY

Chapter 1 led us on an exploration of creation's first light, demonstrating God's Word as a beacon of transformation. It highlighted how God's command brought forth light, piercing through darkness, similarly, His Word shines upon our paths today. This enlightenment transcends the physical, imparting spiritual clarity, direction, and hope amidst our uncertainties.

As we delve into Chapter 2, our gaze shifts from the inception of light to the creation of the sky—a divine intervention that cleaved the waters above from those below. This act on creation's second day bears deep symbolic weight, reflecting our life's moments of division and the ensuing quest for clarity.

My narrative, transitioning from Chad to Pennsylvania, resonates with this theme of divine separation. Immersed in a new country's hustle, I grappled with my 'waters' of conflict—caught between past dreams and present uncertainties. This inner turmoil mirrored the biblical partition of waters, stirring a deep yearning for direction and clear sight.

In my quest, I sought solace in prayer and meditation, looking to a higher power for navigation. This spiritual odyssey echoed the divine separation of the second day of creation, bringing forth not conflict, but clarity—differentiating doubt from faith, fear from hope.

Through this phase of introspection and spiritual seeking, a path gradually unfurled before me. The expansive sky, once a mere backdrop to my dilemmas, transformed into a symbol of limitless potential and liberation. It illustrated that amid life's choppy waters, there lies the promise of serenity and clarity.

Day by day, transformation ensued—confusion gave way to clarity, and uncertainty was replaced by a revitalized purpose. The sky, constant amidst life's flux, stood as a testament to divine guidance, affirming that even the most stormy waters can part to unveil the sky's clarity.

Emerging from this period of change, I was fortified with stronger faith and a crystallized sense of purpose. As God's division of the waters revealed the sky, He navigated me through my doubts and fears, leading me to embrace the vast opportunities that awaited.

Thus, Chapter 2: **Beyond the Divide: Embracing the Sky of Clarity**, unfolds as a personal odyssey towards finding clarity within division, shepherded by the divine architect of both the cosmos and our life's paths. It stands as a homage to the unyielding strength of faith and the assurance of guidance for those who seek clarity amid life's separations.

## THE SOVEREIGN CREATOR'S TAPESTRY

### CRAFTING THE FIRMAMENT

In the unfolding saga of creation, the divine act of parting the waters to reveal the sky marks a pivotal demonstration of God's omnipotence and artistic flair. This creation of the firmament—a limitless vault painted with divine finesse—stands as a tribute to the Creator's command over chaos and cosmos alike. Observing the endless sky above, pristine and tranquil, I found my own life's hurdles cast into sharper relief, gleaning insights about boundaries and the equilibrium essential for growth.

The sky, serving as a demarcation between day and night, paralleled the divisions I faced upon my arrival in Pennsylvania. Initially perceived as formidable divides—spanning past to future, the known to the unknown—these separations, through divine lens, transform into conduits for personal evolution and understanding. In the genesis narrative, God's partitioning act not only sculpts the physical expanse but also symbolizes the significance of delineating spaces in our lives—spaces that safeguard, nurture, and cultivate balance.

The firmament, summoned into being by God's word, cleaves the upper waters from the lower, crafting not merely a physical but a metaphorical boundary. This demarcation underscores the essence of setting limits that shield our well-being, fostering an environment where harmony can burgeon and our souls can align with God's vision for us.

Furthermore, the establishment of the sky underscores a divine blueprint for equilibrium in the cosmos. It nudges us to mirror such balance in our existence—balancing toil with rest, generosity with receiving, expression with reception. As the firmament seamlessly integrates within creation's tapestry, maintaining harmony amidst separation, we too are beckoned to find coherence within life's divisions and adversities. This concord paves the way for our growth, enlightenment, and the fulfillment of our God-given potential.

Each hurdle, each division encountered, reminded me through the majesty of the sky—a testament to God's grandeur—that within every challenge lies the seed for growth and equilibrium. It reinforced that boundaries aren't barricades but avenues to stability, and in the sprawling canvas of our existence, we're gifted the chance to craft our narrative in hues of faith, hope, and love.

Hence, let's heed the firmament's teachings. Let's cultivate healthy limits, strive for balance in every facet of life, and perceive every separation as an opportunity to weave harmony both within ourselves and in our surroundings. By doing so, we pay homage to the Creator's masterpiece, discovering beauty and expansion in the intervals of our journey.

## GUIDING OUR LIVES: NAVIGATING WITH DIVINE PRECISION

Within the grand schema of creation, the firmament stands as more than a mere divider of waters; it emerges as a celestial beacon, guiding avian migrations across the sky in a harmonious ballet. This path, though invisible, is meticulously ordained, reflecting the unseen guidance of God that steered me through the labyrinth of uncertainties inherent in migration and the arduous path towards assimilation. For me, the expanse of the sky evolved from a simple physical domain into a profound emblem of the limitless prospects that beckon when one aligns with God's sovereign plan.

As I endeavored to adjust to a novel culture and surroundings, the firmament overhead remained a steadfast indicator of God's omnipresence and His unwavering direction. Analogous to birds that depend on unseen airflows for their voyage, I too learned to rely on the imperceptible force of God's wisdom to navigate the challenges of forging a new beginning in a foreign territory. It was through this yielding to His will that I unearthed the genuine liberation and elation that stem from entrusting one's journey to the Architect of the universe.

The sky, in its vast and unrestricted scope, symbolized the infinite opportunities God lays before us—opportunities for growth, enlightenment, and making impactful contributions in previously unimaginable ways. It served as a constant reassurance that amid moments of doubt or hesitation, God's guidance is as steadfast as the firmament's perpetual presence above. His designs for us are as boundless and profound as the sky itself, brimming with potential and hope for those brave enough to navigate by His compass.

This epiphany infused my odyssey with a profound sense of tranquility and intent. It fortified me with the courage to tackle the obstacles of acclimatization with optimism and tenacity, secure in the knowledge that God's navigation is flawless and His intentions for me are benevolent. The sky became an everyday prompt to elevate my gaze beyond the immediate, to perceive the grandeur of God's blueprint for my existence.

In our intervals of flux and indecision, let the firmament's lesson resonate within us. Let us entrust our course to the invisible yet unerring hands of God, akin to the birds that glide on faith in the air currents that uplift them. May we open our spirits to the vast possibilities that unfurl with reliance on His divine will. As we charter the skies of our own life stories, may we proceed with the conviction that God's direction ever accompanies us, propelling us to realms beyond our imagination.

## THE DIVINE COMMAND: A REFLECTION OF ORDER PATHWAYS THE UNVEILED

In the grand narrative of creation, God's command to divide the waters is a powerful demonstration of His supreme authority and the intrinsic order within the universe. This divine instruction, which cleaved the waters and set the firmament in place, echoes through our lives in those pivotal moments when we stand at the crossroads of crucial decisions—times when we must choose faith over fear and hope over despair.

As I ventured into the newness of life in Pennsylvania, I encountered several such crossroads, each demanding a leap of faith. The waters of uncertainty loomed large and menacing, ready to engulf me in a sea of doubts. Yet, in these critical junctures, the memory of God's command to part the waters became a beacon of strength. In echoing His command, I learned the profound strength found in obedience, in heeding God's call, even when the way forward was shrouded in mist.

Embracing the divide with faith as my guide, I understood that walking in God's will doesn't shield us from the storm's assault. However, it offers something infinitely more valuable—the assurance of God's presence, shepherding us through the tempest. Much like the Israelites at the Red Sea's brink, I realized that God's intervention in parting the waters of our lives is an invitation into a journey laden with trust and transformation.

The parted waters stand not merely as a symbol of division but as a pathway carved by divine intent, drawing us nearer to our purpose and deepening our faith. This path beckons us to surrender control, to place our trust in God's grand design, and to proceed with the conviction that He is ever by our side, invisibly steering us through every adversity and doubt.

In each decisive moment, with every step taken in faith rather than fear, the concept of the parted waters evolved into a metaphor for the boundless opportunities that emerge from entrusting ourselves to God's sovereign will. They served as a reminder that amidst life's tumultuous seas, there exists a divine order, a marked path forged by God's decree, leading us toward growth, fulfillment, and serenity.

Therefore, let us draw inspiration from the divine command that parts the waters in our journey. Let us face life's crossroads with faith as our guiding star, relying on the Creator's unerring navigation and provision. For in heeding His call, we embark on the sacred path He has charted for us, discovering strength, bravery, and hope on the pilgrimage of faith.


## CRAFTING CLARITY FROM CHAOS

Navigating the transition from the well-trodden paths of Chad to the unknown terrains of Pennsylvania encapsulated a turmoil reminiscent of the tumultuous waters depicted on creation's second day. This significant upheaval unfurled a sea of challenges, often feeling like an overwhelming deluge of uncertainty and fear. Amidst life's churning waters, I sought a beacon of peace and purpose, only to find myself adrift in the tempest of change. Yet, it was within this maelstrom of transition that a profound realization dawned upon me: chaos harbors the seeds of clarity, offering a rare opportunity to forge serenity from the storm.

Prayer and meditation became my sanctuary, my personal firmament delineating the roiling waters of my circumstances from the serene expanse of spiritual peace. These practices transformed into essential lifelines, tethering me to a force mightier than the surrounding upheaval. In moments of prayer or reflection on God's Word, I transcended the tumult, adopting a vantage point bathed in faith.

Mirroring the divine act that cleaved the chaotic waters, my spiritual disciplines echoed the Creator's command, instilling a partition between turmoil and tranquility within my life. This daily enactment of separation served as a reminder of God's omnipotence over our most disordered moments. Just as He commanded the waters to part, introducing order to creation, He was equally poised to infuse my life with clarity and direction. My prayers and meditative pursuits became the conduits for divine calm, where the whispers of God quieted the internal tempests and charted a course towards clearer horizons.

The evolution from chaos to clarity was not a swift transformation but a pilgrimage. Each prayer whispered, each scripture pondered, marked a stride upon the waters, affirming the faith that buoyed me. These acts of devotion did more than merely divide the turbulent from the tranquil; they reshaped the chaos into a divine canvas, upon which God's grace delineated vistas of clarity and purpose.

Through the lens of prayer and meditation, I gleaned an invaluable insight: the chaos that besieges us is not a chasm but a corridor. Within the stormy seas of our existence, God meticulously sculpts clarity, utilizing our trials as the canvas for His most exquisite designs. As we submit to His sovereign will, entrusting Him to segregate the tumultuous from the tranquil, we uncover the expansive skies of His intent for our lives.

Therefore, let us confront our chaos with unwavering faith, assured that our prayers and meditations erect the firmament in our spiritual skies. Allow them to serve as the divine demarcation, leading us to the solace of God's embrace, where chaos is masterfully molded into clarity, and our paths are illuminated by the endless skies of His immutable love and guidance.

## EMBRACING THE SKY'S PROMISE

### THE SKY AS A CANVAS OF HOPE

In the nascent stages of adapting to life in Pennsylvania, there were moments when hope seemed as elusive as the horizon's furthest reach. Amidst those phases, when the heaviness of my new reality obscured my view with veils of doubt, I discovered solace and a profound sense of perspective simply by gazing upward. The sky, sprawling endlessly from one corner of the earth to another, morphed into a canvas of hope, meticulously painted by the Creator's hands.

This vast dome, with its kaleidoscope of colors and boundless scope, whispered of God's limitless grace and grandeur. It served as a reminder that the same Divine Architect who orchestrated the waters' separation to unfurl this majestic canopy also weaves beauty and clarity from the fabric of our life's complexities and uncertainties. Every dawn that stretched across this canvas was a celestial ode, heralding new beginnings and the steadfast companionship of the Creator through each day's trials.

On days enshrouded in clouds of despair and trepidation, the unexpected clearing of skies to unveil the azure beyond stood as a potent metaphor for the clarity God introduces into our obscured lives. Each rift in the clouds seemed to echo God's gentle assurance, signaling that beyond the immediate storms of life, His grace suffices, His plans are intentional, and His presence is unending. The expanse of the sky reminded me of our Creator's infinite ability to bless and guide, transcending the limitations of our immediate troubles and perceptions.

Furthermore, the nocturnal sky, adorned with the glow of stars and the moon's radiance, became a beacon of hope amid darkness, showcasing the splendor that emerges from the gloomiest moments. Every starlight served as a testament to enduring light in darkness, symbols of an unwavering hope that persists even through the deepest night. They stood as celestial affirmations of God's promises—constant and steadfast.

To embrace the sky's promise was to acknowledge my narrative as a thread in a grander tapestry woven by God, where each division serves a purpose, and every cloud of doubt is but transient. It taught me to look beyond the immediate, to anchor hope in the assurance of God's faithfulness, and to lean on the clarity born of His divine guidance.

As we navigate our own seasons of division and ambiguity, let us too turn our gazes skyward, seeing in it a canvas of hope. May it remind us of God's infinite grace, His prowess in sculpting beauty from our life's separations, and His promise of clarity through the clouds. In the sky's vast embrace, we find a visual testament to God's omnipotence and an invitation to elevate our sights above our circumstances, welcoming the hope He offers to each of us.


## SOARING BEYOND LIMITS

The journey of faith is akin to the flight of an eagle, soaring high above the land, transcending the limits of the earth with grace and majesty. In my own life, the act of embracing faith has propelled me into realms beyond my imagination, into spaces once thought unreachable. This lesson became profoundly clear as I navigated the complexities of a new life in Pennsylvania, faced with barriers that seemed insurmountable and challenges that tested my resolve.

The creatures of the air do not doubt their ability to ascend; they simply spread their wings and allow the wind to carry them towards the heavens. Similarly, I learned that faith is not merely a belief in one's ability to overcome but a surrender to a higher power, a trust in the grand design orchestrated by the Creator. With each step taken in faith, each obstacle faced with the assurance of God's presence, I found myself soaring beyond the limits that fear and doubt had placed before me.

This soaring is not without its turbulence; the journey of faith is marked by moments of uncertainty and trials that threaten to pull us back to the ground. Yet, it is in these very moments that the true strength found in surrendering to God's will becomes evident. Just as the eagle uses the resistance of the wind to lift itself higher, I learned to use the challenges I faced as stepping stones, elevating my faith and drawing me closer to the divine.

The sky, with its endless expanse and boundless freedom, became a canvas of hope for me, a visual testament to God's limitless grace and mercy. It served as a reminder that no division is too great, no cloud of uncertainty too thick, that God cannot craft beauty and clarity from. The promise of the sky is not just the assurance of clear days ahead but the realization that, with God, we are capable of reaching heights previously deemed unattainable.

Embracing the freedom found in faith allowed me to navigate the divisions within my soul and the uncertainties of a new beginning. It taught me that the limits we perceive are often self-imposed, barriers that can be transcended through trust in God's grand design. As we learn to spread our wings of faith, we discover that the sky is not the limit but the beginning, a realm of endless possibilities where we are free to soar beyond our fears, doubts, and limitations.

Let us, therefore, embrace the sky's promise with open hearts, allowing the strength found in surrendering to God's will to propel us into the boundless expanse of His grace. May we soar on the wings of faith, transcending the limits of our circumstances, and find freedom in the vast canvas of hope that God paints for us each day.

## THE TRANSFORMATION UNVEILED

### CLARITY AMIDST DIVISION

In life's challenging tapestry, moments of division often obscure our path with doubt, hiding the clarity and purpose we seek. My journey, transitioning from the familiar grounds of Chad to the unfamiliar terrains of Pennsylvania, mirrored the biblical separation of waters—a divine boundary that, though initially daunting, eventually revealed a clearer sky and a unified soul. This transformation was not just a physical change but a deep spiritual awakening, urging me to overcome the internal divisions that disrupted my peace.

The act of divine separation, described on the second day of creation, represents more than the physical parting of waters; it symbolizes the spiritual split between doubt and faith, fear and hope. As God commanded the waters to part, revealing the sky's vastness, I too navigated the turbulent waters of uncertainty. With faith as my guide, I parted the seas of apprehension and emerged with a vision purified by divine light. This journey from doubt to clarity unfolded through moments of quiet reflection, prayer, and steadfast trust in God's plan for my life.

The inner turmoil—conflicting desires, aspirations, and fears—reflected the chaos before the world's creation. Yet, amid this chaos, I discovered a call to unity, a divine invitation to blend the discordant parts of myself into a symphony of faith. This was a call to transcend my fragmented self, to integrate the diverse threads of my identity into a cohesive whole, enriched with divine purpose and grace. This transformation was about finding unity in faith, aligning my will with God's, and embracing a purpose that surpasses personal ambitions to support a higher calling.

Embracing this journey meant surrendering to divine will, recognizing that true clarity and purpose are not found in the absence of division but in the victorious rise above it. As the sky extends boundlessly above the earth, providing a canvas for the sun's morning and evening colors, I learned that my life is also a canvas for God to illustrate His divine narrative. Each challenge and triumph, each joy and sorrow, adds to the masterpiece He intends to reveal.

This transformation is a testament to the power of faith in bringing clarity amidst division. It reminds us that within every challenge lies growth, within every division, a chance for unity, and within every moment of doubt, a call to ascend to the clarity of the sky. As we navigate our life's waters, let us cling to the promise of transformation, trust in God's plan, and let His divine separation guide us to unity, purpose, and clarity.

Let this journey serve as a beacon of hope for all navigating the waters of uncertainty, demonstrating the transformative power of faith to uncover clarity amidst division. May we all find the courage to overcome our internal divisions, embrace the unity and purpose woven into God's grand design, and follow the light of His clarity, guided by the sky's limitless expanse.

## THE SKY'S ENDLESS HORIZON

As I navigated through the tumultuous early days in Pennsylvania, the sky overhead remained constant, a vast expanse stretching far beyond the limits of my vision. It became a profound symbol of the endless possibilities available to those who trust in the divine tapestry woven by the Creator. This endless horizon, with its promise of hope and renewal, encouraged me to look beyond the immediate divisions and uncertainties that clouded my path, urging me to move forward with faith, determination, and an open heart to the grace that orchestrates the universe.

The concept of an endless horizon reflects the boundless nature of God's love and the infinite possibilities He offers to those who seek Him amidst life's challenges. Just as the sky knows no bounds, so too does God's capacity to transform, heal, and lead us to paths of unimagined potential. This realization came to me as I stood, a newcomer in a foreign land, gazing at the vast canvas of the sky, where the interplay of light and clouds painted pictures of divine artistry. It was a visual testament to the fact that beyond every cloud of doubt and every rain of challenge, lies the horizon of hope—a clear sky painted with the promise of new beginnings.

This horizon of hope is not just a distant dream but a tangible reality waiting to be embraced through faith, determination, and the grace that flows freely from our Creator. It taught me that the divisions we face, the barriers that seem insurmountable, are merely veils that temporarily obscure our view of the divine horizon. With each step taken in faith, with each act of determination fueled by trust in God's plan, these veils are lifted, revealing the expansive beauty of God's promises.

The endless horizon also symbolizes the journey of faith itself—a pilgrimage marked not by a final destination but by continual growth, discovery, and transformation under the guidance of the Creator. It invites us to venture beyond the familiar, to explore the depths of our being and the heights of our potential, all while anchored in the knowledge that we are held within the boundless embrace of God's love.

In my journey, the sky's endless horizon became a source of strength and inspiration, a daily reminder that God's possibilities are limitless, and His plans for us are filled with hope and promise. As we embrace this horizon, we find the courage to transcend the divisions that hold us back, to soar on wings of faith toward the destiny that God has prepared for us.

Let this endless horizon inspire us all to move forward with faith and determination, to explore the vastness of God's love and the infinite possibilities it holds. May we trust in the grace of the Creator, allowing it to guide us through the divisions and uncertainties of life, and lead us to the horizon of hope that awaits each one of us. In the embrace of this divine horizon, may we discover the true depth of our potential and the unbounded beauty of a life lived in harmony with God's will.

## CONCLUSION: A NEW DAWN OF POSSIBILITY

As we conclude this chapter, we find ourselves on the brink of a new dawn, gazing upon the expansive sky of clarity that unfolds endlessly before us. This celestial canvas, adorned with the divine hues of sunrise and sunset, serves as a poignant reminder of the Creator's omnipresence and His steadfast promises. It encourages us to view our divisions not as insurmountable barriers but as unique opportunities for personal growth and deeper insight. Within the grand expanse that envelops our world, we are inspired to navigate the tumultuous waters of our existence, guided by the compass of faith and anchored by the hope of new beginnings.

The sky, in its infinite glory, calls us to lift our eyes and hearts upward, transcending the temporary challenges and fears that hold us down. It compels us to spread our wings, embracing the freedom and potential that await us within God's grand design. As we traverse the tapestry of life, let us carry the light of faith—a beacon that guides us through the darkest nights and the stormiest seas.

This new dawn of possibility heralds a journey of transformation, a path lit by divine light that dispels the deepest shadows. It is a call to action, a summons to step into the unknown with confidence and trust in the One who holds the universe in His hands. The ever-expansive and beautiful sky above reminds us of the Creator's infinite love and the endless possibilities that come with communion with Him.

As we turn the pages of our lives, let us cherish each day as a gift, a sacred chance to draw closer to our Creator and to the essence of who we are meant to be. Let us move forward, with hearts lifted to the heavens, eager to explore the unfolding chapters of our divine transformation. In the clarity of the sky, may we find the strength to bridge our divisions, the wisdom to seek understanding, and the courage to step into the dawn of new possibilities.

In this journey of faith and transformation, let us always remember that we are never alone. The same God who parted the waters and revealed the sky watches over us with loving care, guiding us through every trial and rejoicing with us in every victory. Let us advance with renewed hope and steadfast faith, excited to embrace the wonders that lie ahead in the divine narrative of our lives.

May this new dawn of possibility ignite within us a fire of inspiration and a determination to pursue our God-given destiny with passion and purpose. Together, under the vast sky of clarity, let us journey onward, hand in hand with our Creator, into the horizon of endless potential and divine promise.

## THE WATERS GATHERED

As we linger under the vast expanse of the sky, our journey through the tapestry of creation takes a pivotal turn. The sky, now a canvas of clarity and a vault of divine inspiration, serves as a bridge to the next chapter of our spiritual exploration. As we bid farewell to the boundless firmament, our gaze shifts to the waters below, the next frontier in our quest for deeper understanding and connection with the Creator. These waters, summoned by the Almighty's command, beckon us to delve into their mysteries, to unearth the treasures hidden in their depths.

The third day of creation brings us to the edge of the gathered seas, inviting us to contemplate the significance of water in the divine narrative and its role in shaping the contours of our faith. Here, at the water's edge, we stand poised to explore themes of purification, renewal, and life-giving sustenance—themes that resonate deeply with the human experience and our longing for spiritual refreshment.

As we prepare to embark on this new chapter, let us carry with us the lessons learned under the sky of clarity. Let the courage and insights gained from navigating the divisions of our inner and outer worlds guide us as we venture into the depths. The waters gathered by the Creator's hand hold the promise of new revelations, offering us a mirror to reflect on our own lives and the flow of grace that sustains us.

In this next phase of our journey, we are invited to immerse ourselves in the waters of reflection, to let the currents of divine wisdom carry us toward greater understanding and closer communion with God. Together, with hearts open and spirits attuned to the Creator's voice, let us dive into the rich symbolism of the gathered waters. Here, in the embrace of the deep, we will discover the power of God's word to transform and renew, just as it gathered the seas and brought forth life in abundance.

As the narrative unfolds, may we find ourselves drawn ever deeper into the heart of the divine mystery, where every droplet of water tells a story of creation, redemption, and the boundless love of the Creator. Let us journey onward, with anticipation and faith, ready to plunge into the depths where new insights and inspirations await in the gathered waters of God's magnificent creation.

# PART III
# THE EMERGENCE OF LIFE

# CHAPTER 3

# FERTILE BEGINNINGS: THE EMERGENCE OF LAND, SEAS, AND VEGETATION

In Chapter 2, "Beyond the Divide: Embracing the Sky of Clarity," we explored the profound significance of the second day of creation, when God's act of separating the waters above from the waters below unveiled the sky. This chapter mirrored my own journey of seeking clarity amidst life's divisions, finding parallels between the physical divide in the heavens and the internal divides within my own spirit. Through introspection and faith, I found guidance and clarity, much like the sky serves as a canvas upon which the light of dawn breaks, signaling hope and new beginnings.

Once upon a time, amidst the hustle and bustle of a city far from the comforting landscapes of home, I grappled with the daunting task of adapting to an entirely new world. The unfamiliar sight of towering skyscrapers and crowded streets left me yearning for the solace of familiar terrain. Amid this whirlwind of change, I sought refuge in the eternal wisdom of scripture, which offered a beacon of hope and stability.

On the third day of my spiritual journey, as I pored over the verses of Genesis, I was struck by the majestic account of God's creation of the land, seas, and vegetation. This act of divine creation mirrored my own desires for grounding and belonging in a world of chaos. As God commanded the waters to recede and the dry land to emerge, I felt an awakening within my soul—a clear reminder that amidst life's uncertainties, God was meticulously shaping my destiny.

Delving deeper into the events of the third day of creation, I encountered a profound realization: God's omnipotence knows no bounds, capable of fostering life and prosperity out of sheer tumult. This insight propelled me onto a path of faith and self-exploration, anchored in the belief that God's promises are unwavering, even in the face of adversity.

With every passing day, as I delved into the scriptures and embraced the principles of God's word, I experienced a transformation within. The emergence of life from the earth, as ordained by God, mirrored the emergence of hope and purpose within me. Drawing strength from the essence of the third day of creation, I confronted each challenge with newfound courage and resolve, buoyed by the assurance of God's enduring love and support.

Ultimately, it was the transcendent truth of God's word—revealed through the miracle of land, seas, and vegetation—that ushered me into triumph. My journey, fortified by faith, prayer, and an unwavering trust in God's edicts, proved that even in the bleakest moments, His guiding light prevails, ushering us towards a horizon brimming with hope and boundless potential.

As we embark on this chapter, let us immerse ourselves in the lessons of the third day of creation, drawing inspiration from the divine orchestration of life and nature. Through this exploration, we are reminded of our own potential for growth and renewal, guided by the steadfast promise of God's omnipresent light.

# DIVINE MASTERY: GOD'S CREATIVE POWER IN SHAPING THE EARTH

## CRAFTING THE EARTH: THE DIVINE ARCHITECT AT WORK

In the grand tapestry of creation, the third day stands out as a testament to God's unmatched sovereignty and meticulous intentionality. On this day, He commanded the waters to part, unveiling the dry land and summoning an abundance of vegetation to clothe the earth in verdant splendor. This divine act is more than a historical account; it's a vivid illustration of God's power to impose order on chaos, to carve beauty and purpose out of the formless void.

As I found myself adrift in the uncharted waters of a new city, far from the familiar landscapes of Chad, this lesson of divine mastery became my anchor. The upheaval of relocation, much like the chaotic waters before God's intervention, seemed insurmountable. Yet, the story of the earth's emergence served as a powerful reminder that within every moment of disorder lies the potential for creation and renewal. Just as God sculpted the earth and clothed it in greenery, I believed He was at work in my life, shaping my path and nurturing new beginnings from the turmoil.

This understanding of God as the Divine Architect, who brings forth order and purpose from chaos, resonated deeply within me. It offered a fresh perspective on my challenges, transforming them from insurmountable obstacles into opportunities for growth and discovery. Every difficulty became a canvas for God's creative power, each day a chance to witness His intentionality unfold in my journey.

Moreover, this revelation underscored the importance of faith and trust in God's sovereign plan. Just as the earth did not resist the parting of the waters or the calling forth of vegetation, I learned to surrender to God's will, embracing the changes and upheavals with a heart open to His guidance. In doing so, I found peace amidst uncertainty and purpose amidst wandering.

The act of crafting the earth is a profound demonstration of God's desire for order, beauty, and life to thrive amidst the void. It reassures us of His omnipotence and loving intentionality in every aspect of creation, including our lives. As I navigated the complexities of a new environment, the lessons of the third day of creation became a source of strength and inspiration, teaching me that with God, every upheaval is an opportunity for growth and every chaos a potential masterpiece waiting to be revealed.

## EMBRACING CHANGE: A DIVINE INVITATION TO GROW

In the grand tapestry of creation, the emergence of dry land and the birth of vegetation from the previously formless and void earth serve as profound metaphors for the transformative power of change in our lives. Inspired by this divine act, I began to perceive change not merely as a harbinger of upheaval but as a sacred call to growth and expansion. This shift in perspective was born from the realization that, just as seeds are sown into the nurturing embrace of the earth, each new challenge and unfamiliar circumstance I encountered was an opportunity to root myself more deeply in faith.

The act of creation is God's testament to the potential that lies within change. It is a divine assurance that from the depths of chaos and the unknown, life and abundance can emerge. As I navigated the complexities of a new environment, the analogy of seeds taking root became a personal emblem of resilience. Each seed, encapsulating potential, must undergo transformation beneath the soil, away from the light, to eventually break through the surface and reach towards the sun. Similarly, I recognized that the trials I faced were not merely obstacles but fertile ground for spiritual growth and renewal.

The divine orchestration of change in the natural world, where seasons cycle and landscapes evolve, mirrors the dynamic journey of faith. It is a process marked by periods of preparation, growth, blossoming, and, eventually, harvest. Embracing this cycle of change encouraged me to lean into each transition, however daunting, with the assurance that God's providential care is constant, guiding me towards my purpose.

Moreover, this perspective fostered a sense of expectancy and hope. Just as the earth responds to the Creator's command to bring forth vegetation, I learned to anticipate the fruits of faithfulness and perseverance. Change, therefore, became a canvas upon which my faith could paint strokes of trust, patience, and resilience, yielding a landscape rich with the verdant hues of spiritual maturity.

In embracing change as a divine invitation to grow, I discovered the strength to rise above the soil of uncertainty, reaching towards the light of God's presence. Each challenge became a testament to His sovereign ability to bring beauty from ashes and strength from vulnerability. This journey through change, inspired by the divine act of creation, has been an odyssey of becoming—of evolving into a person of deeper faith, rooted in the knowledge that in God's hands, every change holds the promise of new life and endless possibility.

## DIVINE HARMONY: THE SYMPHONY OF CREATION

## INTERCONNECTEDNESS OF LIFE

In the orchestration of creation, where land, seas, and vegetation exist in a delicate balance, there lies a profound message for humanity. This divinely crafted harmony speaks to the interconnectedness of all things and the importance of equilibrium in sustaining life. As I navigated the complexities of a new life far from the landscapes of Chad, I found myself in a dance of adaptation, striving to find a balance between the rich heritage of my past and the unknowns of my present.

This journey of finding balance became a reflection of the divine harmony evident in creation. Just as the land provides a foundation for trees and plants, and the seas offer a home to countless forms of life, I learned to anchor myself in the values and memories of my homeland while embracing the opportunities and challenges of my new environment. This process of integration was akin to the symbiotic relationship between the elements of nature, where each contributes to the health and well-being of the whole.

The beauty of living in a balanced and purposeful symphony with the world around me became increasingly clear. It was not about forsaking one aspect of my identity for another but rather weaving them together into a cohesive tapestry that honored both my origins and my current journey. This realization mirrored the way in which the natural world thrives on diversity and balance, with every species playing a critical role in maintaining the ecosystem's harmony.

Learning to live in harmony with God's creation also meant recognizing the sacredness of the natural world and our responsibility towards it. Just as we are called to find balance in our personal lives, we are also entrusted with the task of preserving the balance of the Earth. This dual process of internal and external harmony became a guiding principle, teaching me the importance of living with intentionality and respect for all of creation.

In embracing this balance, I discovered a deeper sense of peace and purpose. The interplay of elements in creation, from the stability of the earth to the fluidity of the seas and the growth of vegetation, served as a metaphor for my own journey of integration. It underscored the possibility of creating a harmonious life that honors both where we come from and where we are going, rooted in the divine intentionality that governs the universe.

As my story unfolded against the backdrop of a new chapter, the lessons of balance and harmony in creation illuminated my path. They taught me that in every division and every convergence, there lies an opportunity for growth, connection, and the creation of something beautiful and whole. This symphony of creation, with its intricate melodies and rhythms, became a source of inspiration and a reminder of the divine harmony that is possible when we align ourselves with God's grand design.

## Divine Provision: Trusting in God's Sustenance

### GOD'S ABUNDANCE: A TESTAMENT TO FAITH

In the unfolding of creation, the third day brought forth an explosion of life from the earth, a vivid display of God's unfathomable abundance. Vegetation covered the land, not just as a mere act of creation, but as a declaration of God's provision for every living thing. This divine abundance, mirroring the fecundity of the earth, became a powerful reminder of God's steadfast provision in my own life's journey.

From the rich tapestry of the Chad landscapes to the concrete jungles of Pennsylvania, my transition was marked by moments of both scarcity and plenty. Yet, in every circumstance, I witnessed the hand of God moving, providing for me in ways that were often unexpected but always sufficient. The seeds of faith planted in the fertile soil of God's promises grew into a steadfast trust in His provision. Just as the earth yields its harvest in due season, I learned that God's timing is perfect, His resources are boundless, and His willingness to provide is unwavering.

This realization encouraged me to adopt a posture of gratitude and stewardship. Gratitude, for understanding that every breath, every meal, every opportunity was a gift from above. And stewardship, for recognizing that these gifts were not only for my benefit but also to be shared with others. The abundance in my life was a call to extend God's provision to those around me, to be a conduit of His love and generosity.

In moments of scarcity, where the path ahead seemed barren and devoid of life, the memory of the earth's abundance under God's command was a beacon of hope. It taught me to look beyond the immediate challenges and to trust in God's ability to provide, just as He clothes the lilies of the field and feeds the birds of the air. This trust was not passive but active, pushing me to seek out God's purpose in every situation and to align my actions with His will.

As I navigated through the complexities of adapting to a new world, the concept of God's abundance transcended material needs. It encompassed emotional and spiritual sustenance, offering peace in turmoil, strength in weakness, and companionship in loneliness. The knowledge that God's provision is holistic and all-encompassing brought a deeper level of contentment and security, grounding me in the truth that my needs are known and valued by the Creator.

The journey from scarcity to abundance, from uncertainty to trust, mirrors the transformation of the barren earth into a vibrant canvas of life. It is a testament to the power of God's word, a word that still speaks into the depths of our hearts, commanding light to shine out of darkness, and abundance to spring forth from desolation. As I continue on this path, the lessons of God's provision remain a cornerstone of my faith, reminding me to always trust in the divine Sustainer, whose generosity knows no bounds.

## NOURISHING GROWTH: A JOURNEY OF TRANSFORMATION

The narrative of creation, particularly on the third day, when God commanded the earth to bring forth vegetation, serves as a profound metaphor for the spiritual and personal growth I experienced amidst the challenges of adapting to a new environment. This divine command, which transformed barren land into a lush landscape teeming with life, mirrored the transformative journey of my own faith. In the midst of uncertainty and change, embracing God's provision became the very source of nourishment that my spirit desperately sought, fostering resilience and strength within me.

Just as seeds require soil, water, and sunlight to grow, my faith needed the nourishment of God's word, prayer, and community. Each day became an opportunity to delve deeper into the scriptures, discovering the promises of God's unwavering provision and care. In prayer, I laid bare my needs and fears, and in the fellowship of believers, I found the encouragement and support that watered the seeds of faith planted in my heart. This spiritual nourishment led to a flourishing of my inner being, much like the vegetation that covers the earth in an array of colors and life.

The realization that God's provision encompasses more than just material needs but extends to our growth and development was transformative. I learned that God delights in our growth, both spiritually and personally, and He provides the conditions necessary for such growth to occur. This understanding shifted my perspective, teaching me to see every challenge as fertile ground for growth. The once daunting tasks of adapting to a new culture, learning a new language, and establishing a new life were now seen as opportunities to deepen my reliance on God and to witness His provision in action.

As I navigated through this period of growth, I was reminded of the lands in scripture that, once barren, bloomed with life through God's command. It became clear that with God, even the most barren landscapes of our lives can bloom into something beautiful and fruitful. This assurance fueled my courage to embrace change, to step into the unknown, and to trust in the provision of the One who commands the earth to yield its harvest.

This journey of nourishing growth taught me invaluable lessons about God's character: He is a provider, a sustainer, and a gardener who delights in seeing His children grow and thrive. It underscored the importance of remaining rooted in Him, the source of all life and growth. As my faith took root and stretched upwards, reaching for the Son, I witnessed a personal transformation that mirrored the splendor of creation itself.

In reflection, the path of spiritual and personal growth is ongoing, a journey marked by seasons of planting, watering, pruning, and harvesting. Each step, each season, is underpinned by the trust in God's provision. This journey, nourished by God's unfailing love and faithfulness, continues to teach me that with Him, every barren landscape within our lives holds the potential for immense beauty and growth. It is a testament to the power of embracing God's provision, allowing His hands to mold and nourish us into flourishing creations, designed to reflect His glory and grace.

## DIVINE TRANSFORMATION: PERSONAL GROWTH THROUGH FAITH

### SPIRITUAL CULTIVATION: A JOURNEY OF HEART AND FAITH

In the unfolding narrative of creation, the third day presents a vivid illustration of transformation—barrenness giving way to flourishing life. This divine act of preparation and growth resonates deeply with my own journey of faith, particularly as I navigated the complexities of a new environment, surrounded by the starkness of urban life. Just as God meticulously prepared the earth, transforming it into fertile ground capable of supporting diverse forms of vegetation, so too was my heart tilled and readied to receive the seeds of faith that would eventually take root and alter my internal landscape.

This spiritual cultivation was not merely a passive process but an active engagement with God's word and His omnipresent spirit. Each encounter with scripture acted as a plow, breaking up the fallow ground of my heart, turning over fears, doubts, and uncertainties to reveal the rich soil beneath, ripe for sowing. In prayer, I watered these newly planted seeds, and in the presence of God, I found the sunlight needed for growth. The chaos of the city, with its unending concrete expanses, became the backdrop against which this inner transformation unfolded, a testament to the fact that faith can thrive even in the most unlikely places.

The growth process, much like that of the vegetation called forth on the third day, was gradual and required patience, trust, and surrender. There were periods of waiting, moments when it seemed as if the seeds within my heart would never sprout. Yet, in these times of stillness, God's presence was a constant reassurance, a gentle reminder that growth often occurs beneath the surface, unseen to the human eye but known to the Creator. This journey of spiritual cultivation taught me that transformation is as much about the preparation of the ground as it is about the eventual blooming. Each act of faith, each moment spent in God's word, served to enrich my spiritual soil, making it conducive to growth.

As my faith began to take root and stretch upwards, reaching for the divine, I witnessed a transformation within my inner landscape. The concrete and chaos that once seemed overwhelming were now interspersed with moments of grace and beauty, much like patches of greenery in a vast urban sprawl. This growth brought with it a new perspective, a way of seeing the world that was infused with hope, purpose, and a deep sense of belonging. It underscored the truth that, with God, even the most barren areas of our lives can be transformed into fertile ground, bursting with life and potential.

Spiritual cultivation, then, is an ongoing process, a journey that intertwines closely with the act of creation itself. It is a testament to the power of God's word to bring forth life where there was once emptiness, to transform the inner workings of our hearts just as surely as He called forth vegetation from the earth. This transformative process, nurtured by God's word and presence, enables us to thrive amidst any environment, to find strength and vitality in the face of challenges, and to bloom with the resilience and beauty that comes from a deep, abiding faith in the Creator.

## BEARING FRUIT: MANIFESTATIONS OF DIVINE WORK IN DAILY LIFE

In the grand narrative of creation, the third day stands as a poignant symbol of fruition and abundance, a testament to God's power to bring forth life in its myriad forms. This divine principle of growth and multiplication profoundly mirrors my journey of faith, particularly as I navigated the intricacies of adapting to a new life in a foreign land. Just as the earth, once barren, responded to God's command by producing vegetation of all kinds, so too did my life begin to reflect the fruitful outcomes of a heart surrendered to God's will and timing.

The process of bearing fruit was neither immediate nor effortless. It required a steadfast trust in God's timing, a patience cultivated through seasons of waiting and growth. Like a farmer who sows seeds and awaits the harvest, I learned to sow seeds of faith, kindness, and perseverance in the soil of my daily life, trusting in God's provision and care. This trust was not unfounded; in time, I witnessed the sprouting of these seeds in various aspects of my life, from my community engagements to my workplace, and even in my personal development.

In my community, the fruits of God's work within me became evident in the connections and relationships I built. Acts of service and kindness, once sown in faith, began to flourish, creating a network of support and fellowship that echoed the interdependent ecosystem of God's creation. These relationships, rooted in mutual care and understanding, stood as vibrant reminders of God's love manifesting in human connections.

At work, the principles of integrity, diligence, and cooperation I endeavored to live by bore fruit in the form of trust, respect, and opportunities for growth. Just as diverse vegetation adorns the earth with its beauty and utility, so too did my contributions begin to enrich my workplace, reflecting God's creativity and excellence.

In my personal endeavors, whether they were academic pursuits, creative projects, or spiritual goals, I saw the hand of God guiding and multiplying my efforts. This journey of bearing fruit was a vivid illustration of the principle Jesus spoke of in John 15:5 – that abiding in Him, the true vine, results in a life that is fruitful and fulfilling.

Bearing fruit, therefore, became a tangible expression of God's transformative work within me. Each act of kindness, each achievement, and every breakthrough served as a testament to the abundance that follows when we align ourselves with God's will and purpose. This abundance was not limited to material success but extended to the peace, joy, and love that filled my life, mirroring the lushness and variety of creation on the third day.

The journey of bearing fruit, fueled by trust in God's timing and provision, is a continuous cycle of growth, pruning, and harvest. It is a journey that reaffirms the truth that when we commit our ways to the Lord, He will indeed cause our endeavors to thrive, just as surely as He causes the earth to burgeon with life. As I reflect on the manifestation of God's work within me, I am reminded of the call to remain rooted in Him, to trust in His process, and to look forward to the abundant harvest that follows a season of faithful growth

## ACTION AND REFLECTION

As we ponder the meticulous craftsmanship behind the creation of land, seas, and vegetation, we are invited to mirror God's intentionality in nurturing our lives and communities. This chapter serves as a compelling call to action, urging us to engage in responsible stewardship of the earth, reflecting God's care and precision. It encourages us to diligently cultivate our faith, planting seeds of hope, love, and perseverance that will bear fruit in due season. By wholeheartedly trusting in God's provision, we learn to navigate life's challenges with confidence, assured of His unfailing support and guidance.

Let us embrace this invitation to actively participate in the divine rhythm of creation, fostering growth and harmony in every aspect of our existence. This commitment to action and reflection not only deepens our relationship with the Creator but also enriches our lives with purpose and fulfillment. May this chapter inspire us to cultivate a legacy of stewardship, faith, and trust that honors God and blesses those around us.

The story of land, seas, and vegetation on the third day of creation unfolds not merely as an account of the earth's formation but as a profound narrative of possibility, resilience, and divine provision. This chapter, rich with the imagery of burgeoning life and orchestrated balance, imparts to us invaluable lessons: the potential for growth in every crevice of life, the harmony that sustains the world, and the unwavering trust we must place in our Creator's hands. As we close this chapter, let it be with hearts filled with gratitude for the fertile beginnings granted to us and eyes open to the abundance that surrounds us, all under the watchful care and meticulous design of the Almighty.

Now, as we venture forward, our path leads us to the brilliance of the fourth day—when God set the sun, moon, and stars in the firmament of the heavens. This forthcoming chapter invites us into a realm of greater illumination, symbolizing not only the physical light that governs the day and the night but also the spiritual light that guides our steps and enlightens our understanding. Let us carry the lessons of growth, harmony, and trust into this new chapter, emboldened to explore how the Creator's luminous design in the heavens further deepens our faith, enriches our lives, and illuminates our paths. Join me as we step into the light of divine guidance, eager to uncover the boundless wisdom and grace that await us in the unfolding story of creation.

In crafting this chapter, my aim is to draw you deeper into the journey of faith, showing that, like the earth itself, our lives are canvases for God's creative touch. As we move forward, may we do so with hearts open to the transformative power of God's word, finding in His creation a blueprint for our own spiritual growth and renewal.

# CHAPTER 4

# CELESTIAL SYMPHONY: THE CRAFTING OF SUN, MOON, AND STARS

The previous chapter of our journey through "Divine Transformations" revealed the profound interplay of land, seas, and vegetation—a narrative that not only recounts the physical genesis of our world but also maps the contours of spiritual growth and divine provision. We discovered the resilience embedded in creation, a testament to the boundless generosity and meticulous care of our Creator, prompting us to reflect on our roles as stewards of such a magnificent inheritance. Just as the earth was transformed from a formless void into a vibrant habitat, we too are called to embrace transformation, trusting in the Creator's wisdom to guide us through life's tumultuous seas towards fertile shores.

As I embarked on a new chapter in my life, the uncertainties and challenges ahead seemed as vast and impenetrable as the darkness that blanketed the primordial earth. Amidst this uncertainty, I sought solace in scripture, immersing myself in the divine narrative of creation's fourth day—the day God set the sun, moon, and stars in the heavens to light the sky, mark time, and govern the day and night.

This celestial order, with its profound symbolism, offered me a beacon of hope and a reminder of God's omnipresence. The sun's unwavering light became a symbol of hope, guiding me through my doubts and fears, while the moon's serene luminescence reassured me of God's constant vigil, even in the darkest times. The stars, scattered across the vast canvas of the night, reminded me that my life's challenges and triumphs were part of a larger, divine tapestry, each moment intricately woven with purpose and grace.

Reflecting on the creation of these celestial bodies, I realized the depth of God's plans for us—plans that unfold in the fullness of time, governed by a rhythm and order that transcends our understanding. Each obstacle I faced was an opportunity for growth, a stepping stone towards realizing my potential within God's grand design. My meditation on this divine orchestration filled me with strength and purpose, empowering me to face life's adversities with renewed courage and to trust in the guiding light of God's providence.

Thus, the fourth day of creation became a cornerstone of my faith, a reminder that in God's universe, light always prevails over darkness, guiding us towards a destiny filled with hope, purpose, and divine promise.

In the grand narrative of Genesis, the fourth day marks a pivotal moment in the unfolding of creation. God's command brings forth the sun, moon, and stars, entities that do more than merely illuminate the heavens—they symbolize the order, beauty, and wisdom of the Creator's design. This chapter invites us to delve into the significance of these celestial bodies, exploring their role in the physical universe and their deeper spiritual implications for our lives.

As we journey through this chapter, let us keep our hearts open to the lessons of the fourth day of creation, allowing the light of God's celestial symphony to illuminate our paths and guide us towards a deeper understanding of our place within His wondrous creation.

## The Majesty of God's Celestial Creation

### ILLUMINATING THE PATH

In the majestic theater of the cosmos, the sun stands as the lead actor, its brilliant rays extending like the hands of God, reaching out to touch the hearts of those wandering in the shadows. Every morning, it rises without fail, painting the sky with hues of hope, whispering softly to us that after every night's darkness, there is light. This celestial giant, burning with fervent passion, mirrors the boundless love and mercy that God extends to us daily. Its radiant beams penetrate the deepest of shadows, illuminating paths once hidden, guiding lost souls back to the warmth of the divine embrace.

The cyclical journey of the sun, from dawn to dusk, serves as a potent reminder of God's eternal presence in our lives, a testament to His grand design and meticulous care for His creation. Its steadfastness reassures us of the constants in life amidst our temporal woes—the love of God, the promise of His provision, and the certainty of His guidance. As the sun nourishes the earth, bringing life to dormant seeds, so does God's word awaken the slumbering spirit within us, encouraging growth and fostering resilience.

To observe the sun is to witness a fraction of God's glory, a mere glimpse into the infinite power that orchestrates the universe yet cares for each individual heart. It teaches us that no matter how vast the darkness, the light of God's presence is always near, ready to dispel fears and doubts with its pervasive glow. The sun's journey across the sky is a visual hymn of praise, a daily declaration of God's unfailing love and mercy towards us.

In moments of despair, when our paths seem engulfed in fog, let us remember the sun's light, how it finds its way to us, offering direction and clarity. Let this celestial guidance remind us that we are never alone, that God's light is ever-present, guiding our steps towards a brighter tomorrow. With every sunrise, let us renew our faith, emboldened by the knowledge that God's mercies are new every morning, His grace inexhaustible, and His path ever illuminated.

Thus, as we stand under the vast expanse of the sky, witnessing the sun's glory, let it serve as a physical manifestation of God's majesty and a reflection of His celestial creation. Let it strengthen our faith, reminding us of His omnipotence and the meticulous care He invests in each aspect of our lives. For in the majesty of God's celestial creation, we find the strength to face our trials, the courage to persevere, and the hope to continue, assured by the illuminating path set before us by His divine light. *Haut du formulaire*

## COMFORT IN THE DARKNESS

The moon, with its serene glow, emerges as a beacon of divine comfort in the enveloping darkness of night. It stands as a symbol of God's gentle presence in times of uncertainty, casting a soft light that guides through the veil of our troubles. Unlike the sun's vibrant display, the moon's light is subtle, a quiet reminder of the steadfast watchfulness of the Divine. Its consistent cycle, waxing and waning, speaks to the ebb and flow of our lives, reflecting the constant changes we endure, yet it remains a fixed point in the heavens, a source of light in the darkness.

This celestial body, bathing the world in its soft glow, reminds us that we are never truly alone. Even when shadows deepen, and our paths become unclear, the moonlight whispers of God's unending love and comfort. Its gentle illumination is akin to God's whisper in the quiet, a soothing presence that calms fears and dries tears. In its light, we find solace, a divine reassurance that the night is not devoid of guidance.

The moon's presence is a testament to the balance of life, teaching us that there is beauty and purpose in the darkness, and that God's grace is not limited to the day. It encourages us to look beyond our immediate struggles, to the celestial reminder of God's eternal light. As it casts its glow upon the earth, it illuminates our surroundings in a new light, offering us a different perspective, one that finds beauty and hope in the midst of challenges.

In moments of solitude, when the weight of our trials seems most oppressive, the moon serves as a tangible reminder of God's omnipresence. It assures us of His constant vigil, a comforting embrace that holds us through our darkest hours. The soft luminescence invites us to rest in the knowledge that God's guidance is as unfailing as the moon's path across the night sky.

Therefore, let us draw comfort from the majesty of God's celestial creation, particularly in the gentle luminescence of the moon. It is in these quiet moments of reflection that we can feel God's comforting presence most acutely. Let the moonlight be a balm to our weary souls, a celestial reminder that God's love penetrates even the deepest darkness. Through it, we are reminded that no night is too dark, no silence too profound, and no path too obscured for God's light to find us and lead us home.

In embracing the moon's subtle glow, we acknowledge the omnipresence of God, finding comfort in the knowledge that His watchful eyes never leave us. The majesty of God's celestial creation, including the comforting presence of the moon, strengthens our faith, reassuring us that we are enveloped in His eternal light, even in the deepest shadows.

## STARS AS GUIDING LIGHTS

The stars, twinkling in the vast expanse of night, are not merely distant suns but divine beacons, each shining with purpose and precision. They hang in the firmament like jewels adorning the crown of the universe, each placement deliberate, each sparkle a verse in the cosmic hymn of creation. These celestial bodies speak volumes of God's unfathomable creativity and meticulous planning, reminding us that our lives, too, are crafted with intention and care.

Looking up at the night sky, one can't help but feel a sense of awe and wonder at the breadth of God's canvas. The stars, in their silent brilliance, tell a story of creation, of a Master Artist who paints with light and shadow, crafting narratives that span millennia. They serve as a visual testament to God's boundless wisdom, each star a reminder that He orchestrates the universe with a precision that surpasses human understanding.

Amidst life's tumults and trials, the stars offer a perspective that is both humbling and uplifting. They whisper of a world beyond our immediate concerns, a universe vast enough to hold our biggest dreams and deepest fears, yet attentive to the minutiae of our lives. This celestial perspective reassures us that our challenges, while significant, are part of a larger, divine scheme, each moment intricately woven into the fabric of eternity.

The stars' enduring light is a symbol of God's constant guidance and presence. Just as mariners once navigated the seas by the stars, so too can we find direction in life's uncertain waters by looking to these heavenly guides. They remind us that God's light is always shining, offering us navigation through the darkest nights, guiding us towards our true north.

In moments of doubt or despair, the stars encourage us to lift our gaze upwards, to remember that we are part of something greater. They inspire us with the realization that our lives hold infinite potential, carefully placed within the grand tapestry of creation by the Creator's hand. Each star, with its unique place in the sky, mirrors our own individual journeys, uniquely designed, yet interconnected within God's cosmic plan.

Thus, let the stars be a source of comfort and inspiration, reminding us of God's infinite creativity and wisdom. Let their light guide us, not just through the night, but through the challenges of life, reinforcing our faith in the divine plan. For in the majesty of God's celestial creation, amidst the myriad stars, we find a reflection of our own place in the universe—a place filled with purpose, guided by divine light, and held within the loving expanse of God's eternal wisdom.

## RENEWAL WITH EVERY DAWN

The cyclical journey of the sun, from its first tender rays piercing the morning sky to its majestic descent at dusk, serves as a profound metaphor for the cycles of renewal and growth in our spiritual lives. Just as the sun ushers in a new day with promises of fresh beginnings, so does each sunrise offer us a moment to embrace renewal within ourselves, guided by the light of God's Word. This celestial rhythm is a reminder of God's unwavering faithfulness, providing us with daily opportunities to start anew, regardless of the past.

Every sunrise is an invitation from the Divine, a gentle call to shed the remnants of yesterday and step into the light of possibility. It encourages us to open our hearts to the day's potential, to plant seeds of faith, hope, and love, nurtured by the warmth of God's presence. This consistent renewal is not just a chance for personal growth but a divine appointment to align our steps with God's will, to let His light guide us through the day's challenges and opportunities.

The sun's journey across the sky mirrors the path of spiritual enlightenment, moving from the darkness of doubt and fear towards the light of understanding and faith. It teaches us that growth and renewal are constant processes, fueled by the light of God's Word, which illuminates our path and guides our steps. Just as the sun returns each morning, so does the opportunity for us to return to God, to seek His guidance, and to embrace His grace.

This cycle of renewal is a testament to God's endless mercy and compassion. It reassures us that no matter how far we may stray, the dawn brings a new beginning, a fresh start under the watchful eyes of the Divine. It is a call to action, to live each day with purpose, to reflect the light of God in our actions and to spread warmth and love in a world that often feels cold and indifferent.

As we witness the sun rising each day, let it serve as a reminder of our own spiritual journey, of our potential for renewal and growth. Let us embrace the light of God's Word, allowing it to guide our steps, to shape our thoughts and actions, and to illuminate our path towards a closer walk with Him. In the majesty of the sun's daily cycle, we find a reflection of God's promise for renewal, an assurance that with every dawn, we are offered the chance to begin again, to grow closer to the person God has called us to be.

Thus, in the spiritual significance of celestial bodies, particularly the sun's cyclical journey, we discover a powerful metaphor for our own cycles of renewal and growth. It is a daily reminder of God's grace, a symbol of hope and renewal that encourages us to embrace each new day with faith, guided by the light of His Word and the promise of His ever-present love.


## REFLECTION IN THE NIGHT

The moon, with its serene and reflective glow, stands as a celestial symbol for the quiet, introspective moments that are vital for our spiritual growth. Its light, though not its own, is a powerful reminder of the importance of reflection, illuminating our path with the borrowed light of the sun, much like how we, in our moments of contemplation, reflect upon the greater light of God's love and truth. This gentle luminary in the night sky teaches us that even in the absence of the sun's vibrant rays, light persists, guiding us through the darkness with its subtle brilliance.

This borrowed light of the moon serves as a metaphor for the way God's truth can illuminate our lives even when His presence seems distant or obscured. It reassures us that His love is constant, reflecting in our lives through acts of kindness, moments of clarity, and the peace we find in stillness. The moon's phases, from a slender crescent to a full circle of light, remind us of the ebb and flow of our faith journey, high-lighting the importance of trust in God's timing and presence.

In the quiet of the night, when the world slows and the clamor of day fades, the moon offers a silent invitation to pause and reflect. It encourages us to look inward, to examine our hearts and minds under the soft glow of its light, finding there the subtle reassurances of God's guiding hand in our lives. These moments of nocturnal reflection can deepen our connection to the Divine, revealing insights and truths that daylight's hustle might obscure.

The moon's reflective glow teaches us the power of stillness, of finding God's light within ourselves and in the world around us, even when His presence is not immediately apparent. It symbolizes the reflective nature of faith, the way our souls can catch and reflect God's love to those walking in darkness, guiding them towards His eternal light. Just as the moon reflects the sun's light to us in the night, so too can we reflect God's love, becoming beacons of hope and sources of light in the lives of others.

In the spiritual significance of celestial bodies, the moon's reflective glow is a testament to the enduring presence of God's light in our lives, reminding us that darkness is only a canvas for His subtle reassurances. It calls us to embrace the quiet, to seek the power of reflection, and to find comfort in the knowledge that God's love is as constant as the moon's phases. In the tranquility of the night, let us remember that we are never truly in darkness but are always in the presence of God's reflected light, guiding us, comforting us, and calling us to reflect His love and truth in all we do.

Thus, the moon's lesson is one of hope, reflection, and the quiet assurance that even in the absence of visible light, the love of God remains, reflecting through us and illuminating our path forward. Let this celestial guide inspire us to quiet reflection, to seek the whispers of God's voice in the silence, and to remember that His light is always present, gently leading us through the night towards a new dawn.

## NAVIGATION BY THE STARS

The stars, scattered across the night sky in a breathtaking display of celestial majesty, serve as more than just a spectacle for our admiration; they are divine markers, guiding us through the journey of life. Each star, a point of light in the overwhelming expanse of darkness, symbolizes the promises of God—unfailing, guiding, and eternal. As ancient navigators once charted their courses by the stars, so too are we encouraged to navigate the complexities of life with faith as our compass, trusting in the divine patterns set forth by our Creator.

These celestial guides teach us the value of steadfastness and direction. Just as sailors relied on the constancy of the stars to find their way, we, too, can look to the spiritual significance of these heavenly bodies for guidance. The stars remind us that God's light is ever-present, offering illumination in moments of uncertainty and shining brightly amidst the shadows of doubt. They encourage us to keep our gaze fixed on the higher purposes and divine directions, ensuring that we do not lose our way.

In the vastness of God's creation, each star has been meticulously placed, not only serving as a testament to His glory but also as a reflection of His intricate plans for our lives. These luminous points of light remind us that, no matter how aimless or lost we may feel, there is a path laid out for us, illuminated by the light of faith. They are reminders that, within the grand tapestry of the universe, there is order and design, mirroring the structured journey God intends for each of us.

The stars' persistent glow in the darkest nights offers comfort and hope, reinforcing the promise that light prevails over darkness. They teach us the importance of perseverance, of continuing our journey even when the night seems endless, for the dawn is assured. This celestial navigation system, set against the backdrop of the night sky, symbolizes the omnipresence of God's guidance, urging us to trust in the unseen, to follow the subtle nudges of the Spirit, and to walk in faith, not by sight.

By contemplating the stars, we are reminded of the infinite scope of God's promises—each star a distant yet potent reminder of His faithfulness and love. They beckon us to look beyond our immediate circumstances, to the larger story being written across the heavens. In their light, we find the courage to press forward, to chart our course through life's tumultuous seas with confidence and hope.

Thus, the spiritual significance of celestial bodies, especially the stars, enriches our faith journey, offering both a literal and metaphorical navigation system. They inspire us to move forward with conviction, guided by the unchanging light of God's promises. In the silent beauty of the starlit sky, we find a powerful reminder of our Creator's vastness, a call to anchor our lives in the enduring truth of His word, and to trust in the divine navigation He provides.

Let the stars be a constant reminder that we are part of a larger, divine narrative, each of us guided by the light of faith, moving towards our heavenly destination. As we navigate life's complexities, let us look up and remember the guidance offered by these celestial points of light, trusting in the patterns set forth by our Creator, and finding our way by the stars of His promises.

## ACTION: LIVING IN THEIR LIGHT

As we marvel at the sun's brilliance, the moon's serene glow, and the stars' guiding light, let us draw inspiration to live out their lessons in our daily actions. The steadfast journey of the sun teaches us about constancy and faithfulness, urging us to reflect these qualities in our unwavering faith and commitment to our principles. The moon, with its gentle illumination in the darkness, reminds us to be sources of comfort and light to those navigating through life's challenges. Similarly, the stars' guidance across the night sky encourages us to be beacons of guidance and hope for others, helping them find their way in moments of uncertainty.

By embodying the celestial light in our lives, we not only honor the Creator's magnificent design but also become vessels of His love and grace to those around us. Let the luminosity of these heavenly bodies inspire us to brighten the lives of others with acts of kindness, compassion, and understanding. Their unchanging nature in the heavens above serves as a model for us to stay aligned with God's will, navigating through life with purpose and direction.

In essence, living in their light means reflecting the best of their qualities—steadfastness, illumination, and guidance—through our daily actions and interactions. As we embody these celestial lessons, we strengthen our faith and become lights in the world, guiding others towards the warmth and love of God's eternal light. This way, we can ensure that the divine inspiration we draw from the heavens translates into tangible acts of love and service on earth, illuminating paths not just for ourselves but for all who journey alongside us.

In the crafting of the sun, moon, and stars, God spoke into existence more than mere lights in the sky. He created symbols of hope, guides for the night, and reminders of His unfailing presence and love. As we conclude this chapter, let us carry the light of these truths in our hearts, illuminating our paths and guiding us toward a future marked by faith, hope, and divine destiny.

---

**Prayer:** Almighty Creator, in the vastness of Your creation, You have provided us with symbols of Your love and guidance. May we always find in the sun, moon, and stars a reflection of Your glory. Guide us by their light, illuminate our path, and lead us ever closer to You. In Your holy name, we pray, Amen.

As we prepare to transition from the celestial to the tangible, the next chapter beckons us to consider our stewardship of the beautiful world You've entrusted to us. Let us move forward, inspired to turn our faith into a living, breathing commitment to our environment and to each other. This resolve to steward our world faithfully not only honors the Creator but also ensures that the blessings of His creation can be enjoyed by generations to come.

---

# CHAPTER 5

# WINGS AND WAVES: THE DAWN OF BIRDS AND SEA LIFE

In the tapestry of my life, woven with threads of trials and triumphs, I found myself at a juncture where the path forward seemed as vast and unfathomable as the ocean's depths. It was during this phase of introspection and seeking that I stumbled upon the profound narrative of creation's fifth day, a story that resonated deeply with my soul's yearning for purpose and direction.

As I delved into the scriptures, I discovered a mesmerizing depiction of life burgeoning in the skies and seas—birds soaring with unfettered freedom above and sea creatures ruling the watery realms below. This divine act of creation, marked by God's boundless imagination and care, stirred something within me. I saw my reflection in the birds' flight and the sea creatures' exploration, a mirror of my own desires for freedom and a life filled with meaning.

This chapter of my journey, seemingly adrift in life's tumultuous seas, was suddenly alight with the possibility of transformation. The scriptures served as a beacon, guiding me through the darkness of uncertainty. The freedom of the birds in the sky symbolized the liberation I sought from my own constraints, while the dominion of the sea creatures over the depths echoed my quest for control over the direction of my life.

Through prayer and reflection on this divine narrative, I began to perceive my circumstances with renewed clarity. The same Creator who had ordained the birds to fill the skies and the fish to swim in the oceans had also crafted a unique purpose for my life. It was a revelation that imbued me with a newfound sense of empowerment and resolve.

Inspired by the fifth day of creation, I embraced the truth of God's word, stepping boldly into the unknown. With each day of meditation on this scripture, my spirit was fortified with faith and confidence. Like the birds, I was ready to spread my wings and soar above life's challenges, and like the sea creatures, I was prepared to navigate the depths with grace and strength.

This journey, illuminated by the lessons of creation, taught me that within each of us lies the potential for growth and abundance, commanded by God to be fruitful and multiply in every aspect of our lives. The narrative of the fifth day became a testament to victory through faith, prayer, and unwavering trust in God's promises.

As I share this chapter of my story, it is my deepest hope that it serves as a source of encouragement and strength. May it remind you, dear reader, that even when you find yourself adrift, God's word holds the power to illuminate your path, guide you towards your divine destiny, and reveal the boundless possibilities that await when you dare to trust in His provision and purpose for your life.

Embarking on a voyage through the vast and often stormy seas of life, I found my soul adrift, hungering for a beacon of purpose and direction. It was amidst this search that I turned to the divine narrative of creation's fifth day, a day that spoke directly to the essence of my yearning. The scriptures unfurled before me a panorama of freedom and mastery—the birds soaring effortlessly across the heavens and the myriad creatures ruling the mysterious depths of the seas. In their unbounded dominion and grace, I saw a reflection of my own longing for liberation and a life imbued with significance.

This chapter of my odyssey, seemingly engulfed in the fog of uncertainty, began to brighten under the guiding light of scripture. The freedom of the birds, unchained and majestic against the canvas of the sky, mirrored the liberation I sought from my own confines. The sovereign rule of sea creatures over their domain echoed my desire to chart my course with confidence and purpose. Through the divine words of the fifth day of creation, I discovered a lens that revealed not only the potential within me for growth and flourishing but also the steadfast promise of God's unwavering provision.

As I delved deeper into the lessons of the fifth day, my journey transformed from a solitary drift into a purposeful quest. Guided by the scriptures, I embarked on a path lit by the promise of growth, abundance, and divine guidance. This introduction marks the beginning of a chapter where the teachings of creation inspire a reawakening to the possibilities that lay before me, anchored in the faith that with God's provision, I too can soar to new heights and explore the depths of my destiny with boldness and grace.

## A SYMPHONY OF CREATION

On the fifth day of creation, the universe witnessed a magnificent symphony, a divine act that painted the skies and seas with a vibrant tapestry of life. This was the day when the Creator, with a palette rich in diversity, orchestrated a world teeming with creatures, each moving with grace and imbued with purpose. The skies, once silent, now resonated with the flutters and calls of birds, while the seas, tranquil and deep, burst into life with the dance of countless sea creatures. This breathtaking unfoldment of life was a testament to the Creator's love for variety and His intentionality in design, a clear message that every wingbeat in the sky and every ripple in the ocean was part of a grander design.

Amidst the backdrop of life's uncertainties, this symphony of creation stands as a beacon of divine order, a reminder that chaos too has its place in the Creator's plan, leading eventually to harmony and balance. The birds that soar high, defying gravity with their wings, teach us the power of perspective and the freedom that comes with rising above our trials. The sea creatures, navigating the vast and mysterious depths, remind us of the depth of God's mysteries, inviting us to dive deeper into our faith and trust in His unseen guidance.

This cascade of creation is not merely an event of the past but a continuous call to embrace the life we've been granted with joy and a heart full of gratitude. It's an invitation to see beyond the immediate, to appreciate the diversity and complexity of life, and to find our unique purpose within God's intricate design. Just as each bird sings a different tune and each fish swims a distinct path, we too are called to find our voice and chart our course, contributing to the symphony of life with the gifts we've been given.

The fifth day's message is clear: amidst life's tempests and calms, there exists a divine melody, a harmony that binds creation together, orchestrated by a Creator who delights in His work. This understanding encourages us to live fully, embracing each moment with the knowledge that we are part of something greater, a masterpiece in progress. It urges us to live with intention, making every action, every decision, a note that adds richness and depth to the melody of existence.

As we reflect on this divine orchestration, let it fortify our faith, reminding us that we are never alone, always supported by the Creator's loving hand. Let it inspire us to move through life with grace and purpose, just as the creatures of the fifth day do, embracing our roles in this divine symphony with courage and trust. And in moments of doubt or despair, let us remember the fifth day of creation, a vivid reminder of God's omnipotence, creativity, and the order that underpins our lives.

Therefore, let this subsection not only be a narrative of creation's past but also a living testament to God's ongoing work in our lives, a source of strength, encouragement, and unwavering faith. In the grand symphony of creation, each of us has a part to play, a unique melody to contribute, guided by the Conductor's hand, moving towards a crescendo of divine purpose and eternal harmony.

## LESSONS FROM THE SKY

In the vast canvas of the sky, the birds, each adorned with unique feathers and songs, emerged as my inadvertent mentors, teaching me invaluable lessons on individuality and courage. Their daily ballet in the heavens, against the backdrop of shifting clouds, became a metaphor for life's journey—diverse, vibrant, and boundless. Each bird, unfazed by the enormity of the sky, soared with a grace and ease that belied the complexities of flight. Observing them, I began to understand the true essence of embracing one's journey with the distinctiveness that only individuality can bestow.

The birds, masters of the air, knew instinctively when to flap their wings with vigor and when to glide serenely on the winds of change. Their fearlessness in the face of the open sky's vastness spoke volumes to my heart, teaching me that the space above, though immense and daunting, was also a realm of infinite possibilities. It was in their unfettered flight that I discovered the courage to confront my own uncertainties, to challenge the doubts that clung to me as shackles, binding me to the ground.

Each bird, with its unique song, seemed to dance to the rhythm of its own melody, a poignant reminder of the beauty of individuality in the symphony of creation. Their diverse tunes, whether a solitary whistle or a harmonious chorus at dawn, underscored the value of one's voice amidst the cacophony of life. This diversity in unity provided me with the clarity to appreciate my own journey, distinct yet interconnected with the fabric of the larger world.

The way birds soared on the winds of change, utilizing the very force that could have opposed them as a means to lift them higher, taught me the art of turning challenges into opportunities. They did not shy away from the storm clouds; instead, they found pathways through or above them, embodying resilience and adaptability. Their intrepid flight became a source of inspiration, encouraging me to rise above my challenges, to see them not as insurmountable barriers but as winds that could elevate me to new heights.

Moreover, birds, in their communal migrations, exemplified the strength found in unity and the importance of shared journeys. Yet, even within these flocks, each bird maintained its individuality, a balance of self within the collective that mirrored my own search for belonging and independence. This delicate equilibrium between community and individuality illustrated the potential for personal growth alongside collective endeavors.

From the sky's lessons, I learned the importance of perspective— viewing the world from above, problems seemed smaller, and the horizon stretched endlessly, offering a vista of hope and renewal. The birds' fearless ascent into the sky taught me to elevate my gaze, to envision my life beyond the immediate obstacles and doubts, and to trust in the journey's unfolding.

Thus, as I witnessed the birds navigate the boundless skies with individual songs and united flights, I was imbued with a newfound sense of purpose and courage. They taught me that embracing one's journey with authenticity and valor was not merely an act of defiance against fear but a celebration of life's infinite possibilities. In the birds' fearless flight, I found the wings to lift myself above the terrain of doubt, to soar towards the horizons of my dreams with resilience, hope, and an unyielding belief in the power of individuality and courage.

## WISDOM FROM THE DEPTHS

Beneath the vast expanse of the ocean's surface, a world of boundless variety and profound mystery unfolds, home to creatures of every conceivable shape and hue. This underwater realm, teeming with life in its most vibrant and diverse forms, stands as a testament to the complexity and richness of creation. Observing this hidden world, I was struck by a powerful realization: just as the ocean brims with unseen wonders, so too does the landscape of our own lives, particularly in the depths of our faith.

The sea creatures, each with their unique adaptations and roles within the marine ecosystem, serve as living parables of the possibilities that lie beneath the surface of our existence. The way they navigate the depths, each according to its kind, speaks volumes about the individual journey of discovery and growth that each of us is called to undertake. From the majestic whale that traverses the oceans with its colossal grace to the tiniest plankton that forms the foundation of the marine food web, every creature contributes to the tapestry of life in its own unique way.

Their existence, often shrouded in mystery due to the ocean's immeasurable depths, reminded me that much of what is truly valuable in life and in faith lies beneath the surface, waiting to be discovered. Just as the ocean's treasures are hidden from the casual observer, the deepest and most profound aspects of our faith require us to dive deeper, beyond the superficial and into the heart of what it means to believe.

This underwater journey became a metaphor for my own spiritual exploration, urging me to delve into the depths of my soul and uncover the riches that lie within. It was a call to venture beyond the familiar shores of my understanding and plunge into the unknown waters of divine mystery and revelation. The sea creatures, in their silent wisdom, taught me that faith is not merely about skimming the surface but about embracing the depths, where the true essence of our beliefs and convictions are found.

As I contemplated the life forms that dwell in the ocean's depths, I realized that, like them, there are aspects of my faith and my very self that I have yet to explore fully. The sea's hidden realms challenged me to seek a deeper understanding of my relationship with the divine, to uncover the layers of belief and trust that I had yet to fully embrace. This was not a journey of distance but of depth, a descent into the heart of faith where the true richness of spiritual life is discovered.

The variety of the ocean's inhabitants, each uniquely adapted to its environment, also spoke to me of the diversity within the body of faith. Just as no two creatures of the deep are the same, so too are we called to live out our faith in ways that reflect our individuality and unique relationship with the Creator. The sea creatures' ability to thrive in the depths reassured me that, in the vast ocean of faith, there is room for every kind of believer, each with their own way of contributing to the collective understanding and expression of divine love.

Thus, wisdom from the depths became more than just an observation of marine life; it was a profound spiritual lesson in the value of seeking, exploring, and cherishing the depths of our own faith journey. The sea creatures, in their boundless diversity and mystery, became my guides, leading me to discover the unseen depths within myself and the infinite possibilities that faith offers. In their silent wisdom, they called me to dive deeper into the waters of belief, where true understanding and spiritual richness await those brave enough to explore.

## EMBRACING POTENTIAL

Upon reflecting on the fifth day of creation, a profound truth illuminated my thoughts: just like the birds that soar through the heavens and the sea creatures that navigate the mysterious depths, I too am imbued with divine purpose and untapped potential. This realization marked a pivotal moment in my life, sparking a transformation from passive reflection to purposeful action. It was as if the scales fell from my eyes, revealing the vast expanse of possibilities before me, crafted by a Creator who designs with intentionality and care.

This journey of embracing my potential was not merely about recognizing my capabilities, but about moving with conviction towards the fulfillment of my divine purpose. It became clear that I was not created to merely exist, but to actively participate in the unfolding of God's grand design, contributing my unique melody to the symphony of creation. This shift in perspective demanded courage and a deep, unwavering trust in the Creator's plans for me, plans as vast and intricate as creation itself.

The lessons from the sky and the sea became my guiding stars, teaching me that to fulfill my potential, I must learn to soar on the winds of change and dive into the depths of my own being. Like the eagle that rides the thermal currents to reach great heights, I learned the value of resilience and the power of perspective. The eagle's flight taught me that obstacles and challenges, when approached with strength and foresight, can become opportunities to rise above and view the journey from a higher vantage point.

Similarly, the creatures of the deep, each uniquely adapted to thrive in the ocean's vast ecosystem, showed me the importance of embracing my inherent qualities and using them to navigate life's complexities. Just as the octopus adapts its color and form to harmonize with its surroundings, I too learned the significance of adaptability and resourcefulness, of being true to my nature while finding my place within the larger community.

This embrace of potential called for action, for stepping out in faith and moving towards God's calling with determination and trust. It was about letting go of the fear that had once anchored me in place, releasing it as a bird opens its wings to the wind, and trusting that I too could fly. It required a daily commitment to live intentionally, to make choices that align with my divine purpose, and to trust that, in doing so, I would find fulfillment and joy.

Grounded in faith, this journey from introspection to action became a testament to the belief that God's plans for me are woven with threads of grace, challenge, and growth. Each step forward was taken not in isolation, but with the assurance that the Creator who designed the complexities of the universe also intricately designed me. This journey of embracing my potential became a journey of deepening my faith, of learning to see myself through the Creator's eyes, as a vessel of possibility and a bearer of divine light.

As I continue to navigate this path, the lessons of the fifth day remain a constant source of inspiration and courage. They remind me that, in the grand tapestry of creation, I have a unique role to play, a purpose that only I can fulfill. Embracing this truth has propelled me toward a life marked by divine trust and purposeful action, a life where introspection leads to impactful living, guided by the unwavering belief in the potential that God has planted within me.


## THE CALL TO STEWARDSHIP

Reflecting on the intricacies of creation, particularly the roles of birds in the sky and creatures in the sea, I experienced a profound realization: we are all stewards of this magnificent creation that God has generously entrusted to us. This insight was not merely an observation but a clarion call to action, reminding us that our existence is deeply intertwined with the natural world and that we bear a sacred responsibility to care for it.

The birds, with their melodies gracing the morning skies, and the sea creatures, with their silent dance in the ocean's depths, serve not only as marvels of creation but as custodians of the earth's delicate balance. They perform essential roles in the ecosystems they inhabit, from pollinating plants to maintaining the health of marine environments. Their existence is a testament to the interconnectedness of life, a complex web that we are part of, not apart from.

The birds, with their melodies gracing the morning skies, and the sea creatures, with their silent dance in the ocean's depths, serve not only as marvels of creation but as custodians of the earth's delicate balance. They perform essential roles in the ecosystems they inhabit, from pollinating plants to maintaining the health of marine environments. Their existence is a testament to the interconnectedness of life, a complex web that we are part of, not apart from.

This realization illuminated my own role in this grand design. Just as each bird and fish contributes to the harmony of nature, so too do my actions reverberate through the web of creation. It was a revelation that our stewardship is not merely a choice but a duty, an integral part of our faith and our relationship with the Creator.

Acknowledging this duty, I understood that stewardship extends beyond mere conservation; it is an act of worship, a demonstration of our reverence for the Creator by caring for His creation. It involves making conscious choices that promote sustainability and protect the environment, from the food we eat to the products we use, each decision reflecting our commitment to the divine mandate of stewardship.

This call to stewardship also highlighted the impact of our actions on the world and its inhabitants. The way we treat the earth and its creatures speaks volumes about our respect for the Creator. Neglect and abuse of the environment are not just physical acts but spiritual failings, a disregard for the divine gift of creation.

Embracing my role as a steward, I began to see opportunities for action in everyday life, from reducing waste to supporting conservation efforts. Each small step became part of a larger journey toward fulfilling my God-given responsibility to care for the earth. It was a journey marked by learning and growth, as I sought to better understand the needs of the environment and how I could contribute to its well-being.

This journey of stewardship also became a path of spiritual growth, deepening my connection with God through the care of His creation. It reinforced the idea that faith is lived out in action, in the choices we make and the ways we interact with the world around us. Caring for creation became a tangible expression of my faith, a daily testament to my commitment to follow God's call.

As I continue to walk this path of stewardship, I am constantly reminded of the beauty and fragility of the world God has entrusted to us. It is a world that demands our care and respect, a world where each of us plays a critical role in its preservation. This reflection on creation and our call to stewardship is an invitation to all believers to recognize their part in the divine command to care for the earth. It is a reminder that our faith is not just about personal salvation but about living out God's love in our actions, in our stewardship of the incredible world He has made.

## LIVING IN HARMONY

The fifth day of creation unfolds as a masterclass in harmony, presenting a vision of existence where every creature, from the smallest fish in the ocean's depths to the birds that navigate the boundless skies, plays a pivotal role in the symphony of life. This divine orchestration, where each being contributes to the balance and beauty of nature, served as a profound lesson on the essence of harmony in our lives. It underscored the necessity of living in synchrony with the natural world and in peaceful coexistence with our fellow beings, a harmonious blend that enriches the tapestry of creation.

As I delved deeper into this reflection, I realized that living in harmony is not merely cohabiting the earth but actively nurturing an environment that allows every form of life to thrive. This realization brought with it a sense of responsibility—to live not as a disruptor but as a contributor to the world's harmony. It inspired a commitment to act with intentionality, ensuring that each choice and action of mine resonates with the underlying melody of creation, adding beauty and balance rather than discord.

This understanding transformed my perspective on interaction with the natural world and fellow humans. It became clear that every decision, from the simplest daily habits to larger life choices, holds the potential to either uphold or disturb the delicate equilibrium of life. This consciousness guided me to embrace practices that sustain and protect the environment, recognizing that the health of our planet directly impacts the well-being of its inhabitants.

Moreover, this blueprint for existence emphasized the interconnectedness of all life forms. It revealed that harmony extends beyond environmental stewardship to encompass our relationships with others. Just as the birds and sea creatures coexist within their ecosystems, supporting the cycle of life, so too are we called to live in a manner that fosters mutual respect, understanding, and support among our communities.

Living in harmony, as exemplified by creation, also deepened my appreciation for diversity. The myriad forms of life, each unique yet integral to the whole, illustrated the beauty that diversity brings to our world. This diversity within unity became a model for human society, teaching that our differences, when embraced and valued, contribute to the richness and vibrancy of our collective existence.

This commitment to harmony inspired a more mindful way of living, one that recognizes the impact of our actions on the world around us. It encouraged practices of conservation, empathy, and altruism, rooted in the belief that a life lived in harmony with creation is a testament to the Creator's intent for a world where all can flourish.

The lesson of living in harmony, drawn from the fifth day of creation, thus became a guiding principle for my life. It shaped a path of intentional living, where each step is taken with consideration for its ripple effects on the natural world and on the lives of others. This path is marked by a desire to contribute positively to the world's symphony, ensuring that my presence adds to its harmony rather than detracts from it.

In embracing this blueprint for existence, I found a deeper sense of purpose and fulfillment. The pursuit of harmony became not just an ecological or social endeavor but a spiritual one, reflecting a commitment to align my life with the divine design. It is a journey that continually challenges me to act with compassion, mindfulness, and a deep respect for the interconnected web of life, fostering an environment where all creation can truly flourish in harmony.

## ACTION AND REFLECTION

In the quiet moments of reflection inspired by the dawn of birds and sea life, we find ourselves standing at the crossroads of contemplation and action. This natural spectacle serves as a poignant reminder of the vibrant potential that resides within each of us, urging us to not only recognize our individual capacities but to actively employ them in ways that contribute positively to the tapestry of life. It beckons us to live intentionally, to weave purpose into every decision and action, ensuring that our presence enriches the world.

This reflection challenges us to examine our interactions with the environment and with each other, fostering a spirit of stewardship and compassion that transcends mere existence. It calls for a commitment to embrace our potential, to unfold our wings like the birds at dawn, and to dive into the depths of our capabilities, as do the creatures of the sea. By doing so, we align ourselves with a greater purpose, one that advocates for the flourishing of all creation.

Let us, therefore, step forward with renewed resolve, carrying the lessons of action and reflection into our daily lives. May we engage in actions that nurture and sustain, that protect the delicate balance of nature, and promote the well-being of every living being. In embracing this call, we not only honor the divine blueprint of creation but also fulfill our role as caretakers of the earth, contributing to a legacy of harmony and flourishing for generations to come.

The narrative of the fifth day is not just a story of creation but a directive for living—a call to embrace our potential, live in harmony, and steward the gifts we've been given. As we close this chapter, let us carry forward the lessons learned, inspired to soar to new heights and dive into the depths of our purpose, guided by the Creator's hand.

---

**Prayer:** Heavenly Father, we stand in awe of Your creation—from the birds of the air to the fish of the sea. Thank You for the lessons they teach us about freedom, potential, and stewardship. Guide us to live in harmony with Your creation, fulfilling our role as stewards with grace and dedication. Amen.

As we turn the page, we're called to face the environmental challenges that threaten our world. Our journey of stewardship is just beginning, urging us to act with wisdom and courage for the healing and renewal of our planet.

---

# PART IV
# ENVIRONMENTAL STEWARDSHIP

# CHAPTER 6

# HEALING OUR WORLD: ADDRESSING ENVIRONMENTAL CHALLENGES

On the sixth day of creation, a day marked by divine artistry and profound purpose, God meticulously shaped the land animals and, in a pinnacle act of creativity, fashioned humankind in His own image. This act, so pivotal in the narrative of creation, mirrored a critical juncture in my personal journey—an intersection of self-discovery and purpose that beckoned me to explore deeper the essence of my existence.

Navigating through life's intricate maze, I often found myself wrestling with profound questions about my worth and purpose. Amidst the diversity of life, akin to the myriad land animals each uniquely crafted by the Creator, I yearned for clarity about my place in the vast tapestry of existence. My soul ached to uncover my distinct role and to contribute meaningfully to the world that envelops me. It was during this period of soul-searching and introspection that I sought refuge in the immutable truths of scripture, longing for guidance to illuminate my path through the shadows of uncertainty.

As I delved into meditation on the events of the sixth day of creation, I was profoundly moved by the realization that humanity was created in the very image of God. This revelation was a beacon of light, cutting through the fog of self-doubt and insecurity, reminding me of my intrinsic value and dignity as a beloved child of God. Liberated from the chains of self-deprecation, I began to embrace my identity with a newfound confidence, acknowledging that I was intricately designed for a purpose far beyond my understanding.

Through prayer and contemplation of this momentous day of creation, I garnered the strength and courage to boldly step into my divine calling. Just as the first humans were blessed with dominion and tasked with stewardship over the creation, I recognized that I, too, was endowed with influence and responsibility within my realm. This epiphany ignited a renewed sense of empowerment and accountability within me, as I wholeheartedly accepted the divine mandate to cultivate and steward the earth, imbuing it with goodness and grace.

Ultimately, it was the immutable truth of God's Word, as manifested in the creation narrative, that guided me to triumph over the tumult of my soul. Through meditation on His Word and adherence to His divine will, I found the pathway to a life brimming with purpose and fulfillment. Surrendering to God's sovereign plan for my existence, I discovered unparalleled joy and contentment in serving as His ambassador, disseminating love, kindness, and hope in every stride.

This journey, inspired by the divine act of creation on the sixth day, transformed not only my understanding of identity and purpose but also my approach to life. As I continue to walk in alignment with God's plan, I am constantly reminded of the honor and responsibility that comes with being made in His image. Embracing this calling, I am committed to living a life that reflects His love and fulfills the unique purpose for which I was divinely crafted.

## RECAP OF CHAPTER 5: WINGS AND WAVES: THE DAWN OF BIRDS AND SEA LIFE

Chapter 5 immersed us in the splendor of the fifth day of creation, where the skies and seas were filled with life. It was a journey of self-discovery, mirroring the boundless freedom of birds in flight and the depth of sea creatures. As we marveled at the diversity and intricacy of life, we were reminded of our call to stewardship—to protect, cherish, and nurture the abundant life God has placed within our care. Now, as we transition to Chapter 6, our focus shifts towards understanding the gravity of our responsibility and the urgency of the environmental challenges that confront our world.

## INTRODUCTION: RECOGNIZING OUR ROLE IN CREATION'S NARRATIVE

As stewards of God's creation, we find ourselves at a pivotal moment in history. The beauty and balance of the world, so vividly celebrated on the fifth day of creation, are under threat from pollution, climate change, and habitat destruction. This chapter serves as a call to action, reminding us that our stewardship has profound implications not only for birds and sea creatures but for the entire web of life that sustains our planet.

We are entrusted with a magnificent and diverse world, a testament to divine artistry and intention. Each element of creation, from the smallest microorganism to the vast oceans, plays an integral role in maintaining the ecological balance that supports life. As inheritors of this legacy, it is our duty to ensure that this balance is not disrupted but rather enhanced by our actions.

The challenges we face are daunting but not insurmountable. By recognizing our role within the broader narrative of creation, we can begin to enact change. This involves not only understanding the impacts of our actions on the environment but actively seeking ways to mitigate them. It requires a shift from passive observance to proactive participation in the preservation and restoration of the world around us.

As we move through this chapter, let us reflect on the responsibility bestowed upon us and embrace our role as caretakers. This is not merely an obligation but a sacred trust, calling us to act with wisdom, compassion, and courage. Let us stand as stewards of creation, committed to restoring the harmony and vitality of the Earth, ensuring that it remains a thriving home for all forms of life, now and for future generations.

## ADDRESSING THE CLIMATE CRISIS: A CALL TO STEWARDSHIP AND ACTION

At the heart of our narrative lies a pressing and formidable challenge that confronts humanity with a stark reality—the climate crisis. This phenomenon, characterized by rapid and unprecedented changes in the Earth's climate, emerges as a formidable adversary against the delicate tapestry of ecosystems. It alters weather patterns with an intensity seldom seen and causes sea levels to rise with devastating consequences. The evidence is irrefutable, and the message is clear: our planet, this magnificent creation entrusted to our care, is in jeopardy.

As stewards of this creation, the call to action has never been more urgent. This crisis demands not just awareness but immediate, concerted efforts aimed at curtailing the emissions of greenhouse gases, the invisible culprits accelerating this change. It beckons us to move beyond mere acknowledgment of the problem to adopting sustainable energy sources that promise a greener, more hopeful future.

Our responsibility in this era of environmental upheaval is profound. As individuals of faith, we are tasked with advocating for policies and practices that weave respect and protection for our planet into the fabric of society. This advocacy is not a passive wish but a dynamic and purposeful endeavor to realign humanity's relationship with the Earth. It is a testament to our commitment to honor the divine mandate of stewardship, acknowledging that the Earth is not ours to exploit but a sacred trust to nurture and preserve for future generations.

The climate crisis is more than an environmental issue; it is a moral imperative that challenges us to question our values and the legacy we wish to leave behind. It calls us to stand at the forefront of change, to lend our voices in the halls of power and in our communities, championing the cause of environmental justice and sustainability. In this fight, every action counts, from the reduction of personal carbon footprints to the support of global initiatives aimed at mitigating climate change.

This pivotal moment in history offers us an opportunity to redefine our relationship with the Earth. It invites us to envision a world where human activity harmonizes with nature rather than disrupts it, where the bounty of the Earth is shared equitably, ensuring that no one is left vulnerable to the ravages of climate change. As bearers of faith, we are imbued with hope, a powerful force that compels us to believe in the possibility of transformation and renewal.

In embracing this challenge, we are called to be visionaries, to imagine and work towards a future where the beauty and diversity of creation are preserved for all to marvel at and enjoy. This journey of stewardship is a journey of faith in action, a tangible expression of our reverence for the Creator manifested in our care for His creation. It is a path that demands courage, resilience, and an unwavering commitment to the common good.

As we navigate through the complexities of the climate crisis, let us hold fast to the conviction that, with collective action and divine guidance, we can forge a sustainable path forward. This section of our narrative is not just about identifying the challenges but about rallying a call to action—a call to rise, mobilize, and effectuate change that honors the delicate balance of our planet. In this endeavor, our faith serves as both our anchor and our compass, guiding us to act justly, love mercy, and walk humbly with our God as we seek to heal our world.

## POLLUTION AND ITS TOLL ON LIFE

In the unfolding narrative of our planet's history, a somber chapter emerges, one that details the pervasive and insidious nature of pollution. This challenge, manifested through contaminated air, water, and soil, casts a long shadow over the health and vitality of our Earth and its myriad inhabitants. The images are poignant and distressing: oceans suffocated by plastic, landscapes marred by waste, and skies clouded with toxins. The toll of unchecked pollution is not merely an environmental concern; it is a clarion call to humanity, urging immediate action to safeguard the sanctity of creation.

As stewards of this Earth, we are confronted with the urgent task of reversing the tide of pollution. This endeavor is monumental, requiring a paradigm shift towards sustainability and ecological responsibility. The journey begins with a commitment to minimizing waste, a simple yet profound act that challenges the throwaway culture that pervades our society. By reducing our consumption and opting for products that are designed to last, we contribute to a decrease in the demand for disposable goods, thereby reducing the volume of waste generated.

Embracing recycling emerges as a crucial strategy in our arsenal against pollution. This process not only diverts waste from landfills and oceans but also conserves natural resources and reduces the need for raw materials. Recycling transforms what was once considered rubbish into valuable resources, closing the loop in a circular economy that prioritizes sustainability over disposability.

The call to action extends beyond individual efforts, reaching into the realms of industry and governance. Advocating for cleaner, greener industries is paramount. This advocacy involves supporting policies and practices that reduce emissions, regulate pollutants, and encourage the development of renewable energy sources. It is a call for a collective awakening to the realities of environmental degradation and the need for systemic change.

Addressing pollution and its toll on life is not merely an environmental duty; it is a moral imperative that resonates with the core tenets of faith. It speaks to our responsibility to care for the Earth as a sacred trust, to protect the vulnerable who suffer most from environmental injustice, and to pass on a healthier, more vibrant planet to future generations.

The consequences of inaction are dire, but the potential for transformation is immense. By adopting sustainable practices, advocating for environmental stewardship, and fostering a culture of respect for the Earth, we can begin to heal the wounds inflicted by pollution. This healing process is not instantaneous, nor is it easy, but it is within our reach if we commit to purposeful action and persistent advocacy.

This subsection, "Pollution and Its Toll on Life," serves not only as a diagnosis of one of our planet's most pressing challenges but also as a blueprint for change. It invites readers to reflect on their relationship with the Earth, to recognize the interconnectedness of all life, and to take up the mantle of stewardship with renewed vigor. In this endeavor, faith serves as both a motivation and a source of strength, guiding us to live in harmony with creation and to strive for a world where life in all its forms can flourish.

Let this be a rallying cry for all who cherish the Earth and its inhabitants. May our actions reflect our commitment to healing our world, embracing the principles of sustainability and stewardship that are essential for the well-being of our planet. Together, through faith and action, we can address the challenge of pollution and pave the way for a future marked by ecological harmony and respect for the sacredness of life.

## HABITAT DESTRUCTION AND BIODIVERSITY LOSS: A CALL TO ACTION

In the grand tapestry of creation, each thread—every species, every ecosystem—plays a critical role in the health and balance of our planet. Yet, as we chart the course of human progress, we find ourselves at a precarious juncture where the relentless expansion of our activities has begun to unravel this intricate weave. Habitat destruction and the subsequent loss of biodiversity stand as stark indicators of the profound impact our actions have on the Earth. This challenge, borne of an insatiable appetite for land and resources, not only diminishes the beauty and variety of life but also threatens the very systems that sustain us.

The destruction of natural habitats, from the deforestation of tropical rainforests to the draining of wetlands, eradicates the homes of countless species, pushing them towards extinction. This loss of biodiversity—a catastrophic consequence of habitat destruction—erodes the resilience of ecosystems, diminishing their ability to provide essential services such as pollination, water purification, and carbon sequestration. The repercussions of this loss extend far beyond the environmental realm, affecting agricultural productivity, human health, and global food security.

Addressing the dual crises of habitat destruction and biodiversity loss necessitates a paradigm shift in how we interact with the natural world. Protecting and restoring natural habitats must become a cornerstone of our efforts to maintain the planet's health. This commitment to conservation represents not merely an act of preservation but a recognition of the intrinsic value of all life forms and their right to exist.

Efforts to safeguard natural habitats and halt biodiversity loss must be both global and local in scope. On a global scale, this involves supporting international conservation initiatives and agreements that aim to protect endangered species and ecosystems. Locally, it calls for the adoption of sustainable land use practices that balance human needs with the imperative to preserve natural habitats. This includes promoting responsible agriculture and forestry, establishing protected areas, and restoring degraded landscapes.

The path to achieving this balance requires innovation, collaboration, and a deep commitment to stewardship. It challenges us to envision a future where human development does not come at the expense of the natural world but rather coexists harmoniously with it. This vision compels us to rethink our consumption patterns, to embrace sustainable technologies, and to advocate for policies that prioritize the health of the planet.

As individuals of faith, we are called to lead by example, embodying the principles of stewardship in our daily lives. This entails making conscious choices that reflect our respect for creation, from supporting environmentally friendly products and services to engaging in community conservation efforts. By doing so, we not only contribute to the preservation of biodiversity but also inspire others to join in this vital cause.

The challenge of habitat destruction and biodiversity loss is daunting, yet it also presents an opportunity for transformation. It invites us to renew our commitment to the Earth, to act with intentionality and compassion, and to forge a legacy of stewardship that honors the Creator's gift of life in all its diversity. In this endeavor, our faith offers both motivation and solace, reminding us that through collective action and divine guidance, we can heal our world and safeguard the marvels of creation for generations to come.

This subsection, "Habitat Destruction and Biodiversity Loss," not only lays bare the challenges we face but also serves as a call to action—a reminder that the stewardship of our planet is a sacred responsibility entrusted to us. Let us rise to this challenge with courage and determination, embracing conservation efforts and sustainable practices as expressions of our deepest convictions and our hope for a restored world.

## THE POWER OF SUSTAINABLE LIVING

In the narrative of our journey toward healing the planet, the transition to sustainable living emerges not merely as a chapter of choice but as an imperative chapter of necessity. This transition represents a profound act of stewardship, a tangible expression of our respect for the Creator's work, and a commitment to the well-being of future generations. The principles of sustainable living—conserving energy, utilizing renewable resources, reducing waste, and supporting eco-friendly products—serve as the cornerstones upon which we can build a healthier, more vibrant world.

Adopting sustainable practices transcends the bounds of individual action; it becomes a collective testament to our capacity for change and our dedication to preserving the planet's delicate balance. The act of conserving energy, whether through simple measures like turning off unused lights or more significant commitments like investing in energy-efficient appliances, reflects a conscious decision to reduce our environmental footprint. Similarly, the choice to use renewable resources—such as solar or wind power—marks a step towards reducing our reliance on fossil fuels and mitigating the impacts of climate change.

Supporting eco-friendly products is another pillar of sustainable living. By choosing goods that are produced in environmentally responsible ways, we vote with our wallets for a cleaner, greener future. This support not only fosters the growth of sustainable industries but also encourages innovation in the creation of products that are kinder to the earth.

Yet, the power of sustainable living extends beyond the environmental benefits it brings. It also serves as a catalyst for social and economic transformation, promoting practices that are not only ecologically sound but also equitable and just. Sustainable living encourages us to consider the broader implications of our consumption choices, including the impact on workers, communities, and ecosystems around the world.

Moreover, sustainable living is an act of faith in action. It embodies the biblical call to care for creation, recognizing that the earth is a precious gift entrusted to our stewardship. Through each sustainable choice we make, we honor this divine mandate, contributing to the restoration and preservation of the natural world.

Each action, no matter how small, is a ripple in the pond of global change. From the decision to recycle or compost, to the choice to bike rather than drive, every effort counts. These actions, when multiplied by millions, have the power to effect significant environmental healing, demonstrating that individual responsibility can lead to collective impact.

Embracing sustainable living also involves education and advocacy. It requires us to not only adopt eco-friendly practices in our own lives but also to share the message of sustainability with others. By raising awareness and advocating for policies that support environmental protection, we can inspire a broader shift towards sustainability in our communities and beyond.

In conclusion, the power of sustainable living lies not only in its ability to mitigate environmental degradation but also in its capacity to unite us in a common purpose. It challenges us to live more mindfully, to consider the legacy we wish to leave behind, and to act with intentionality for the sake of our planet and future generations. As we embrace the solutions that sustainable living offers, let us do so with hope, knowing that each step we take is a step towards healing our world. This journey towards sustainability is a journey of faith, a journey that reaffirms our commitment to stewardship, and a journey that holds the promise of a renewed earth.

## ADVOCACY FOR ENVIRONMENTAL JUSTICE: A PROFOUND MISSION IN HEALING OUR PLANET

In the quest to heal our planet, the journey extends beyond the mere adoption of sustainable practices to encompass a deeper, more profound mission—advocacy for environmental justice. This mission recognizes the stark reality that the burden of environmental challenges does not fall equally upon all shoulders. The world's most vulnerable populations, often the least responsible for the degradation of our planet, suffer disproportionately from polluted air and water, toxic waste, and the devastating effects of climate change. In the face of this injustice, our faith does not allow us to remain silent spectators. Instead, it compels us to action, to raise our voices in defense of those who bear the weight of environmental harm.

Advocacy for environmental justice is a clarion call to ensure that every community, regardless of economic status, race, or geography, has access to the essentials of life: clean air, water, and land. It is a commitment to fight against the disparities that leave marginalized communities more exposed and less protected against environmental hazards. This commitment is rooted in the understanding that the health of our planet is inextricably linked to the well-being of its inhabitants, and that true stewardship involves caring for both creation and our fellow human beings.

Our faith teaches us that every individual is created in the image of God, deserving of dignity, respect, and a healthy environment. Standing in solidarity with those affected by environmental injustice means advocating for policies and practices that do not merely address the symptoms of degradation but tackle its root causes. It involves challenging the systems and structures that perpetuate inequality and working towards a future where environmental benefits and burdens are shared equitably.

This call to advocacy demands courage, persistence, and compassion. It requires us to educate ourselves and others about the realities of environmental injustice, to listen to the stories of those who live with its consequences, and to amplify their voices in the halls of power. It means partnering with affected communities to build resilience and advocate for change, ensuring that their needs and perspectives are central to the solutions we pursue.

Moreover, advocacy for environmental justice is an expression of hope. It is a belief in the possibility of change, in the power of collective action to transform societies and restore the environment. This hope is not naive; it is grounded in the conviction that with God's guidance and the commitment of people of faith, we can overcome the challenges that face us.

In embracing solutions to environmental challenges, our advocacy for environmental justice becomes a tangible manifestation of our faith. It is a demonstration of love for our neighbor, obedience to the call to stewardship, and a reflection of God's justice. By standing with the vulnerable and working towards a just and sustainable world, we live out the gospel in a way that heals not only the planet but also the divisions and inequalities that mar human society.

As we move forward in this journey, let us do so with the knowledge that our actions can make a difference. Let our faith inspire us to advocate for environmental justice with passion and perseverance, knowing that in doing so, we honor the Creator and contribute to the healing of our world. This subsection, "Advocacy for Environmental Justice," is not just a part of our narrative—it is a call to live out our faith in the world, making it a better place for all its inhabitants.

## ENGAGING IN CONSERVATION EFFORTS: A FAITH-DRIVEN CALL TO ACTION

In the tapestry of creation, each strand—every species, every habitat—plays a crucial role in maintaining the balance and beauty of our world. Yet, as we witness the alarming rate of environmental degradation, the call to engage in conservation efforts has never been more urgent. This call is not merely a suggestion but a clarion demand for action, inviting us to play an active role in the protection of endangered species and the preservation of natural habitats. It resonates deeply with our faith, which teaches us to be stewards of the Earth, caretakers of its wonders, and defenders of its treasures.

Supporting organizations dedicated to conservation is one of the tangible ways we can contribute to this vital cause. These organizations work tirelessly on the front lines, combating habitat destruction, advocating for environmental policies, and conducting research to further conservation goals. By offering our support—be it financial, vocal, or through volunteerism—we empower their efforts and become co-laborers in the mission to safeguard our planet's future.

Volunteering for restoration projects presents another avenue through which we can directly impact conservation efforts. These projects, often community-led, aim to restore ecosystems to their natural state, reestablish native plant species, and provide habitats for local wildlife. Engaging in such endeavors not only helps heal the planet but also deepens our connection to the natural world, offering profound lessons in humility, patience, and the intrinsic value of every form of life.

Moreover, promoting biodiversity in our own communities is a testament to the understanding that conservation starts at home. Whether by planting native species in our gardens, creating wildlife-friendly spaces, or advocating for green spaces in urban areas, we contribute to a broader ecological network that supports diverse forms of life. These efforts, though seemingly small, accumulate to form a mosaic of habitat patches essential for the survival of many species.

The call to engage in conservation efforts is deeply intertwined with our faith. It reflects our acknowledgment of the divine in all creation and our responsibility to protect and preserve it. Through active participation in conservation, we answer a sacred call to stewardship, one that honors the Creator by cherishing and safeguarding His creation.

This subsection, "Engaging in Conservation Efforts," is not merely a call to action; it is an invitation to embody our faith through the care of the Earth. It challenges us to look beyond our immediate concerns and to invest in the future of our planet. By taking up this mantle of responsibility, we participate in a greater story of renewal and hope, contributing to the healing of our world and ensuring its beauty and diversity endure for generations to come.

Let us, therefore, embrace conservation as a core element of our faith practice, recognizing in it the opportunity to serve, to learn, and to witness the power of collective action. In doing so, we not only work towards the preservation of endangered species and habitats but also cultivate a deeper appreciation for the intricacy and interdependence of all life. Our engagement in conservation efforts stands as a powerful testament to our commitment to stewardship, a reflection of our reverence for life, and a contribution to the legacy of a healthier, more vibrant planet.

## ACTION: MOVING FORWARD WITH PURPOSE

As we stand at the crossroads, facing the environmental challenges that threaten the fabric of our world, it is imperative that we draw upon our deepest convictions—faith, hope, and love—to forge a path forward.

These challenges, daunting as they may be, present us with an unparalleled opportunity to embody the principles of stewardship that are central to our faith. In this critical moment, let us recommit ourselves to being agents of change, to advocating for sustainable practices, and to living in ways that honor and preserve God's magnificent creation.

Faith, the bedrock of our journey, empowers us to look beyond the immediate and see the potential for transformation. It instills in us the belief that, with divine guidance and unwavering commitment, we can confront the environmental crises of our time and emerge victorious. Faith calls us to trust in the Creator's design, to recognize our role within it as caretakers, and to act with conviction in fulfilling that role.

Hope, the beacon that guides us, illuminates the path through the darkest of times. It assures us that our efforts, no matter how small, contribute to the tapestry of change. Hope encourages us to envision a world where harmony between humanity and nature is restored, where the scars of environmental degradation are healed, and where future generations can thrive. It reminds us that with every action we take, we sow the seeds of a more sustainable and just world.

Love, the force that propels us, calls us to extend our compassion to all corners of creation. It urges us to consider the lilies of the field and the birds of the air, recognizing their value and working tirelessly to protect their habitats. Love compels us to stand in solidarity with the most vulnerable among us, those who bear the brunt of environmental injustice, ensuring that our pursuit of sustainability is inclusive and equitable.

As agents of change, we are tasked with advocating for policies and practices that reflect our commitment to sustainability. This advocacy takes many forms, from supporting renewable energy initiatives to campaigning for the protection of endangered species and natural habitats. It involves engaging with our communities, raising awareness about the importance of environmental stewardship, and inspiring others to join in the collective effort to safeguard our planet.

Living in a manner that honors God's creation requires intentional choices in our daily lives. It means adopting sustainable habits, reducing our consumption, recycling, and reusing whenever possible, and making informed decisions that prioritize the well-being of the environment. It is a holistic approach that encompasses every aspect of our existence, from the food we eat to the products we buy and the way we travel.

As we move forward with purpose, let us do so with the understanding that our collective efforts are vital to paving the way for a healthier, more sustainable world. Let this journey be marked by a spirit of collaboration, as we join hands with fellow stewards of the earth, drawing strength from our shared commitment to making a difference.

In embracing solutions and taking action, we are not only responding to the call of stewardship but also deepening our faith, nurturing our hope, and expressing our love for God's creation. Our path forward is clear: to live with purpose, to act with courage, and to inspire change through our example. In doing so, we affirm our belief in a future where humanity and nature exist in harmony, a testament to the power of faith, hope, and love in action.

## CONCLUSION: A CALL TO STEWARDSHIP

As we close the chapter on our exploration of embracing solutions for the environmental challenges that confront us—grounded in faith, propelled by hope, and guided by love—we stand on the precipice of a profound transition. Chapter 6 has beckoned us to become agents of change, to weave sustainability into the fabric of our daily lives, and to advocate passionately for the protection of God's magnificent creation. Our journey through these pages has been one of awakening and action, a clarion call to stewardship that resonates with the deepest echoes of our faith.

Yet, as we turn the page, we enter a space of contemplation and reverence in Chapter 7, titled "Divine Rest: Sanctifying the Seventh Day." Here, we are invited to reflect on the rhythm of creation itself, a rhythm established by the Creator who, after six days of creative work, rested on the seventh day, sanctifying it as a day of rest for all creation. This transition from action to rest, from labor to reflection, is not merely a cessation of activity but an integral aspect of our stewardship and our spiritual journey.

In this next chapter, we delve into the significance of rest in the divine narrative and its implications for us as caretakers of the earth. The sanctification of the seventh day serves as a reminder that our efforts to heal and protect the planet must be balanced with moments of rest and renewal, both for ourselves and for the world around us. It underscores the importance of pausing to celebrate the fruits of our labor, to recharge our spirits, and to deepen our connection with the Creator and His creation.

"Divine Rest: Sanctifying the Seventh Day" challenges us to embrace the concept of Sabbath not just as a day of rest but as a principle of living that honors the natural limits and cycles of the earth. It encourages us to consider how our lifestyles and choices can reflect a respect for these limits, promoting sustainability not only through our actions but also through our rest. This chapter invites us to explore practices of rest and Sabbath-keeping that renew our commitment to environmental stewardship, nourish our souls, and draw us closer to the heart of God.

As we transition from the active engagement of addressing environmental challenges to the sacred observance of rest, let us carry forward the lessons learned and the commitments made. Let us hold in our hearts the understanding that true stewardship encompasses both diligent action and intentional rest, both of which are acts of worship and expressions of our love for the Creator. In sanctifying the seventh day, we acknowledge the divine wisdom in rest, reaffirming our trust in the One who sustains all things and inviting His restorative peace into our lives and our world.

Join us in Chapter 7 as we explore the depths of divine rest and its sanctifying power, a journey that promises to enrich our spiritual lives and enhance our role as stewards of God's creation.

**Prayer:** For Healing and Renewal

Heavenly Father, we pray for the healing of our planet and the wisdom to steward Your creation with care and love. Grant us the courage to face the environmental challenges of our time and inspire us to take action for the good of all Your creatures. In Your holy name, we pray, Amen.

Our journey through stewardship and environmental challenges has prepared us for the next chapter: living out our faith in action, as we seek to make a tangible difference in the world around us. Let us step into this call with determination and hope, ready to transform our faith into deeds that heal and renew the earth.

As we move forward, let this prayer guide us to act with conviction and compassion. May we embody the stewardship entrusted to us, caring for the earth and advocating for its preservation. With every step we take, let us remember the power of collective action and the impact of individual dedication. Together, inspired by faith and driven by a shared vision of restoration, we can work towards a healthier, more sustainable world for future generations.

# CHAPTER 7

# DIVINE REST: SANCTIFYING THE SEVENTH DAY

In the grand narrative of creation, where each day unfolds with a divine purpose, the seventh day holds a unique and profound significance. It is a day marked by God's rest, a sacred pause in the continuum of creation that invites us to reflect, to renew, and to realign with the divine rhythm that orchestrates the universe. This pause, this divine rest, is not a mere cessation of activity but a celebration of completion, an acknowledgment of the goodness that permeates the fabric of the world.

As we transition from the vibrant call to action and stewardship in Chapter 6, where we grappled with the pressing environmental challenges of our time, we find ourselves at a pivotal moment in our journey. It is here, at the threshold of Chapter 7, that we pause to draw breath, to reflect on the path we have traversed, and to embrace the profound lessons of the Sabbath.

The story of our engagement with the world's environmental challenges is one of commitment, hope, and relentless pursuit of sustainability. We've explored the avenues through which we can contribute to the healing of our planet, from advocating for sustainable practices to embracing conservation efforts with zeal. Our journey has been marked by a deepening understanding of our role as stewards of God's creation, a role that demands action, awareness, and an unwavering commitment to the preservation of the natural world.

Yet, as we embark on this new chapter, we are reminded that our stewardship is not solely defined by our actions but also by our capacity to rest, to honor the sacred rhythm that God himself modeled on the seventh day of creation. This chapter is a story of realization and spiritual renewal that begins with a pivotal juncture in my own journey—a moment of profound revelation as I contemplated the divine act of creation and God's rest.

On the seventh day, as I reflected on the tapestry of life that God had woven across the span of six days, I found myself at a crossroads, a moment ripe with potential for deep spiritual insight. It was a time to contemplate not just the act of creation but the sanctity of rest, the divine pause that punctuates the cycle of life with a silent yet eloquent testament to the importance of reflection, rejuvenation, and reverence.

Embracing the Sabbath became a journey of discovery, a deliberate step towards aligning my life with the divine rhythm of work and rest. It was a conscious decision to prioritize rest and reflection, trusting in God's provision and sovereignty over my life. This commitment to observing the Sabbath emerged not from obligation but from a desire to draw closer to God, to find solace and strength in His presence, and to realign my priorities in accordance with His will.

Through prayer and contemplation on the sanctity of the seventh day, I experienced a transformation—a deep sense of peace and contentment that suffused my being, a solace found only in the sacred space of rest. The Sabbath revealed itself as a time for spiritual renewal and rejuvenation, a period where my faith was fortified, and my spirit was refreshed by the profound truth of God's enduring presence.

As we delve into the rich tapestry of Chapter 7, let us carry with us the lessons learned from our active engagement with the challenges of our world. Let us explore the sacred significance of the Sabbath, understanding it as a divine gift of rest that offers us a chance to renew our strength, to deepen our faith, and to continue our journey with renewed purpose and hope.

In this chapter, we are invited to embrace the rhythm of divine rest and to explore the ways in which the Sabbath can transform our approach to life, our stewardship of the planet, and our relationship with the Creator. Let this exploration be a source of encouragement and strength, a reminder that in the act of divine rest, we find the resilience to face the challenges ahead and the grace to continue our stewardship with renewed vigor and faith.

## THE DIVINE GIFT OF REST

### HONORING GOD'S RHYTHM OF WORK AND RENEWAL

In the intricate design of creation, where each day unfolds a new layer of God's masterpiece, the seventh day stands out as a profound testament to the balance between work and rest. Sanctified and blessed by God, this day serves as a sacred model, beckoning us to embrace a rhythm of life that is often lost amidst the relentless pace of modern existence. It is a rhythm that honors the need for rest, not as an afterthought but as a vital component of our well-being and spiritual growth.

God's rest on the seventh day is more than a divine pause; it is an invitation into a space of renewal and reflection. It highlights the importance of setting aside our labors to seek rejuvenation of body, mind, and spirit. This divine model challenges us to reevaluate our understanding of productivity and success, urging us to consider rest as fundamental to our health and as a reflection of our trust in God's providence.

By sanctifying the seventh day, God imbues it with a significance that goes beyond mere cessation of work. It becomes a sacred time for emotional and spiritual renewal, an opportunity to deepen our connection with the Creator and to recharge our souls. This act of sanctification is a call to honor our inherent need for rest, acknowledging that in doing so, we align ourselves more closely with God's design for our lives.

Embracing God's rhythm of work and renewal requires a deliberate shift in our priorities. It invites us to pause and consider how we can integrate moments of rest into the fabric of our daily lives. This might mean setting aside specific times for prayer and meditation, engaging in activities that replenish our energy and spirit, or simply being still and present in the moment, allowing ourselves to be refreshed by God's presence.

The challenge to adopt this rhythm is counter-cultural, pushing against the tide of a society that often values constant activity and productivity above all else. Yet, in choosing to honor God's model of rest, we find a counterintuitive truth: that in rest, our capacity for work is enhanced, our creativity is nurtured, and our effectiveness is increased. Rest, therefore, becomes not an obstacle to our productivity but a catalyst for it.

Moreover, embracing this divine rhythm is an act of faith. It reflects our trust in God's sovereignty and His provision for our lives. It is an acknowledgment that we are not the masters of our fate but are held in the loving care of a Creator who knows our needs and provides for them. By setting aside time for rest, we express our reliance on God, trusting that He will sustain us and that our work, grounded in periods of rest, will bear fruit according to His will.

This divine invitation to rest and renewal is a gift, one that offers freedom from the weariness that comes from an unceasing cycle of work. It is a reminder that our value is not determined by our productivity but by our identity as beloved children of God. In accepting this invitation, we open ourselves to the transformative power of rest, allowing it to shape our lives in ways that reflect a deeper understanding of success—one that is rooted in balance, well-being, and a profound connection with the divine.

As we journey through this section on the divine gift of rest, let us be encouraged to embrace God's rhythm of work and renewal. May we find in it a source of strength and rejuvenation, a wellspring of peace and contentment, and a guide to living a life that honors both our need for productivity and our profound need for rest.

## CREATING SPACE FOR GOD TO WORK

In the sacred pause of rest, we open a door to the divine, creating space for God to move and work within the deepest recesses of our beings. This act of ceasing from our labors, of deliberately stepping away from the demands and toils that fill our days, is far more than a mere cessation of activity. It is a profound spiritual practice, a deliberate cultivation of openness to the transformative power of God's presence in our lives. By embracing rest, we are not showing weakness or neglecting our duties; rather, we are engaging in a deep act of faith, recognizing that true strength and renewal flow from God.

Resting, in the divine context of the Sabbath, becomes a testament to our trust in God's provision and sovereignty. It is an acknowledgment that our efforts alone are insufficient without the sustaining and life-giving power of God's grace. In laying down our burdens and ceasing our work, we are not abandoning our responsibilities but placing them in the hands of the One who commands the wind and the waves. This trust is not passive but active, a choice to believe in God's ability to provide, protect, and lead, even in our absence or silence.

The Sabbath invites us into a rhythm of grace, where rest and work dance in harmony, each giving meaning and value to the other. In this rhythm, we find balance—a balance that nourishes our physical selves, yes, but more importantly, rejuvenates our spirits and renews our strength. It is in these moments of rest that we often hear God's voice most clearly, speaking peace to our turmoil, offering guidance through our confusion, and whispering reassurance to our doubts.

This sacred practice of creating space for God to work within us through rest is a journey into the heart of faith. It challenges our modern sensibilities, which often equate value with productivity and worth with accomplishment. Yet, the divine economy operates on different principles, where rest is valued as highly as labor, and inactivity can be as fruitful as action. For in the quiet, in the stillness, God works in ways that defy our understanding, shaping our character, guiding our thoughts, and molding our spirits to reflect His own.

Honoring the Sabbath and embracing rest as a spiritual practice require intentionality. It means consciously setting aside time and space in our lives to disconnect from the demands of the world and connect with God. This may involve physical rest, yes, but it also calls for a quieting of the mind and heart, a laying aside of the endless list of tasks and concerns, to be present with God. In this space, we are not idle; we are actively engaging in the work of the soul, allowing God to refresh, renew, and restore us.

The benefits of this practice extend beyond our personal renewal. As we are filled with the peace and contentment that come from resting in

God, we are better equipped to extend that peace and contentment to others. Our relationships are enriched, our perspectives are broadened, and our capacity for compassion and empathy is deepened. We become vessels of God's peace in a world desperately in need of it.

In creating space for God to work within us through rest, we are participating in a divine exchange. We offer our time, our silence, and our stillness, and in return, God fills us with His strength, His peace, and His presence. This exchange is at the heart of the Sabbath—a gift of rest from God to us, and a gift of trust from us to God.

As we explore this subsection on creating space for God to work, let us be encouraged to embrace rest not just as a physical necessity but as a vital spiritual practice. May we discover the joy and peace that come from laying down our burdens and allowing God to work within us, renewing our strength and refreshing our spirits.

## EMBRACING THE SACRED SABBATH

## A TIME OF REST AND REFLECTION

The Sabbath, in its divine wisdom, extends an invitation to a deeper, more profound experience than mere cessation from labor. It beckons us into a sacred space—a sanctuary in time where the soul is nourished, the spirit is rejuvenated, and the heart is realigned with the eternal. This day of rest and reflection is a gift, intricately woven into the fabric of creation, reminding us that to fully embrace life, we must pause, reflect, and connect with the source of all life.

In setting aside our work and worries, we are not merely pausing our regular activities; we are actively creating a space for God to speak into our lives. The Sabbath offers a unique opportunity to step back from the relentless pace of daily existence, to breathe deeply of the presence of God, and to meditate on His goodness. It is in these moments of quiet reflection that we often hear God's voice most clearly, guiding us, comforting us, and reminding us of His unfailing love.

This sacred space for reflection allows us to examine our lives through the lens of God's will, encouraging us to consider whether our priorities reflect His priorities, whether our paths align with the path He has set before us. The Sabbath, therefore, becomes a pivotal point in our week—a time to reassess, to realign, and to renew our commitment to living according to God's design.

Moreover, the Sabbath as a time of rest and reflection serves as a commandment, a divine directive that underscores the importance of rest in God's plan for humanity. It is a commandment that speaks of God's desire for His children to experience the fullness of life, to enjoy a rhythm of work and rest that is both life-giving and life-sustaining. This commandment is born out of love, a reminder that we are not created for endless toil but for a harmonious existence that includes rest, reflection, and worship.

Embracing the Sabbath is thus an act of obedience, an acknowledgment of our need for God's wisdom and provision in our lives. It is a declaration of trust, affirming that we can lay down our work for a day because we believe in the God who provides, the God who sustains, and the God who invites us into His rest. In this act of obedience, we find freedom—freedom from the tyranny of the urgent, freedom from the idolatry of productivity, and freedom to rest in the assurance of God's care.

The Sabbath also invites us to experience the fullness of life that God intends for us, a life marked by joy, peace, and contentment. In the rhythm of rest and work that the Sabbath establishes, we discover the balance that is essential for a healthy, holistic life. We are reminded that our value is not measured by our accomplishments but by our identity as beloved children of God. The Sabbath reorients us to the truth that our worth is intrinsic, bestowed by God, and not earned by our efforts.

As we embrace the sacred space of the Sabbath, let it be a time of rich reflection and spiritual nourishment. Let us draw near to God, meditating on His goodness and realigning our priorities with His will. In doing so, may we find the rest for our souls that Jesus promises, and may we experience the fullness of life that comes from walking in obedience to God's commandments. The Sabbath stands as a beacon, guiding us to the peaceful shores of divine rest and reflection, where we are renewed, restored, and reminded of the boundless grace of God.

## THE PRACTICE OF SABBATH-KEEPING

The practice of Sabbath-keeping is a deliberate journey into the heart of divine rest, a sacred act of obedience that echoes our deep desire to honor God. This ancient ritual, rooted in the very rhythm of creation, calls us to pause, to disconnect from the ceaseless demands of our daily lives, and to enter into a space of renewal and reverence. In a world that often measures worth by productivity and success by busyness, Sabbath-keeping stands as a countercultural act of faith, affirming our commitment to God's design for a balanced life of work and rest.

Embracing the Sabbath requires intentional choices and actions, a conscious decision to set aside the time and space for rest and worship. For many, this may involve a physical disconnect from the technologies that tether us to work and the wider world, offering a precious opportunity to quieten the noise that fills our days. In the silence left in technology's wake, we find the space to listen, to reflect, and to connect with God in a more profound and intimate way.

Spending time in nature is another powerful expression of Sabbath-keeping, reminding us of the beauty and majesty of God's creation. In the rustling of leaves, the flowing of streams, and the tranquility of natural landscapes, we encounter the divine artist behind it all. These moments in nature not only restore our souls but also reaffirm our place within the broader tapestry of life, inspiring a deeper appreciation for the world God has entrusted to our care.

Participation in worship, whether in a communal setting or a personal time of prayer and reflection, is a cornerstone of Sabbath observance. It's in these sacred gatherings or solitary moments that we lift our hearts and voices in praise and thanksgiving, drawing near to God and being refreshed by His presence. Worship, in its many forms, acts as a bridge between the divine and the human, renewing our spirit and grounding us in the truth of God's word.

Engaging in activities that restore our souls is uniquely personal, varying greatly from one individual to another. For some, it may be reading and meditating on Scripture, for others, creating art or music, and yet for others, it might be serving those in need. These activities, whatever they may be, are not about escapism but about engagement with practices that fill our souls, draw us closer to God, and reflect His love and beauty back into the world.

Sabbath-keeping, in all its expressions, is a tangible manifestation of our desire to live according to God's will, honoring Him not just with our words but with our time and our deeds. It's a practice that not only benefits us personally, providing rest and renewal, but also impacts those around us, as we emerge from the Sabbath more centered, more compassionate, and more reflective of Christ's love.

This act of obedience and reverence is, at its core, a declaration of trust in God's provision and care. It acknowledges that our lives are not solely defined by what we produce but by whom we cherish, serve, and worship. As we embrace the sacred practice of Sabbath-keeping, let it be a weekly reminder of our covenant with God, a covenant rooted in love, sustained by grace, and celebrated through rest.

In embracing the Sabbath, we are invited to rediscover the joy of God's creation, the peace of His presence, and the rhythm of life that balances work with rest, activity with renewal. Let this practice of Sabbath-keeping strengthen our faith, deepen our relationship with God, and inspire us to live in a way that honors the sacred rhythm He has established for our lives.

## A TIME OF REST AND REFLECTION: CREATING SPACE FOR GOD TO WORK THROUGH SABBATH REST

In the sacred pause of rest, we open a door to the divine, creating space for God to move and work within the deepest recesses of our beings. This act of ceasing from our labors, of deliberately stepping away from the demands and toils that fill our days, is far more than a mere cessation of activity. It is a profound spiritual practice, a deliberate cultivation of openness to the transformative power of God's presence in our lives. By embracing rest, we are not showing weakness or neglecting our duties; rather, we are engaging in a deep act of faith, recognizing that true strength and renewal flow from God.

Resting, in the divine context of the Sabbath, becomes a testament to our trust in God's provision and sovereignty. It is an acknowledgment that our efforts alone are insufficient without the sustaining and life-giving power of God's grace. In laying down our burdens and ceasing our work, we are not abandoning our responsibilities but placing them in the hands of the One who commands the wind and the waves. This trust is not passive but active, a choice to believe in God's ability to provide, protect, and lead, even in our absence or silence.

The Sabbath invites us into a rhythm of grace, where rest and work dance in harmony, each giving meaning and value to the other. In this rhythm, we find balance—a balance that nourishes our physical selves, yes, but more importantly, rejuvenates our spirits and renews our strength. It is in these moments of rest that we often hear God's voice most clearly, speaking peace to our turmoil, offering guidance through our confusion, and whispering reassurance to our doubts.

This sacred practice of creating space for God to work within us through rest is a journey into the heart of faith. It challenges our modern sensibilities, which often equate value with productivity and worth with accomplishment. Yet, the divine economy operates on different principles, where rest is valued as highly as labor, and inactivity can be as fruitful as action. For in the quiet, in the stillness, God works in ways that defy our understanding, shaping our character, guiding our thoughts, and molding our spirits to reflect His own.

Honoring the Sabbath and embracing rest as a spiritual practice require intentionality. It means consciously setting aside time and space in our lives to disconnect from the demands of the world and connect with God. This may involve physical rest, yes, but it also calls for a quieting of the mind and heart, a laying aside of the endless list of tasks and concerns, to be present with God. In this space, we are not idle; we are actively engaging in the work of the soul, allowing God to refresh, renew, and restore us.

The benefits of this practice extend beyond our personal renewal. As we are filled with the peace and contentment that come from resting in God, we are better equipped to extend that peace and contentment to others. Our relationships are enriched, our perspectives are broadened, and our capacity for compassion and empathy is deepened. We become vessels of God's peace in a world desperately in need of it.

In creating space for God to work within us through rest, we are participating in a divine exchange. We offer our time, our silence, and our stillness, and in return, God fills us with His strength, His peace, and His presence. This exchange is at the heart of the Sabbath—a gift of rest from God to us, and a gift of trust from us to God.

As we explore this subsection on creating space for God to work, let us be encouraged to embrace rest not just as a physical necessity but as a vital spiritual practice. May we discover the joy and peace that come from laying down our burdens and allowing God to work within us, renewing our strength and refreshing our spirits.

## THE PRACTICE OF SABBATH-KEEPING: CULTIVATING DIVINE REST

In the sacred pause of rest, we open a door to the divine, creating space for God to move and work within the deepest recesses of our beings. This act of ceasing from our labors, of deliberately stepping away from the demands and toils that fill our days, is far more than a mere cessation of activity. It is a profound spiritual practice, a deliberate cultivation of openness to the transformative power of God's presence in our lives. By embracing rest, we are not showing weakness or neglecting our duties; rather, we are engaging in a deep act of faith, recognizing that true strength and renewal flow from God.

Resting, in the divine context of the Sabbath, becomes a testament to our trust in God's provision and sovereignty. It is an acknowledgment that our efforts alone are insufficient without the sustaining and life-giving power of God's grace. In laying down our burdens and ceasing our work, we are not abandoning our responsibilities but placing them in the hands of the One who commands the wind and the waves. This trust is not passive but active, a choice to believe in God's ability to provide, protect, and lead, even in our absence or silence.

The Sabbath invites us into a rhythm of grace, where rest and work dance in harmony, each giving meaning and value to the other. In this rhythm, we find balance—a balance that nourishes our physical selves, yes, but more importantly, rejuvenates our spirits and renews our strength. It is in these moments of rest that we often hear God's voice most clearly, speaking peace to our turmoil, offering guidance through our confusion, and whispering reassurance to our doubts.

This sacred practice of creating space for God to work within us through rest is a journey into the heart of faith. It challenges our modern sensibilities, which often equate value with productivity and worth with accomplishment. Yet, the divine economy operates on different principles, where rest is valued as highly as labor, and inactivity can be as fruitful as action. For in the quiet, in the stillness, God works in ways that defy our understanding, shaping our character, guiding our thoughts, and molding our spirits to reflect His own.

Honoring the Sabbath and embracing rest as a spiritual practice require intentionality. It means consciously setting aside time and space in our lives to disconnect from the demands of the world and connect with God. This may involve physical rest, yes, but it also calls for a quieting of the mind and heart, a laying aside of the endless list of tasks and concerns, to be present with God. In this space, we are not idle; we are actively engaging in the work of the soul, allowing God to refresh, renew, and restore us.

The benefits of this practice extend beyond our personal renewal. As we are filled with the peace and contentment that come from resting in God, we are better equipped to extend that peace and contentness to others. Our relationships are enriched, our perspectives are broadened, and our capacity for compassion and empathy is deepened. We become vessels of God's peace in a world desperately in need of it.

In creating space for God to work within us through rest, we are participating in a divine exchange. We offer our time, our silence, and our stillness, and in return, God fills us with His strength, His peace, and His presence. This exchange is at the heart of the Sabbath—a gift of rest from God to us, and a gift of trust from us to God.

As we explore this subsection on creating space for God to work, let us be encouraged to embrace rest not just as a physical necessity but as a vital spiritual practice. May we discover the joy and peace that come from laying down our burdens and allowing God to work within us, renewing our strength and refreshing our spirits.

## THE PRACTICE OF SABBATH-KEEPING

### A SACRED ACT OF OBEDIENCE AND RENEWAL

The practice of Sabbath-keeping is a deliberate journey into the heart of divine rest, a sacred act of obedience that echoes our deep desire to honor God. This ancient ritual, rooted in the very rhythm of creation, calls us to pause, to disconnect from the ceaseless demands of our daily lives, and to enter into a space of renewal and reverence. In a world that often measures worth by productivity and success by busyness, Sabbath-keeping stands as a countercultural act of faith, affirming our commitment to God's design for a balanced life of work and rest.

### EMBRACING THE SABBATH

Embracing the Sabbath requires intentional choices and actions, a conscious decision to set aside time and space for rest and worship. For many, this may involve a physical disconnect from the technologies that tether us to work and the wider world, offering a precious opportunity to quiet the noise that fills our days. In the silence left in technology's wake, we find the space to listen, to reflect, and to connect with God in a more profound and intimate way.

### NATURE AND WORSHIP

Spending time in nature is another powerful expression of Sabbath-keeping, reminding us of the beauty and majesty of God's creation. In the rustling of leaves, the flowing of streams, and the tranquility of natural landscapes, we encounter the divine artist behind it all. These moments in nature not only restore our souls but also reaffirm our place within the broader tapestry of life, inspiring a deeper appreciation for the world God has entrusted to our care.

Participation in worship, whether in a communal setting or a personal time of prayer and reflection, is a cornerstone of Sabbath observance. It's in these sacred gatherings or solitary moments that we lift our hearts and voices in praise and thanksgiving, drawing near to God and being refreshed by His presence. Worship, in its many forms, acts as a bridge between the divine and the human, renewing our spirit and grounding us in the truth of God's word.

## PERSONAL SOUL-RESTORING ACTIVITIES

Engaging in activities that restore our souls is uniquely personal, varying greatly from one individual to another. For some, it may be reading and meditating on Scripture; for others, creating art or music; and yet for others, it might be serving those in need. These activities, whatever they may be, are not about escapism but about engagement with practices that fill our souls, draw us closer to God, and reflect His love and beauty back into the world.

## IMPACT AND TRUST IN GOD

Sabbath-keeping, in all its expressions, is a tangible manifestation of our desire to live according to God's will, honoring Him not just with our words but with our time and our deeds. It's a practice that not only benefits us personally, providing rest and renewal, but also impacts those around us, as we emerge from the Sabbath more centered, more compassionate, and more reflective of Christ's love.

This act of obedience and reverence is, at its core, a declaration of trust in God's provision and care. It acknowledges that our lives are not solely defined by what we produce but by whom we cherish, serve, and worship. As we embrace the sacred practice of Sabbath-keeping, let it be a weekly reminder of our covenant with God, a covenant rooted in love, sustained by grace, and celebrated through rest.

## INVITATION TO REDISCOVER

In embracing the Sabbath, we are invited to rediscover the joy of God's creation, the peace of His presence, and the rhythm of life that balances work with rest, activity with renewal. Let this practice of Sabbath-keeping strengthen our faith, deepen our relationship with God, and inspire us to live in a way that honors the sacred rhythm He has established for our lives.

## THE SABBATH AS A CATALYST FOR CHANGE

### TRANSFORMING OUR APPROACH TO LIFE

The Sabbath, a divine institution woven into the fabric of creation, holds within it transformative power that extends far beyond a single day of rest. It stands as a profound counter-narrative to the prevailing ethos of our time, which measures worth by productivity and equates success with unceasing activity. By embracing the Sabbath, we embark on a journey of transformation, one that invites us to reconsider the very foundations upon which we build our lives.

In integrating the principles of Sabbath-keeping into our daily existence, we undertake a radical act of resistance against the cultural currents that drive us towards burnout and disconnection. The Sabbath beckons us to a different way of living, one that values rest and rejuvenation as essential to our well-being. It challenges us to set aside time for God, for ourselves, and for our loved ones, fostering relationships and activities that nourish our souls.

This transformative shift in perspective requires a conscious decision to prioritize rest, not as a luxury, but as a necessity. In doing so, we affirm the intrinsic value of our humanity, recognizing that we are not merely the sum of our achievements but beloved creations of God, defined by our relationship with Him. The Sabbath reminds us that our identity is rooted in Whom we belong to, not what we accomplish.

By observing the Sabbath, we send a powerful message to the world around us. We declare that our time is not solely for production but for reflection, not just for doing but for being. This stance not only challenges societal norms but also invites others to reconsider their own priorities and the relentless pace at which they live their lives.

The practice of Sabbath-keeping serves as a catalyst for change, transforming not only our individual lives but potentially the fabric of society. It proposes a model of living that values balance, honors creation, and acknowledges our need for spiritual sustenance. This change in approach can lead to healthier communities, more sustainable lifestyles, and a deeper sense of contentment and peace.

Furthermore, the Sabbath offers a space for us to reconnect with God's creation, appreciating the beauty and wonder of the natural world. It encourages us to step away from the screens and schedules that dominate our lives and to engage in restorative activities that remind us of the joy of simply being. In these moments of rest, we find clarity and purpose, guided by the still, small voice of God that speaks in the silence.

The transformative power of the Sabbath extends to our work as well. By resting one day a week, we approach our tasks with renewed energy and creativity. The Sabbath teaches us that rest is not the opposite of productivity but its complement. It is in the rhythm of work and rest that we find our most fulfilling and effective engagement with the world.

In embracing the Sabbath as a catalyst for change, we open ourselves to a life marked by balance, purpose, and deep connection with the divine. This sacred day offers us a vision of what life can be when we align ourselves with God's intentions for rest and renewal. It is an invitation to live in a way that honors our Creator, nourishes our souls, and brings light to a world in desperate need of hope and healing.

As we reflect on the transformative potential of the Sabbath, let us be inspired to integrate its principles into our lives, challenging the status quo and embracing a new way of being. In doing so, we will discover the true essence of our humanity, rooted in rest, rejuvenation, and our sacred identity in God.

## RENEWAL AND RESISTANCE: EMBRACING THE SABBATH AS A TRANSFORMATIVE ACT

In the sacred rhythm of the Sabbath lies a powerful form of resistance—a stand against a world that too often prioritizes profit over people, the sanctity of the earth, and the very essence of our well-being. Sabbath-keeping emerges not just as a practice of faith but as a revolutionary act, asserting that our time, our health, and the environment are sacred gifts, not commodities to be exhausted in the relentless pursuit of more. It's a declaration of our values, a testament to what we hold dear, and a commitment to protect and preserve what is truly important.

This act of resistance is profound in its simplicity. By choosing to rest, we counteract a consumerist culture that devalues creation and commodifies every moment of our time. Sabbath-keeping becomes a quiet rebellion against the notion that our worth is measured by our productivity, that success is quantified by accumulation, and that busyness is synonymous with importance. In resting, we affirm the intrinsic value of life itself, honoring the Creator by cherishing creation.

The Sabbath, then, is more than a day of rest; it's a stance against exploitation and environmental degradation. It stands in solidarity with those who bear the brunt of a world that sacrifices the well-being of the many for the gain of the few. By observing the Sabbath, we align ourselves with the oppressed and the marginalized, acknowledging their struggles and joining in their fight for justice and dignity.

This practice of renewal and resistance challenges us to reflect on our own lifestyles and the impact they have on others and the planet. It invites us to consider the ways in which we might unwittingly contribute to systems of exploitation and to seek alternatives that promote equity and sustainability. In choosing rest, we choose to step off the treadmill of consumption and to find value in being rather than having.

Moreover, Sabbath-keeping as an act of resistance calls us to communal action. It's a practice that, when shared, has the potential to foster a collective consciousness about the importance of rest, the value of time, and the sanctity of our environment. Together, we can create spaces of rest that serve as sanctuaries from the demands of a profit-driven world, offering support and strength to those in need.

In the quiet of the Sabbath, we also find the strength to resist the despair that can come from witnessing the degradation of our world. It is a day that renews our hope and rejuvenates our spirits, enabling us to continue the work of caring for creation with renewed vigor and optimism. The Sabbath reminds us that, despite the challenges we face, we are not alone, and that rest itself is a form of resilience, a source of the strength we need to continue the fight for a better world.

As we embrace the Sabbath as an act of renewal and resistance, we are reminded of the power of collective action and the importance of standing up for what we believe. This practice reaffirms our commitment to a world that values people and the planet over profit, urging us to live in ways that honor the sacredness of life and creation. It's a call to live counter-culturally, to embody the values of the Kingdom of God in a world that often seems to have forgotten them.

In this subsection on "Renewal and Resistance," we explore the Sabbath not just as a day of rest but as a profound statement of faith and defiance against the forces that seek to diminish the value of life and creation. Let this idea encourage and strengthen our faith, urging us to engage deeply with the practice of Sabbath-keeping as both a source of personal renewal and a form of resistance against the exploitation and degradation of our world.

## CONCLUSION: EMBRACING DIVINE REST

As we close this chapter on divine rest, let us carry with us the lessons of the Sabbath—a reminder of God's provision, a call to rest and renewal, and a challenge to live in harmony with the divine rhythm of work and rest. May we embrace the Sabbath with intention and reverence, allowing its sacred rhythm to shape our lives, deepen our faith, and renew our commitment to stewardship and care for all of creation.

---

**Prayer:** Heavenly Father, thank You for the gift of the Sabbath, for the rest and renewal it brings to our lives. Help us to honor this sacred day, to find rest in Your presence, and to live in the rhythm of Your grace. May our observance of the Sabbath deepen our relationship with You and with Your creation. Amen.

As we transition from the reflections and actions proposed in this chapter, we move forward with a renewed sense of purpose, ready to embody the principles of divine rest and to carry its peace into the world around us. Through our continued practice of Sabbath-keeping, let us serve as beacons of rest and rejuvenation, advocating for a lifestyle that values peace, sustains well-being, and honors the interconnectedness of all life. In doing so, we not only uphold the sanctity of divine rest but also contribute to a more compassionate and sustainable world.

# CHAPTER 8

# REFLECTIONS ON MODERN FAITH

In the heart of a bustling city, amidst the relentless pace of modern life, I witnessed an extraordinary event one tranquil evening. The sky, a vast canvas of twilight, suddenly erupted in a spectacle of colors more vibrant than any I had ever seen. Around me, people from all walks of life, usually engrossed in their digital worlds, paused to gaze upward in collective wonder. This phenomenon, soon to be known as the "Celestial Mural," marked the beginning of a profound personal journey, bridging the ancient narrative of creation with the pulse of my contemporary faith.

As an environmental scientist, I had long wrestled with reconciling my deep faith with the empirical realities of my profession. However, the Celestial Mural seemed to whisper a profound truth to me: the beautiful harmony that exists between the divine act of creation and the pursuit of scientific understanding.

Motivated by this insight, I set out to explore how the principles of creation could inform and enrich my faith, guiding me to new understandings of environmental stewardship, scientific exploration, and societal values. My journey revealed that the story of creation, far from being an outdated myth, offered meaningful guidance for today's world.

## ENVIRONMENTAL STEWARDSHIP: A SACRED DUTY

The narrative of creation, as depicted in the sacred texts, paints a picture of the world as an exquisite masterpiece of divine artistry, a vibrant tapestry woven by the hands of the Creator. Within this narrative, I discovered a profound calling, a divine mandate that resonated deeply within my soul: the call to environmental stewardship. This revelation was not merely an awakening to the beauty and intricacy of the natural world but an acknowledgment of the sacred duty entrusted to us—to care for this earth, to nurture it, and to safeguard its splendor for the generations that follow.

Embracing this call transformed my perspective. I began to view every river, mountain, and forest, every creature that roams the earth or swims in its vast oceans, as a testament to God's creativity and love. The realization that this magnificent creation was entrusted to our care filled me with a sense of responsibility and purpose. It became clear that caring for the earth was not just an environmental imperative but an act of worship, a tangible expression of our love for the Creator and a reflection of our gratitude for His countless blessings.

Motivated by this newfound understanding, I initiated community clean-up efforts, recognizing that the stewardship of our local environments was a critical first step in the broader mission of caring for the planet. These efforts brought together individuals from diverse backgrounds, united by a common purpose—to restore beauty and balance to our immediate surroundings. Together, we reclaimed spaces overrun by waste, transforming them into vibrant areas of natural beauty once again reflective of the divine artistry that surrounds us.

I also championed the cause of sustainable living, advocating for lifestyles and practices that minimize harm to the environment and promote the well-being of all creation. This involved not only personal changes in my daily habits and choices but also efforts to raise awareness within my community. By leading by example and sharing knowledge, I hoped to inspire others to see the value in sustainable living—not merely as a means of conservation but as a way of life that honors God's creation.

Furthermore, I contributed to the development of green technologies, supporting innovations that promise to reduce our environmental footprint and lead us towards a more sustainable future. I recognized that technology, when guided by the principles of stewardship and sustainability, could be a powerful tool in our efforts to care for the earth. By investing in and advocating for green technologies, I sought to bridge the gap between human advancement and environmental preservation, ensuring that our progress as a society does not come at the expense of the planet's health.

Through these actions, my life became a testament to the conviction that environmental stewardship is indeed a sacred duty. It is a commitment that extends beyond the confines of personal faith to touch the heart of our collective existence on this earth. By caring for the planet, we honor the Creator, acknowledging His sovereignty and expressing our reverence for His creation. We also embrace our role as caretakers, entrusted with the noble task of preserving the beauty and diversity of the world for generations to come.

This journey of stewardship is not a solitary path but a shared pilgrimage, inviting each of us to contribute our unique gifts and talents to the noble cause of caring for the earth. It challenges us to look beyond our immediate concerns and to act with foresight and compassion, ensuring that the legacy we leave is one of reverence, care, and hope. As we walk this path, let us do so with the knowledge that in every effort to protect and preserve God's creation, we draw closer to the Creator Himself, fulfilling our sacred duty and strengthening our faith through the act of stewardship.


## SCIENTIFIC DISCOVERY: A DIVINE EXPLORATION

The Celestial Mural, a breathtaking tapestry of stars and galaxies, served as a catalyst, reigniting my passion for exploring the universe's mysteries. In every scientific discovery, I began to see not just the workings of nature but glimpses of divine genius, each revelation a verse in the grand poem of creation. This realization spurred me to organize forums that convened individuals from diverse faith backgrounds alongside scientists, fostering a space where spirituality and empirical knowledge could converge in harmony rather than conflict.

These gatherings unveiled a profound truth: faith and science, far from being adversaries, are allies in our quest to understand the cosmos and our place within it. Dialogues bridged the chasm that has historically divided these realms, revealing that a symbiotic relationship exists between them. Through these conversations, it became clear that science offers tools and methodologies to unravel the physical mysteries of the universe, while faith provides a lens through which we can comprehend its deeper meaning and purpose.

The interplay between faith and scientific inquiry enriched our collective understanding, allowing us to appreciate the world and the Creator in a more holistic light. It underscored the notion that the pursuit of knowledge, whether through telescopes or scriptures, is a divine exploration, a journey that draws us closer to the mysteries of the divine. This exploration is not just an academic endeavor but a spiritual practice that enhances our faith, offering us a fuller, more nuanced appreciation of the Creator's craftsmanship.

As we delve deeper into the intricacies of the universe, let us do so with the conviction that every discovery is a step closer to understanding the mind of God. Let this journey of discovery strengthen our faith, reminding us of the limitless wonder of creation and the boundless genius of the Creator. In the convergence of faith and science, we find not contradiction but confirmation—a harmonious chorus that celebrates the beauty and complexity of the world and invites us to continue our exploration with reverence and awe.


## RECONCILING FAITH WITH MODERN SOCIETAL VALUES

My journey of faith took me into the heart of a pluralistic society, a melting pot of diverse values, beliefs, and worldviews. Amidst this mosaic of cultures and ideologies, I found myself confronted with the challenge of living out my faith authentically while respecting the tapestry of diversity that surrounded me. Inspired by the themes of harmony and balance woven throughout the narrative of creation, I felt called to contribute towards building a more just and peaceful world.

This calling led me to engage in various initiatives aimed at promoting social justice, human rights, and peace. Drawing from the rich well of ancient wisdom found in my faith, I sought to address the pressing issues of our time—inequality, injustice, and conflict—with a spirit of compassion and solidarity. I became an advocate for recognizing the divine image in every person, a principle that compels us to treat one another with dignity, respect, and love.

In my efforts, I championed policies and actions that reflect the core values of compassion, equality, and justice. Through dialogues, community service, and advocacy, I worked to bridge the gap between faith and societal challenges, demonstrating how the teachings of old can offer guidance in navigating the complexities of modern life. My engagement in these causes was not just about addressing societal issues but about manifesting the kingdom values in the here and now—values that promote the well-being of all creation.

My journey revealed that reconciling faith with modern societal values is not only possible but necessary. It showed that faith, when lived out with intention and openness, can be a powerful force for positive change in the world. By grounding our actions in the timeless principles of our faith—love, justice, and mercy—we can foster a society that reflects the harmony and balance of creation itself.

This path of reconciling faith with contemporary societal values strengthened my own beliefs and deepened my commitment to living out my faith in a way that is responsive and relevant to the needs of our time. It affirmed that ancient wisdom, when applied with discernment and compassion, can illuminate the way forward, guiding us in our collective pursuit of a more just, peaceful, and equitable world.

In sharing this part of my journey, I hope to encourage and strengthen your faith, inspiring you to see the opportunities for living out your beliefs in a pluralistic society. Let us be advocates for a faith that transcends cultural and ideological divides, a faith that actively engages with the world to bring about transformation and healing. Together, we can demonstrate how the principles of our faith can guide us in addressing the challenges of modern life, fostering a faith that is both deeply rooted and expansively relevant.

## A LIVING FAITH FOR TODAY

My journey, sparked by the awe-inspiring Celestial Mural, embodies the essence of a modern faith that draws deeply from the well of creation's narrative. This ancient story, far from being a relic of the past, teems with insights and principles that resonate profoundly with the complexities of contemporary life. It has the power to illuminate our path, guiding our understanding and practice of faith, spirituality, and ethics in today's rapidly evolving world.

By delving into the narrative of creation, I discovered a rich tapestry of divine wisdom that informs our approach to environmental stewardship, scientific discovery, and the reconciliation of faith with modern societal values. This exploration revealed that our spirituality need not be confined to the private realms of personal belief but can extend its roots into the very fabric of our communal life and the broader challenges of our time.

In embracing environmental stewardship, we acknowledge our sacred duty to care for the earth as God's cherished creation. This commitment transforms our relationship with the planet from one of exploitation to one of stewardship, reflecting a spirituality that honors the divine in all aspects of life. Similarly, engaging with scientific discovery becomes an act of faith in itself, revealing the intricacies of God's creation and inspiring a sense of wonder and reverence for the natural world.

Seeking reconciliation between faith and contemporary societal values challenges us to navigate the complexities of living out our beliefs in a pluralistic society. It calls us to embody a faith that is both inclusive and compassionate, advocating for justice, peace, and the dignity of all people. This aspect of our journey invites us to reflect on how ancient wisdom can guide us in addressing the ethical dilemmas and social challenges of our era.

My experience, therefore, is not just a personal narrative but an invitation to all of us to explore the relevance of the creation story for our lives today. It encourages us to cultivate a living faith that is vibrant, thoughtful, and attuned to the divine calling of our era—a faith that does not shy away from the challenges of the modern world but engages with them head-on, armed with the wisdom of our spiritual heritage.

This living faith for today is an ongoing journey of discovery, reflection, and action. It invites us to constantly seek the divine in the ordinary, to find sacredness in our everyday interactions with the world, and to live out our faith in ways that are responsive to the needs of our time. It challenges us to be bearers of light in a world that often seems shrouded in darkness, to be agents of transformation in a society yearning for change, and to be voices of hope in an age often marked by cynicism and despair.

In embracing this living faith, we join a community of believers who are navigating the complexities of faith in the 21st century. Together, we can discover in the creation story a source of wisdom for our times, a wellspring of inspiration for living out our beliefs in ways that are meaningful, relevant, and deeply connected to the divine purpose for our lives and our world.

## BRIDGING CREATION WITH CONTEMPORARY FAITH

In an age where technology and societal norms evolve at an unprecedented pace, the ancient narrative of creation provides a beacon of wisdom, guiding us through the complexities of modern life. It reminds us that, amidst rapid change, the foundational truths of our existence and our relationship with the divine remain constant. The story of creation, with its profound simplicity and depth, invites us to rediscover the essence of our faith in the Creator and the purpose of our stewardship on Earth.

As we navigate the digital landscape, where virtual connections often replace physical ones, the creation story calls us to remember the intrinsic value of the natural world and our interconnectedness with it. It challenges us to look beyond the immediate convenience of technology and consider the long-term impact of our actions on the planet. In doing so, it fosters a sense of responsibility and humility, encouraging us to use our technological advancements in ways that honor the Creator's intentions for His creation.

The narrative of creation also offers insights into the nature of human creativity and innovation, reflecting the image of the Creator within us. It suggests that our capacity to create and innovate is a divine gift, meant to be used for the betterment of the world and the glorification of God. This perspective inspires us to approach scientific discovery and technological innovation with a sense of wonder and reverence, recognizing them as opportunities to explore the complexities of the universe and contribute to the flourishing of all creation.

Furthermore, the creation story serves as a powerful reminder of the unity and diversity within the world. It portrays a universe where every element has its place and purpose, encouraging us to embrace diversity and work towards unity in our communities. This message is particularly relevant in today's pluralistic society, where differences often lead to division. By reflecting on the harmonious diversity of creation, we are motivated to seek common ground and foster a culture of respect and collaboration.

The principles of creation also have profound implications for our ethical decisions and moral values. They call us to consider the consequences of our actions, not just for ourselves but for the entire web of life. This awareness leads to a more compassionate and just approach to issues such as poverty, inequality, and environmental degradation. It challenges us to live out our faith through actions that reflect our stewardship of the Earth and our love for our neighbors.

In practical terms, the story of creation encourages us to integrate sustainable practices into our daily lives, from reducing waste to supporting renewable energy. It urges us to engage in dialogues that bridge the gap between faith and science, deepening our understanding of the world and enriching our spiritual journey. It also calls us to be active participants in our communities, advocating for policies and practices that promote justice, peace, and the well-being of all creation.

The narrative of creation offers a rich tapestry of insights for bridging contemporary faith with the challenges and opportunities of the modern world. By reflecting on the lessons of creation, we can cultivate a faith that is both deeply rooted in ancient wisdom and actively engaged with the pressing issues of our time. This journey of reflection and action invites us to experience a more vibrant, thoughtful, and responsive faith, capable of transforming our lives and the world around us.

## ENVIRONMENTAL STEWARDSHIP: A CALL FROM CREATION

The narrative of creation unfolds a vision of the world as a breathtaking masterpiece, intricately designed by the divine. It reveals the Earth not as a mere backdrop for human activity but as a sacred canvas, painted with care and intentionality. Entrusted to humanity's stewardship, this divine artistry calls us to a profound responsibility: to protect and preserve the beauty and balance of our planet for generations yet unborn.

In today's era, marked by rapid environmental degradation, the creation story emerges not just as a tale of origins but as a pressing call to action. It challenges us to see beyond the immediate conveniences of our lifestyles to the long-term impacts of our choices on the planet's health. This stewardship, as outlined in the creation narrative, is not an optional task but a sacred duty, a tangible expression of our faith and reverence for the Creator.

The degradation of our environment – from the air we breathe to the water that sustains life – poses one of the most critical challenges of our time. Climate change, pollution, and habitat destruction threaten the very fabric of global ecosystems, placing countless species, including our own, at risk. The creation story, in its beauty and simplicity, renews the call for sustainable living and environmental responsibility, urging us to act not out of fear but out of faith.

This sacred narrative compels believers to view environmental stewardship as a direct reflection of their faith. It's a call to honor the Creator by caring for His creation, recognizing that every action taken against pollution, habitat destruction, and climate change is an act of worship, a testament to our respect for the divine handiwork that surrounds us.

Responding to this call means embracing sustainable practices in our daily lives, from reducing waste to conserving energy and supporting eco-friendly initiatives. It involves educating ourselves and others about the importance of biodiversity and the critical roles different species and ecosystems play in maintaining the balance of our planet.

Moreover, environmental stewardship encourages us to advocate for policies and practices that protect the Earth's natural resources and ensure the well-being of all its inhabitants. It's about making conscious choices that promote environmental justice, recognizing that the impacts of environmental degradation often fall most heavily on the poor and marginalized.

In engaging with the creation narrative, we are invited to reflect on our relationship with the environment. We are reminded that every element of the natural world has been endowed with purpose and value by the Creator. This perspective challenges us to see the world not as a resource to be exploited but as a gift to be cherished and protected.

The call from creation is a call to transformation – a shift in how we view our role in the world and how we live out our faith in action. It's an invitation to join a global community of caretakers, working together to heal and preserve the Earth. By answering this call, we participate in a sacred mission, aligning our efforts with the divine intention for harmony, sustainability, and respect for all life.

As believers, embracing environmental stewardship is a profound way to live out our faith, demonstrating our love for the Creator by caring for His creation. It's an act of hope, contributing to the healing and restoration of the world. In doing so, we not only honor the Creator's work but also ensure that future generations can witness and enjoy the divine artistry of our shared home.

## SCIENTIFIC DISCOVERY: THE QUEST FOR UNDERSTANDING

The narrative of creation, as presented in sacred texts, is not just a story of the beginning but a profound invitation to explore the marvels of the universe. It portrays the universe's formation with such poetry and depth, urging believers to pause and ponder the complexity and beauty that surrounds us. This account, far from standing in opposition to scientific inquiry, acts as a bridge, connecting the realms of faith and science in a harmonious relationship.

This intertwining of faith and science opens up a world where the quest for understanding is celebrated, where the intricacies of God's creation are not just observed but deeply explored. Scientific discovery becomes a sacred journey, a means to appreciate the vastness and detail of the Creator's work. Through engaging with various scientific disciplines, from the grand scale of cosmology to the minute details of biology, believers are invited to deepen their understanding and appreciation of the divine ingenuity that orchestrates the universe.

The exploration of the cosmos, with its galaxies, stars, and planets, reveals the grandeur of creation, showcasing a universe designed with precision and care. This cosmic journey inspires awe and wonder, as believers contemplate the vastness of space and the delicate balance that allows life to exist. Similarly, the study of biology, with its examination of life at the molecular and cellular levels, unveils the complexity and beauty of living organisms, each reflecting the Creator's ingenuity in their design and function.

Such scientific engagements nurture a faith that is informed and expansive, one that sees the hand of the Creator in the laws of physics, the beauty of mathematical patterns, and the complexity of biological systems. It is a faith that understands scientific progress as a means to delve deeper into the mysteries of creation, celebrating each discovery as a testament to the Creator's genius.

The relationship between faith and science, therefore, is not one of conflict but of mutual enrichment. Science offers tools and methodologies to explore the world, while faith provides a deeper context and purpose for these explorations. This synergy encourages believers to approach scientific inquiry with curiosity and humility, recognizing that our understanding of the universe is continually evolving.

This perspective also challenges believers to engage with contemporary scientific issues, from environmental conservation to medical ethics, viewing them through the lens of faith. It prompts a reflection on how scientific advancements can be aligned with the values and principles of our faith, ensuring that progress benefits humanity and honors the Creator.

Furthermore, this approach to faith and science fosters a community that values dialogue and collaboration. It encourages conversations between scientists and believers, each bringing their insights and perspectives to enrich the understanding of our world. These dialogues can bridge gaps, dispel misconceptions, and build a shared appreciation for the wonder of creation.

In embracing the intricate relationship between faith and science, believers are invited to witness the Creator's handiwork in every aspect of the natural world. This journey of discovery does not diminish the mystery or majesty of creation; rather, it enhances our wonder and deepens our reverence. It is a journey that reaffirms our faith, reminding us that in the vastness of the universe and the intricacy of life, we see reflections of the divine.

As we explore the universe from the macroscopic galaxies to the microscopic strands of DNA, we are constantly reminded of the Creator's mastery and creativity. Each scientific discovery, each glimpse into the workings of the universe, is an opportunity to celebrate the divine intelligence that underpins all of creation. It is a call to a faith that is vibrant and dynamic, embracing scientific progress as a pathway to greater understanding and appreciation of God's magnificent creation.

In this light, the days of creation become not just a historical account but a living narrative that continues to unfold before us. They invite us into an ongoing exploration of the universe, encouraging us to see the hand of the Creator in the laws that govern the cosmos, the life that populates the Earth, and the matter that forms the physical world. This exploration is an act of faith, a testament to our belief in a Creator who invites us to know and appreciate the work of His hands. Through this journey, our faith is strengthened, and our sense of wonder and reverence for the natural world is deepened, fostering a relationship with the Creator that is informed, awe-inspired, and ever-growing.


## RECONCILING FAITH WITH MODERN SOCIETAL VALUES

In our journey through life, especially within the tapestry of a pluralistic society, the narrative of creation provides profound insights that can help bridge the gap between ancient faith and modern societal values. This sacred story is not just about the origins of the universe but also about cohabitation, respect, and the sanctity of life. It paints a vision of a world where harmony and balance are not ideals but inherent qualities that guide our interactions and decisions.

This narrative encourages believers to view the diversity of life and human culture as a reflection of the divine, a manifestation of God's creativity and love for variety. Every person, every creature, and every part of this Earth is a piece of a larger divine puzzle. Recognizing the divine image in every individual, the creation story calls us to embrace equality, justice, and peace. These are not just societal aspirations but expressions of a faith deeply engaged with the complexities of the world.

In navigating contemporary issues such as human rights, social justice, and ethical dilemmas, the creation narrative offers us a compass. It urges us to approach each challenge with compassion and wisdom, inspired by the understanding that all creation is interconnected and sacred. This perspective shifts our approach from one of judgment to one of empathy, recognizing that each person's experiences and beliefs are part of the diverse fabric of humanity God has woven.

The story of creation reminds us that every individual bears the divine image, a profound truth that compels us to fight for justice and equality. It challenges us to confront societal structures that marginalize and oppress, advocating for systems that uplift and empower. In this light, faith becomes a catalyst for social change, inspiring believers to work tirelessly for a world that reflects the divine principles of love and justice.

Furthermore, the creation narrative encourages us to cultivate peace, both within ourselves and in our communities. It teaches us that harmony with one another and with the environment is not only possible but essential for the flourishing of life. This peace is not passive but active, requiring us to engage in dialogue, to listen deeply, and to seek understanding across divides. It is through these efforts that we can build bridges of empathy and compassion, uniting us in our shared humanity.

Moreover, the story of creation calls us to stewardship, to care for the Earth and all its inhabitants as a sacred trust. This responsibility extends beyond environmental conservation to include advocating for policies and practices that ensure the well-being of all people. It is a call to action that challenges us to consider the impact of our choices on the most vulnerable among us, urging us to live in a way that honors the divine image in everyone.

In dealing with ethical dilemmas, the creation narrative serves as a moral guide, providing principles that can help us make decisions that align with our faith and values. It invites us to reflect on the consequences of our actions, to choose paths that promote life, dignity, and respect for all creation. This reflective approach to ethics encourages us to seek solutions that are just, compassionate, and equitable, drawing on our faith as a source of wisdom and strength.

By engaging with the world's complexity through the lens of creation, believers are empowered to be agents of change. We are called to be voices for the voiceless, defenders of the oppressed, and caretakers of the planet. This engagement is an expression of our faith, a testament to our belief in a God who loves diversity, seeks justice, and desires peace for all creation.

In conclusion, the narrative of creation offers invaluable lessons for reconciling faith with modern societal values. It challenges us to see the divine image in everyone, to embrace diversity with respect and love, and to navigate the complexities of contemporary issues with compassion and wisdom. Through this lens, our faith becomes a living, breathing entity, deeply interconnected with the world around us. It becomes a force for good, inspiring us to build a more just, peaceful, and harmonious world. This journey of reconciliation is not easy, but it is one of the most profound expressions of our faith, demonstrating our commitment to living out the values of the creation narrative in every aspect of our lives.

## PRACTICAL IMPLICATIONS FOR DAILY LIVING

### EMBRACING SUSTAINABLE PRACTICES:

Embracing sustainable practices in our daily lives serves as a tangible expression of our stewardship, reflecting our commitment to caring for the creation entrusted to us. Rooted in the narrative of creation, this stewardship invites us to live in a way that honors the intricate balance and beauty of the world. By incorporating simple, yet impactful, sustainable actions into our routines, we actively participate in the preservation and nurturing of the Earth.

## REDUCING WASTE

A critical first step in this journey is mindfulness about what we consume and how we dispose of our resources. Opting for reusable products, recycling, and composting lessens our footprint and contributes to a healthier planet. These actions, though small, echo the principle of valuing what has been given to us.

## CONSERVING ENERGY

Another vital aspect of living sustainably involves simple changes such as switching to energy-efficient light bulbs, unplugging devices when not in use, and maximizing natural light. These practices significantly reduce our energy consumption and align with our stewardship, reminding us of our dependence on and responsibility to the natural world.

## SUPPORTING ECO-FRIENDLY INITIATIVES

Extending our commitment to stewardship can also mean participating in local conservation projects, supporting businesses that prioritize sustainability, or advocating for environmental policies. Our engagement makes a difference. It's a way to connect with our communities, share our values, and make a collective impact.

These sustainable practices are more than just actions; they are expressions of a faith that respects and cherishes the divine creation. They challenge us to consider how our daily choices affect the world around us and encourage us to live in a manner that reflects our gratitude for the Earth. Through these practices, we embody a stewardship that is conscious, deliberate, and deeply rooted in our faith.

## ADOPTING SUSTAINABLE HABITS

This requires intentionality and sometimes a shift in perspective. It asks us to look beyond convenience to the broader implications of our actions. This perspective is not about sacrifice but about embracing a lifestyle that fosters harmony, balance, and respect for creation.

## INCORPORATING SUSTAINABILITY INTO DAILY LIFE

This is an ongoing journey, one that evolves as we learn and grow. It's a path marked by small decisions that, collectively, have a profound impact. As we walk this path, we are reminded of our role as caretakers of the Earth and the legacy we leave for future generations.

In conclusion, living sustainably is a practical way to live out our faith in daily life. It reflects a deep respect for the Creator and a commitment to the stewardship of His creation. Through simple, sustainable practices, we not only contribute to the well-being of the planet but also cultivate a lifestyle that is reflective of our values and beliefs. This journey of stewardship is a powerful expression of our faith, demonstrating that our daily choices can honor the divine and contribute to a more sustainable and just world.

## ENGAGEMENT WITH SCIENCE: FOSTERING CURIOSITY AND LEARNING

Fostering a culture of curiosity and learning within our faith communities is vital for deepening our understanding of both creation and the Creator. By engaging with the scientific fields, we open ourselves to a world of discovery that can enrich our appreciation for the divine craftsmanship behind the universe. This engagement is not about questioning our faith but about expanding it, exploring the breadth and depth of God's creation with awe and reverence.

Encouraging dialogue between faith and science can demystify misconceptions that the two are in conflict. Instead, this conversation reveals how scientific discovery and spiritual understanding can complement and enhance one another. Such dialogues can take place in study groups, workshops, or through inviting experts to speak at community events, creating a bridge between these two worlds.

By exploring scientific concepts, from the vastness of the cosmos to the intricacies of biology, we gain insights into the complexity and beauty of the universe. This understanding can lead to a deeper appreciation of the Creator's ingenuity, encouraging us to see His handiwork in the laws of physics, the structure of DNA, and the rhythms of ecosystems. These discoveries invite us to marvel at the Creator's power and wisdom, fostering a profound sense of wonder and worship.

Promoting scientific literacy within faith communities also equips believers to engage more thoughtfully with the world around them. Understanding the basics of science and technology can empower individuals to make informed decisions about issues that impact our lives and our planet, from environmental stewardship to medical ethics. This informed engagement reflects our responsibility to care for the creation and to navigate complex moral landscapes with wisdom and compassion.

Furthermore, embracing science as a complement to faith can inspire the next generation. It encourages young believers to pursue careers in science and technology, viewing these fields as avenues to explore and steward God's creation. This perspective nurtures a generation that holds both a deep faith and a rigorous scientific understanding, poised to make meaningful contributions to society and to the church.

Creating spaces for scientific engagement within faith communities also challenges the false dichotomy that one must choose between faith and reason. It asserts that intellectual exploration and spiritual devotion can coexist, enriching rather than diluting one another. This balance fosters a holistic approach to understanding our world and our place within it, grounded in both knowledge and faith.

Fostering a culture of curiosity and learning about science within faith communities is a practical way to deepen our understanding of the divine. It encourages us to approach God's creation with both wonder and inquiry, bridging the gap between faith and science. Through this engagement, we not only enrich our spiritual lives but also equip ourselves to be thoughtful stewards of the world we inhabit. This journey of discovery is a testament to our faith, affirming that the pursuit of knowledge, guided by wisdom and reverence, is a form of worship that honors the Creator.

The narrative of creation, brimming with timeless wisdom and divine craftsmanship, serves as a beacon for those navigating the intricate landscape of modern faith. It lays before us a rich tapestry of insights, guiding us through the challenges and opportunities that define our era. By delving into this sacred story, believers are invited to explore a spirituality that is both deeply anchored in ancient truths and dynamically intertwined with the complexities of today's world.

## ENVIRONMENTAL STEWARDSHIP

As derived from the creation narrative, urges us to adopt a lifestyle of care and respect for the natural world. This commitment reflects a profound understanding of our role as custodians of the Earth, entrusted with its care by the Creator. It is a call to action that resonates with the urgency of our times, encouraging us to live in harmony with the environment and to safeguard it for future generations.

## ENGAGEMENT WITH SCIENTIFIC DISCOVERY

Another facet of the creation narrative, enriches our faith by expanding our understanding of the universe. It invites us to marvel at the intricacies of creation, seeing in every scientific breakthrough a glimpse of the Creator's ingenuity. This harmonious relationship between faith and science fosters a curiosity that is both spiritually fulfilling and intellectually stimulating, challenging us to embrace the wonders of the cosmos as expressions of divine artistry.

## RECONCILING FAITH WITH CONTEMPORARY SOCIETAL VALUES

Perhaps the most challenging aspect of the creation narrative requires us to engage with the world around us in ways that are compassionate, just, and reflective of the divine image in every individual. This aspect of the narrative urges us to confront social injustices, to advocate for peace and equality, and to navigate ethical dilemmas with wisdom and integrity. It is a call to live out our faith in the public square, to be a voice for the voiceless, and to embody the principles of love and justice in our actions.

Through this reflective journey, inspired by the story of creation, believers are equipped to cultivate a faith that is vibrant and thoughtful. It is a faith that does not shy away from the challenges of the modern world but engages with them head-on, seeking solutions that are informed by spiritual wisdom and compassion. This approach to faith does not offer easy answers but invites us into a deeper exploration of what it means to live in accordance with divine will.

The ancient narrative of creation continues to be a source of inspiration and guidance for believers seeking to navigate the complexities of modern faith. By embracing the calls to environmental stewardship, scientific engagement, and societal reconciliation, we can foster a spirituality that is both deeply rooted in tradition and expansively connected to the world around us. This journey of reflection and action enables us to respond to the calling of our time with a faith that is alive, responsive, and transformative. It reminds us that, in the face of ever-changing landscapes, the timeless wisdom of the creation narrative remains a steadfast compass, guiding us towards a more just, compassionate, and sustainable world.

# CHAPTER 9

# THE ROLE OF HUMANITY IN CREATION

Amid the rush of everyday life, I found myself on a journey that would profoundly reshape my understanding of my place in the world. It began unexpectedly, on a day that seemed no different from any other, when a documentary about the breathtaking beauty and fragile state of our planet caught my attention. As I watched, something within me stirred—a deep, compelling call to action. This moment marked the beginning of my transformative journey into understanding the role humanity plays in creation, a journey that revealed to me the sacred duty we hold as stewards of the Earth.

As I delved deeper into the creation narrative, I discovered that it was not just a story about the beginnings of the universe and life but a divine mandate for humanity. It became clear that we are entrusted with a unique responsibility and privilege: to care for the Earth and all its inhabitants. This realization was both humbling and empowering, prompting me to reflect on how my actions and choices intersect with environmental ethics, social justice, and the very fabric of daily living.

The call to stewardship, I learned, is a call to transition from exploitation to guardianship. Facing the accelerating environmental crises—climate change, deforestation, and the loss of biodiversity—I felt an urgent need to reconsider my relationship with the natural world. It was a profound shift in perspective, from viewing the Earth as a resource to be used to seeing it as a sacred trust to be protected. This guardianship respects the intrinsic value of all creation and challenges me to adopt sustainable practices that ensure the Earth's resources are preserved and regenerated for future generations.

Moreover, I recognized that my role in creation extends beyond environmental stewardship to include social justice. The interconnectedness of all creation means that how we treat the environment is deeply intertwined with issues of equity, poverty, and human rights. I saw that environmental degradation disproportionately affects the world's most vulnerable populations, exacerbating issues of scarcity, displacement, and inequality. Embracing my role as a caretaker, I felt called to advocate for policies and practices that promote not only ecological health but also economic and social well-being.

In my daily living, this understanding translated into conscious consumption, community engagement, educational advocacy, and spiritual reflection. I began to reflect on my personal consumption habits and their impact on the environment, choosing sustainable products, reducing waste, and supporting ethical businesses. I participated in local initiatives aimed at environmental conservation and social justice, ranging from community gardening projects to campaigns advocating for policy change. I also committed to informing and educating myself and others about the importance of environmental stewardship and its link to social justice, understanding that knowledge empowers us to make informed decisions and advocate effectively.

Integrating the principle of stewardship into my spiritual practice deepened my commitment to the care of the Earth and all its inhabitants. Contemplating my place within creation, I felt a renewed sense of connection to the divine work of sustaining and nurturing the world. This journey of discovery, reflection, and action has been transformative, challenging me to live with greater intentionality, compassion, and reverence for all creation.

My exploration of the creation narrative and humanity's role within it has not merely been an academic exercise but a profound personal journey. It has reshaped my understanding of myself as a caretaker of the Earth, entrusted with a sacred duty that spans the protection of the environment, the promotion of social justice, and the mindful conduct of my daily life. Embracing this role has challenged me to live with purpose and passion, participating in the divine work of caring for the world—a privilege that inspires action and reflection in equal measure.

## STEWARDS OF THE EARTH: A DIVINE MANDATE

The narrative of creation presents humanity with a profound role—stewards of the Earth, a position entrusted to us from the onset of existence. This divine mandate weaves through the essence of our being, closely intertwined with our moral fiber, environmental ethics, and pursuit of social justice.

As guardians of creation, our stewardship extends beyond mere supervision; it demands a deep reverence for the natural world, recognizing its intrinsic value and our duty towards its preservation and renewal. This mandate challenges us to transform our interaction with the planet from exploitation to a sustainable relationship that respects all life.

This stewardship is not merely a burden but a sacred trust, reflecting the divine confidence in our capacity for compassion and wisdom. It compels us to balance today's needs with tomorrow's welfare, ensuring that the Earth's resources are not merely consumed but cherished and restored. Our decisions and actions thus become a tribute to our respect for the Creator and His creation, forming a legacy of care and protection for future generations.

The implications of this divine mandate reach every corner of our daily lives—from the food we eat to the products we purchase and the energy we consume. Each choice mirrors our commitment to this role, prompting us to consider not just the immediate benefits but also the long-term impacts on the environment and future generations.

However, our role in creation spans beyond environmental stewardship to encompass broader social justice concerns. The health of our planet is tightly linked to the welfare of its inhabitants. Environmental degradation, climate change, and biodiversity loss disproportionately impact the world's most vulnerable communities, exacerbating poverty, displacement, and inequality.

Therefore, our caretaking role also involves advocating for policies and practices that promote ecological health alongside economic and social well-being. It urges us to combat injustice, support those most affected by environmental damage, and seek solutions that are fair, equitable, and sustainable.

Embracing this divine mandate invites us to live intentionally and purposefully. It challenges us to reflect on our place within creation, rethink our relationship with the natural world, and reaffirm our commitment to stewardship daily. In doing so, we not only fulfill the Creator's trust but also contribute to the healing and flourishing of the Earth and all its inhabitants.

In summary, the narrative of creation grants us a role of unmatched importance—as the Earth's stewards. This divine charge, intertwined with environmental ethics and social justice, summons us to a life of care, respect, and advocacy. It enriches our lives, deepens our faith, and underscores our duty to protect and nurture the planet. As we embrace this role, we join in the ongoing work of creation, partnering with the Divine in the sacred task of sustaining and cherishing the Earth and all its marvels.

## ENVIRONMENTAL ETHICS: GUARDIANSHIP OVER EXPLOITATION

The clarion call of stewardship, echoing through the creation narrative, compels us to transition from exploitation to guardianship of our natural world. This shift is a divine mandate, becoming increasingly urgent as we face escalating environmental crises such as climate change, rampant deforestation, and the alarming loss of biodiversity. These challenges are not distant concerns but immediate threats that jeopardize the very fabric of life on Earth.

Our stewardship necessitates a profound reevaluation of our interactions with the planet. It requires moving away from viewing the Earth as merely a repository of resources to be exploited and encourages us to foster a relationship of care and respect, recognizing the Earth as a living, breathing entity that sustains all forms of life. This new perspective transforms our role from dominators to guardians, charged with preserving the intrinsic value and beauty of our surroundings.

Embracing this guardianship involves committing to sustainable practices that not only preserve but also regenerate the Earth's resources for future generations. It demands action at all levels—from individual decisions to community initiatives and global policies—all aimed at ensuring the health and vitality of our planet. This commitment challenges us to rethink our lifestyles and make choices that lessen our environmental impact while promoting the planet's well-being over short-term gains.

Implementing sustainable practices means making deliberate choices in our daily lives, such as reducing waste, conserving energy, supporting renewable resources, and protecting natural habitats. These actions reflect a deeper recognition of the delicate balance of life and acknowledge that every decision we make affects the health of our planet.

Moreover, the shift towards guardianship and sustainability is not solely an environmental imperative but also a moral one. It reflects our values and ethics, affirming the sanctity of creation and recognizing every aspect of the natural world—forests, rivers, mountains, and creatures—as a testament to the Creator's artistry.

This ethical approach to environmental stewardship also acknowledges the interconnectedness of all life. Environmental degradation impacts human well-being, disproportionately affecting the most vulnerable communities. Therefore, our guardianship extends beyond ecological concerns to encompass issues of social justice, ensuring that our efforts to preserve the planet also promote equity and well-being for all its inhabitants.

In our journey toward embracing environmental ethics and guardianship, we are called to be leaders and advocates for change. It is our responsibility to educate ourselves and others about the environmental challenges we face and to take concrete steps to address them. By doing so, we not only respond to the stewardship mandate but also inspire others to join this vital mission.

In conclusion, the shift from exploitation to guardianship is central to environmental ethics, deeply embedded within the narrative of creation. As stewards, we are privileged and responsible for ensuring that the planet's resources are preserved and enhanced for future generations. This divine mandate compels us to live in a manner that honors the Creator, advocating for lifestyles and policies that prioritize the health of our planet. By answering this call, we embrace our role as guardians of the Earth, participating in the divine task of sustaining and enriching the world's beauty and bounty.

## SOCIAL JUSTICE: THE INEXTRICABLE LINK

The divine narrative of creation intricately weaves the threads of environmental stewardship and social justice into a single tapestry, highlighting the profound interconnectedness of all creation. This connection underscores a vital truth: our treatment of the environment and our commitment to equity and justice are not separate endeavors but are deeply intertwined. The role humanity plays in the vast expanse of creation extends far beyond the caretaking of the earth's natural resources; it encompasses the moral imperative to uphold justice, dignity, and equity for all people.

Environmental degradation—a consequence of unchecked exploitation and negligence—casts long shadows over the world's most vulnerable communities. It exacerbates the challenges of poverty, scarcity, and displacement, widening the chasm of inequality. The loss of biodiversity, climate change, and pollution do not affect all equally; they disproportionately harm those who are least able to protect themselves against such threats. This imbalance calls into question our commitment to stewardship and justice, urging us to consider the broader implications of our actions on the fabric of society.

Embracing our role as caretakers of creation, therefore, demands that we advocate for policies and practices that foster not only the health of our planet but also the well-being of its people. It is a call to recognize that true stewardship extends to ensuring economic stability, access to resources, and the protection of rights for all members of the global community. This comprehensive approach to caretaking challenges us to dismantle systems of exploitation and to build in their place structures that promote sustainability, equity, and respect for all life.

The pursuit of social justice within the context of creation care involves addressing the root causes of environmental degradation and its social implications. It means championing initiatives that aim to reduce carbon emissions, protect natural habitats, and ensure clean air and water for all, recognizing these as fundamental human rights. Moreover, it involves supporting sustainable development goals that aim not only to protect the environment but also to elevate the quality of life for people everywhere, especially those who face the brunt of environmental crises.

Our advocacy for social justice and environmental stewardship reflects a holistic understanding of our faith and its teachings on compassion, mercy, and justice. It compels us to act not out of obligation but out of a deep sense of love and responsibility towards our fellow human beings and the world we share. This commitment to action is an expression of our faith, a tangible demonstration of our belief in a Creator who calls us to care for both the earth and its inhabitants.

In this journey toward integrating social justice and environmental stewardship, education plays a crucial role. By informing ourselves and others about the interconnectedness of these issues, we empower individuals and communities to make informed decisions that promote the common good. Community engagement and grassroots activism become avenues through which we live out our commitment to stewardship, working hand in hand with others to effect meaningful change.

In conclusion, the inextricable link between social justice and environmental stewardship is a fundamental aspect of our role as caretakers of creation. It challenges us to view stewardship through a broader lens, one that encompasses the well-being of the entire global community. By embracing this comprehensive approach to caretaking, we answer the divine call to advocate for a world that reflects the values of equity, sustainability, and compassion. This commitment to justice and care for the environment is a profound expression of our faith, a reflection of our dedication to following the path laid out by the Creator for the betterment of all creation.

## Implications for Daily Living

### CONSCIOUS CONSUMPTION

The divine mandate of stewardship calls for a transformation not just in our hearts but in the very fabric of our daily lives. This transformation begins with conscious consumption, a principle that urges us to reflect deeply on our personal consumption habits and their broader impact on the environment. It's a call to mindfulness, to recognize that every purchase we make, every item we use, and every piece of waste we generate has consequences for the planet.

Choosing sustainable products is one of the most direct ways we can embody our role as caretakers. This means prioritizing items that are produced responsibly, using processes and materials that minimize environmental harm. It's about looking beyond the immediate appeal of products to consider their lifecycle—from production to disposal—and opting for those that support the health of the planet.

Reducing waste is another critical aspect of conscious consumption. Our throwaway culture has led to a crisis of pollution and resource depletion, but as individuals, we have the power to make a difference. By minimizing our waste—whether through recycling, composting, or simply buying less—we take a stand against the disposable mindset and contribute to a more sustainable world.

Supporting ethical businesses is also a crucial step in living out our stewardship. These are businesses that not only care for the environment but also uphold fair labor practices and contribute positively to their communities. By choosing to spend our money with these businesses, we encourage a model of commerce that aligns with our values of care, respect, and responsibility for the earth and its inhabitants.

Conscious consumption, therefore, is not merely a series of actions but a manifestation of our faith and commitment to stewardship. It reflects a deliberate choice to live in a way that honors the Creator by respecting His creation. This approach to daily living challenges us to be intentional about our choices, to seek out information, and to make decisions that reflect our dedication to safeguarding the planet for future generations.

In embracing conscious consumption, we recognize that our individual actions can collectively lead to significant environmental and social change. We become part of a movement towards sustainability that transcends cultural and geographical boundaries, united by a shared commitment to the well-being of our planet. This shift in how we consume is a powerful expression of our faith, a testament to our belief in a Creator who entrusts us with the care of His creation.

Conscious consumption is an integral part of living out our role as caretakers of the earth. It's a practical application of our faith, demonstrating our commitment to stewardship in the choices we make every day. By choosing sustainable products, reducing waste, and supporting ethical businesses, we not only lessen our environmental impact but also contribute to a more just and sustainable world. This approach to daily living is a reflection of our dedication to fulfilling the divine mandate of stewardship, honoring the Creator by caring for His creation with thoughtfulness and intentionality.


## COMMUNITY ENGAGEMENT:

Community engagement serves as a powerful conduit through which we can live out our faith and fulfill our divine mandate as caretakers of the Earth. This involvement not only amplifies our individual efforts but also fosters a collective spirit of stewardship and compassion within our communities. By participating in or supporting local initiatives aimed at environmental conservation and social justice, we embody the practical implications of our role in creation, translating our beliefs into tangible actions that make a difference in the world around us.

Community gardening projects, for example, offer a unique opportunity to connect with the Earth, providing spaces where individuals can come together to cultivate food, beauty, and biodiversity. These gardens become living classrooms, teaching participants about sustainability, cooperation, and the importance of local ecosystems. They are also a testament to the power of collective action, showing how small, localized efforts can contribute to broader environmental and social well-being.

Campaigns advocating for policy change represent another critical area of community engagement. These initiatives allow us to lend our voices to the call for laws and policies that prioritize the health of the planet and the rights of its inhabitants. Whether it's advocating for clean energy, protecting natural habitats, or promoting social equity, our involvement in these campaigns demonstrates a commitment to systemic change—a reflection of our belief in the interconnectedness of all creation and our responsibility to safeguard it.

Supporting local initiatives, whether through active participation or financial contributions, is an expression of our faith in action. It acknowledges that stewardship extends beyond personal lifestyle choices to include active involvement in the public sphere. Through these actions, we join with others in our community to address environmental challenges and social injustices, creating a ripple effect that can inspire further action and awareness.

Community engagement also strengthens our sense of connection—to each other, to our local environments, and to the larger global community. It reminds us that we are not alone in our efforts to care for the Earth and advocate for justice. This sense of solidarity is vital, as it encourages perseverance, provides support, and fosters a shared vision for a better world.

In conclusion, our engagement with local initiatives for environmental conservation and social justice is a critical aspect of living out our divine mandate as caretakers. It is a way to put our faith into practice, embodying the values of stewardship, compassion, and justice in our daily lives. By participating in community gardening projects, advocating for policy change, or supporting local environmental and social justice efforts, we actively contribute to the healing and flourishing of our planet and its people. This community engagement is not just an implication for daily living; it's a call to action that resonates with our deepest beliefs and values, urging us to work together for the common good of all creation.

EDUCATIONAL ADVOCACY:

Educational advocacy plays a pivotal role in the stewardship of creation, serving as a beacon that illuminates the path toward sustainability and justice. By committing ourselves to both learning and teaching about the critical issues at the intersection of environmental stewardship and social justice, we wield knowledge as a tool for transformation. This commitment to education underpins our ability to make informed decisions and to advocate for change that honors the divine mandate to care for the Earth and its inhabitants.

In the quest for environmental stewardship, understanding the intricate dynamics of our planet's ecosystems, the impacts of climate change, and the principles of sustainable living is crucial. This knowledge not only enlightens us about the challenges we face but also highlights the opportunities for action. It empowers us to adopt practices in our own lives that reduce harm to the environment and to support broader initiatives that seek to do the same.

Equally important is the recognition of the deep connection between environmental health and social justice. Learning about this link sheds light on how environmental degradation disproportionately affects marginalized communities, contributing to issues of poverty, health disparities, and displacement. Such understanding compels us to broaden our advocacy, striving not only for ecological well-being but also for the upliftment of those who are most vulnerable.

Educational advocacy extends beyond personal enrichment to the sharing of knowledge within our communities. Hosting workshops, participating in discussions, and utilizing social media are ways we can disseminate information and spark conversation about these critical issues. Through these efforts, we foster a community-wide awareness that can drive collective action and influence public policy.

The role of faith communities in educational advocacy cannot be overstated. Churches, mosques, synagogues, and temples have the potential to be centers of learning and activism, where the moral imperatives of stewardship and justice are explored and embraced. By integrating these topics into sermons, study groups, and community programs, faith communities can play a significant role in mobilizing action for the care of creation.

Empowering the next generation is also a fundamental aspect of educational advocacy. Engaging children and youth in environmental education and social justice initiatives not only prepares them to be informed caretakers of the planet but also instills in them values of compassion, responsibility, and equity. These young stewards will carry forward the legacy of care and advocacy, making lasting contributions to the health of the planet and the well-being of its people.

In conclusion, educational advocacy is an essential component of living out our faith in the context of creation care. By informing ourselves and others about the importance of environmental stewardship and its connection to social justice, we build a foundation for informed decision-making and effective advocacy. This journey of learning and teaching not only deepens our understanding but also strengthens our faith, as we witness the power of knowledge to inspire change and bring about a more just and sustainable world. Through educational advocacy, we fulfill our divine mandate to be caretakers of the Earth, equipped with the wisdom and conviction to make a meaningful impact.

## SPIRITUAL REFLECTION:

Integrating the principle of stewardship into our spiritual practice and reflection opens a profound avenue for deepening our faith and understanding of our role within creation. This practice of contemplation not only enriches our spiritual lives but also strengthens our commitment to caring for the Earth and all its inhabitants. It invites us to see the world through a lens of interconnectedness and divine responsibility, where every aspect of creation is valued and protected.

Spiritual reflection on stewardship encourages us to consider the magnificence of creation and our place within it. It prompts us to ask ourselves how we can live in harmony with the natural world, in ways that reflect our gratitude and respect for the gifts we have been given. This process of reflection can lead to a profound sense of awe and wonder, fostering a deeper appreciation for the complexity and beauty of the environment that sustains us.

By integrating stewardship into our daily spiritual practices—whether through prayer, meditation, scripture study, or participation in religious services—we make space for considering how our faith calls us to act in the world. This intentional inclusion helps to ground our environmental and social justice efforts in our spiritual beliefs, making our commitment to stewardship a natural extension of our faith.

Contemplating our role as caretakers within creation also challenges us to confront the ways in which our actions contribute to environmental degradation and social injustice. It compels us to consider the ethical implications of our lifestyle choices, from the products we buy to the energy we consume. This level of introspection can lead to meaningful changes in behavior, aligning our daily lives more closely with the principles of care and respect for the Earth.

Spiritual reflection on stewardship also offers solace and strength. In a world where environmental crises can feel overwhelming, turning to our faith can provide a sense of hope and a reminder of the power of collective action inspired by shared values. It reassures us that, in our efforts to protect and preserve the Earth, we are not alone but are part of a larger community of believers who are also called to this sacred duty.

Moreover, this integration of stewardship into our spiritual life encourages us to share our journey with others, fostering a sense of community and mutual support. It invites conversations about faith and environmental responsibility, creating opportunities for learning and growth. Through these discussions, we can inspire one another to take action, reinforcing the idea that stewardship is a shared responsibility that transcends individual beliefs and backgrounds.

In conclusion, the implications of integrating the principle of stewardship into our spiritual reflection are profound and far-reaching. It enriches our faith, deepens our commitment to environmental and social justice, and aligns our daily actions with our spiritual values. This holistic approach to stewardship serves as a powerful reminder of our responsibility to care for the Earth and all its inhabitants, driving us to live in a way that honors the Creator and sustains His creation for generations to come. Through spiritual reflection, we cultivate a deeper connection to the divine mandate of stewardship, empowering us to make a meaningful difference in the world.

The culmination of this chapter is not merely the end of a discussion but an open door to a continuous journey of discovery and action. It serves as an emphatic invitation to all readers, particularly those navigating the complexities of modern existence, to delve deeper into the intersection of science, faith, and our inherent role within creation. This exploration is an opportunity to affirm our commitment to stewardship, community, spirituality, and creativity in the context of our contemporary world.

We are beckoned to view the Earth not as a mere backdrop for human activity but as a sacred trust bestowed upon us. This trust calls for a transformation in how we interact with our planet—urging us from exploitation to a guardianship that honors and preserves. Our journey into understanding our place in creation reveals a profound responsibility: to care for this world with the reverence it deserves, ensuring its beauty and resources endure for future generations.

Moreover, this chapter invites us to rediscover our connection to both creation and community. In a world increasingly defined by digital interactions and fast-paced living, the creation narrative offers timeless lessons on unity, care, and mutual support. It urges us to engage actively in our local communities, to contribute to conservation efforts, and to foster relationships that bridge divides, reminding us of our shared responsibility in the stewardship of creation.

Spirituality emerges as a pivotal pathway to encountering the divine, with the natural world acting as a catalyst for deeper reflection and connection. Through moments of quiet contemplation in nature, participation in ecological pilgrimages, or the integration of creation-focused practices in our spiritual life, we are invited to a profound communion with the Creator. This spiritual engagement with the world around us deepens our appreciation for its mystery and majesty, encouraging a life lived in reverence and wonder.

Creativity, too, is highlighted as a divine gift, encouraging us to mirror the Creator's ingenuity in our endeavors. Whether through artistic expression, scientific exploration, or the simple acts of daily problem-solving, our creative efforts are a testament to our participation in the ongoing story of creation. By embracing this gift, we contribute to the world's beauty and complexity, adding our voice to the chorus that celebrates the marvels of the universe.

As we navigate the implications of the creation narrative in the modern context, we are reminded of the joy and purpose found in living in harmony with the divine design. This chapter is not just a reflection on our roles as stewards, community members, spiritual seekers, and creators; it is a call to action—a prompt to live intentionally and passionately, embracing the legacy of creation in every aspect of our lives.

In closing, this narrative extends an invitation to all readers to engage with the world through the lens of creation. It encourages a journey of exploration, reflection, and action, guided by the wisdom embedded in the creation narrative. As you continue reading, may you find inspiration to deepen your commitment to stewardship, to foster meaningful community connections, to enrich your spiritual life, and to embrace your creativity. Let the story of creation guide your steps, inspiring you to act with wisdom, compassion, and creativity, as we collectively strive to make the world a reflection of the divine vision of peace, beauty, and harmony.

Reflecting on our impact leads to a renewed commitment to stewardship. As we look forward, we consider the legacy we wish to leave, focusing on the future generations who will inherit the Earth and continue the work we've begun.

# CHAPTER 10

# SCIENTIFIC PERSPECTIVES ON CREATION

In a small, dimly lit room filled with stacks of books and the soft hum of a computer, I found myself at a crossroads of curiosity and faith. My journey had always been one of seeking understanding, trying to reconcile the expansive universe described by my telescopes and textbooks with the intimate creation spoken of in moments of prayer and reflection. Here, in this room, I embarked on a quest not just for knowledge, but for wisdom—the wisdom to see the tapestry of time and light through both the lens of science and the eyes of faith.

I delved into the realms of modern cosmology, where the origins of the universe were not merely theoretical constructs but a narrative of staggering age and expansiveness. The Big Bang theory, with its explosive inception from a singularity and the subsequent unfurling of the cosmos, did not diminish my reverence for the Genesis narrative. Instead, it expanded my understanding of "In the beginning," inviting me to marvel at the grandeur of God's creation on a scale beyond human comprehension. Far from seeing this as a challenge to my faith, it became a source of awe—a reflection of the meticulous order and vastness crafted by the Creator's hand.

My exploration then took me to the symphony of evolution, the scientific study of life's origins on Earth. The diversity and complexity of life, from the simplest organisms to the rich tapestry of ecosystems we see today, unfolded before me not as a contradiction but as a divine methodology. This perspective allowed me to appreciate the divine creativity and patience in life's gradual emergence, revealing a Creator who delights in diversity and complexity.

This journey through science and faith taught me the complementarity of these two ways of understanding the world. Science provided me with tools and methodologies to uncover the workings of the natural world, while my faith offered a framework to interpret these discoveries within the context of divine purpose and intention. Together, they painted a fuller picture of the universe, one that reflected the Creator's power, wisdom, and love.

As I sat there, surrounded by the tools of my quest—books, papers, and the ever-glowing screen—I realized that my unique position in the universe came with a dual responsibility. Not only was I a steward of creation, called to protect and cherish the natural world, but I was also a steward of knowledge. My pursuit of scientific inquiry, tempered with humility and ethical integrity, was a sacred task, one that had profound implications for my understanding of creation and my role within it.

In practical terms, this meant advocating for educational initiatives that bridged the gap between science and faith, promoting a holistic understanding of the universe. It meant applying scientific insights to promote sustainable living practices, viewing environmental stewardship as an extension of my spiritual duty. It also meant supporting ethical scientific research that sought the betterment of humanity and the world.

In conclusion, my journey into the dialogue between science and faith did not lead me to contention but to a harmonious exploration that deepened my awe and appreciation for the intricacies of creation. By embracing the insights offered by both science and faith, I cultivated a deeper understanding of the universe as an intricate, divine creation. This journey affirmed my commitment to stewardship and wonder, guiding me to live in awe of the mysteries that unfold in the vast expanse of the cosmos and the depth of the human spirit.

## EMBRACING THE CONFLUENCE OF SCIENCE AND FAITH

The journey to understand the universe and the origins of life on Earth has often been navigated through the complementary lenses of science and faith. Rather than viewing these perspectives as conflicting, this exploration reveals a rich landscape where scientific discovery and spiritual wonder merge, creating a tapestry of understanding that enriches our perspective on existence.

Science, with its empirical methods, unveils the laws governing the cosmos, from subatomic particles to expansive galaxies, revealing a universe marked by intricate order and complexity. This pursuit, driven by curiosity, mirrors the spiritual journey that seeks understanding beyond the tangible, reaching for truths that transcend the material.

Faith interprets the meaning and purpose behind scientific facts, offering a connection to the Creator who imbues the universe with significance. It deepens our reverence for creation, enhancing our understanding with awe at the cosmos's vastness and the intricate design of life on Earth.

The confluence of science and faith enriches our understanding by connecting knowledge with meaning. Scientific advancements inspire awe that resonates with our spiritual wonder, deepening faith and allowing us to perceive the Creator's hand in the universe's elegance.

This relationship between Genesis and modern science can be seen as complementary. Genesis provides a foundational understanding of the world as divine creation, while science offers insights into the processes shaping it. Together, they present a holistic view that encompasses both the mechanisms and the purpose of existence, inviting us to marvel at the grandeur of both creation and its Creator.

Embracing this confluence challenges us to broaden our understanding, integrating scientific knowledge with spiritual insights. It calls us to be stewards of creation, informed by science and inspired by faith, engaging with the world in a way that reflects reverence for its Creator. This integration fosters a culture of curiosity, respect, and awe for the natural world and its divine origins.

Practically, this means advocating for education that explores both scientific and spiritual perspectives, supporting ethical research aimed at bettering humanity, and engaging in environmental stewardship as an expression of care for creation. It involves living in a way that respects the world's complexity and sanctity, inspired by the knowledge that it is the work of a Creator who delights in revealing Himself through both the pages of Scripture and the phenomena of nature.

The quest to understand the universe's origins and workings invites us into a deeper exploration of both science and faith, in a harmonious search for truth that unites empirical inquiry with spiritual reflection. By embracing the confluence of these domains, we open ourselves to a fuller appreciation of creation's majesty and the wonder of its Creator, enriching our lives with deeper understanding and profound awe.

## THE UNIVERSE'S ORIGINS: A TAPESTRY OF TIME AND LIGHT

Modern cosmology unveils a universe that stretches far beyond the reaches of our imagination, a boundless expanse birthed from the singularity known as the Big Bang. This scientific narrative, rather than clashing with the spiritual journey of faith, enriches the Genesis account, inviting believers to explore the origins of the universe not as a tale of conflict between science and faith, but as a harmonious exploration of divine creativity. The description of the universe's inception and its expansive evolution over billions of years offers a profound expansion of our understanding of "In the beginning," allowing us to marvel at the vastness of cosmic history through a lens of faith.

The Big Bang theory describes a universe emerging from an infinitesimal point, expanding across the vastness of space—a concept that mirrors the awe-inspiring power of creation depicted in religious texts. This perspective encourages believers to marvel at the grandeur of God's creation, recognizing the divine hand not only in the moment of creation but also in the laws that govern the universe's expansion. The meticulous order and structure that underpin the cosmos, from the laws of physics to the formation of stars and galaxies, suggest a universe infused with intention and beauty, rather than randomness.

Viewing the origins of the universe through this integrated lens of science and faith enhances our appreciation for the complexity and order of creation. It invites us into a state of awe and wonder, where the scientific understanding of the universe's vastness and the eons of cosmic history enhance our spiritual appreciation. This perspective does not view science as an adversary to faith but as a complementary pathway that can deepen our understanding of the Creator's work.

The narrative of cosmic evolution, from the fiery births of stars to the delicate dance of galaxies, can be seen as a divine tapestry woven from time and light. Each thread, representing the laws of physics and the milestones of cosmic development, contributes to the beauty and complexity of the whole. This tapestry invites believers to look beyond the surface, recognizing the Creator's hand in the intricate patterns and structures of the cosmos.

The narrative of the universe's origins, as revealed by modern cosmology, challenges us to expand our understanding of creation. It encourages us to embrace the vastness and age of the universe as expressions of the Creator's power and majesty. This expanded perspective does not undermine the Genesis narrative but deepens our appreciation for it, allowing us to see the biblical account of creation in the light of the incredible history and structure of the universe that science reveals.

The exploration of the universe's origins offers an opportunity for believers to integrate the insights of modern cosmology with their faith. This journey does not detract from spiritual truth but enhances our sense of wonder and reverence for the Creator. By viewing the universe's inception and expansion through the lens of faith, we can appreciate the grandeur of God's creation in a way that enriches our spiritual understanding and deepens our awe for the meticulous order and vastness of the cosmos. This approach affirms that exploring the universe's origins can be a profound act of faith, revealing the universe as a divine tapestry of time and light, woven by an omnipotent Creator.


## LIFE ON EARTH: THE SYMPHONY OF EVOLUTION

The scientific study of evolution offers a breathtaking panorama of life's unfurling on Earth, from the simplest single-celled organisms in ancient oceans to the complex tapestry of ecosystems we observe today. This journey through time, illuminated by evolutionary biology, does not pose a challenge to the creation narrative but profoundly complements it, inviting a deeper appreciation of the divine methods employed in populating the Earth with a diverse array of life.

Viewing evolution through the lens of faith allows us to see it as divine orchestration, a testament to the Creator's ingenuity and foresight. The complexities uncovered by science do not diminish our awe of God's creation; rather, they enhance our appreciation for His work. This perspective recognizes the divine creativity and patience in the gradual unfolding of life, revealing a Creator who delights in diversity and complexity.

The narrative of evolution, marked by epochs of gradual change and moments of rapid diversification, mirrors the dynamism and resilience imbued in creation. It speaks to a Creator who is continually nurturing and shaping life, delighting in the myriad ways life can adapt and thrive in changing environments. This dynamic view of creation highlights God's pleasure in variety and His ongoing involvement in the natural world.

Understanding evolution also deepens our appreciation for the interconnectedness of all life. The intricate web of ecosystems, where plants, animals, and microorganisms interact, reflects a divine blueprint of interdependence. This interconnectedness reminds us of our place within creation—not as dominators but as stewards called to protect and preserve the natural world.

The study of evolutionary processes encourages believers to reflect on God's detailed involvement in creation. It portrays a Creator active not only in grand acts like forging galaxies but also in the subtle details of genetic variation and natural selection. This view emphasizes God's meticulous attention to detail and His commitment to sustaining life in all its forms.

Embracing the symphony of evolution enriches our spiritual life by broadening our understanding of how God interacts with His creation. It challenges us to recognize His hand in both miraculous events and everyday natural processes. This realization fosters a deeper sense of reverence and humility as we contemplate the vastness of God's creativity and the depth of His love for all creation.

Practically, this appreciation for evolutionary processes can inspire believers to engage more fully with the natural world. It motivates us to learn about and protect endangered species and habitats and to advocate for policies that preserve biodiversity. It encourages us to value all forms of life, recognizing each creature's role in the ecosystem and its intrinsic worth as part of God's creation.

In conclusion, the symphony of evolution, as revealed through the study of life's origins and diversity on Earth, offers a profound opportunity for believers to deepen their faith. Instead of viewing scientific discoveries as challenges to the creation narrative, we can embrace them as insights into the methods God used to enrich our world with life. This approach allows us to celebrate the divine creativity and patience evident in the unfolding of life, fostering greater appreciation for the Creator who delights in diversity and complexity. By integrating this understanding into our spiritual lives, we affirm our commitment to stewardship and deepen our awe in the face of the mysteries of creation.

## THE COMPLEMENTARITY OF SCIENCE AND FAITH

Exploring the universe has often been depicted as a journey along two divergent paths: one forged by science and the other illuminated by faith. Yet, this portrayal overlooks the profound complementarity that exists between these realms. By embracing both science and faith, believers gain a more comprehensive perspective of creation, merging empirical discovery with spiritual insight, thus enhancing our appreciation for the universe's grandeur in ways neither domain could achieve alone.

Science equips us with rigorous methodologies and a relentless pursuit of knowledge, uncovering the mechanisms and laws that govern everything from the microscopic intricacies of DNA to the vast expanses of interstellar space. These revelations spark wonder and curiosity, pushing us deeper into the universe's mysteries.

Conversely, faith provides a framework to interpret these discoveries, offering meaning and purpose. It encourages looking beyond the material to contemplate the divine intentions underlying existence, thus enriching our understanding with a spiritual dimension.

This convergence portrays the universe as a divine masterpiece, reflecting the Creator's glory and majesty. It does not diminish the value of scientific inquiry or spiritual belief; instead, it enriches both by presenting a universe rich in both matter and meaning.

This integrated perspective urges believers to engage with the world with intellectual rigor and spiritual depth. It allows us to appreciate astronomical phenomena through the lens of astrophysics while recognizing them as manifestations of divine splendor. It compels us to explore the natural world's complexities, seeing in its diversity a testament to divine creativity.

Furthermore, this approach affirms our unique role as creation's stewards, endowed with the intellect to unravel the universe's mysteries and the soul to appreciate its spiritual significance. This dual capacity is a gift, accompanied by the responsibility to use our knowledge and faith to serve the world and its Creator.

Practically, this means supporting scientific endeavors that heal, protect, and enhance the natural world as expressions of faith in action. It calls for advocating environmental stewardship as a spiritual duty informed by scientific understanding.

In conclusion, exploring the universe does not require choosing between science and faith. Instead, it can be a harmonious exploration that leverages both disciplines' strengths. Together, science and faith offer a fuller understanding of creation, celebrating the natural world's intricate designs as expressions of divine power, wisdom, and love. This complementary approach not only deepens our appreciation for the universe's majesty but also reinforces our commitment to stewardship, recognizing our role in preserving and honoring the splendor of creation.

## THE ROLE OF HUMANITY: STEWARDS OF SCIENCE AND CREATION

Humanity's unique position in the universe endows us with profound dual responsibilities: as stewards of both creation and knowledge. This privilege enables us to explore the cosmos, unravel life's mysteries, and apply our scientific understanding in service to Earth. As stewards of creation, we are tasked with the sacred duty of nurturing and protecting every aspect of the natural world—from every leaf and creature to every water drop—as manifestations of the divine.

Our role as Earth's protectors compels us to leverage scientific insights to safeguard the environment. This involves understanding and preserving the ecological networks that sustain life, combatting pollution, conserving biodiversity, and addressing climate change impacts to ensure the planet remains a hospitable home for all its inhabitants, now and in the future.

Simultaneously, as stewards of knowledge, we bear the responsibility of pursuing scientific inquiry with humility and ethical integrity. This stewardship recognizes that our explorations and discoveries carry profound implications—not only for our understanding of the physical world but also for our comprehension of our place and purpose within it. Each breakthrough and insight offers a glimpse into the mechanics of creation, while also posing ethical dilemmas and spiritual questions that demand careful consideration.

Our pursuit of knowledge must be guided by ethical principles, ensuring that our scientific endeavors honor the sanctity of life and the integrity of creation. This includes conducting research that respects the dignity of all beings, employing technologies that enhance rather than harm the quality of life, and making decisions that reflect a balance between innovation and preservation.

The role of humanity as stewards also extends to how we share and apply our knowledge. Educating others about environmental conservation, advocating for policies that protect the natural world, and developing sustainable technologies are all expressions of our stewardship. Through these actions, we not only contribute to the well-being of the planet but also inspire a collective commitment to its care.

Moreover, our stewardship calls us to reflect on the spiritual dimensions of our relationship with creation. It invites us to view the natural world not as a resource to be exploited but as a sacred trust to be honored. This perspective deepens our appreciation for the beauty and complexity of Earth, fostering a sense of wonder and gratitude for the opportunity to explore and understand the universe.

In embracing our role as stewards of science and creation, we acknowledge the interconnectedness of all life and the interdependence of our scientific and spiritual pursuits. We recognize that our actions have consequences that ripple through ecosystems and communities, affecting not only the present but also future generations. This awareness compels us to act with foresight and compassion, aligning our efforts with the greater good.

In conclusion, humanity's role as stewards of science and creation is a calling of unparalleled significance. It challenges us to wield our knowledge and capabilities with care, to protect the natural world, and to pursue scientific inquiry with ethical integrity. By fulfilling this dual responsibility, we honor our unique position in the universe and contribute to the ongoing work of creation. This stewardship is not just a duty but a privilege, offering us the chance to participate in the divine act of nurturing and sustaining the world, guided by a spirit of humility, reverence, and love.

## PRACTICAL APPLICATIONS IN DAILY LIFE

## EDUCATIONAL ENRICHMENT

Incorporating the interplay between science and faith into our daily lives begins with a commitment to educational enrichment. This endeavor involves advocating for and actively participating in educational initiatives that treat science and faith not as opposing forces but as complementary perspectives, each enriching our understanding of the universe. By fostering environments where questions about the cosmos and life's origins are explored through both scientific inquiry and spiritual reflection, we cultivate a holistic view of creation as an intricate masterpiece of both physical laws and divine intention.

Educational enrichment in this context means seeking out, creating, and supporting learning opportunities that bridge the gap between science and faith. This could involve organizing community workshops that feature speakers from both scientific and religious backgrounds, participating in discussion groups that delve into topics at the intersection of science and spirituality, or advocating for curricula in schools that reflect the harmony between these fields. These initiatives encourage a dialogue that respects the methodologies and insights of science while acknowledging the depth and wisdom that faith brings to our understanding of the universe.

By engaging in this form of educational advocacy, we challenge the misconception that science and faith must exist in separate realms. Instead, we showcase the beauty of their interaction, how scientific discoveries about the universe—from the vastness of galaxies to the intricacies of cellular life—can inspire awe and wonder that resonate with our spiritual beliefs. This approach does not dilute the rigor of scientific inquiry or the profundity of spiritual insight; rather, it highlights how each can illuminate the other, enriching our appreciation for the complexity and majesty of creation.

Promoting a holistic understanding of the universe as both a physical and spiritual creation also has profound implications for how we view our place and purpose within it. It fosters a sense of responsibility and stewardship, encouraging us to care for the natural world not just as a valuable resource but as a sacred trust. This perspective motivates us to engage in sustainable practices and to advocate for policies that protect the environment, driven by a conviction that doing so is both a scientific imperative and a spiritual duty.

Furthermore, educational enrichment that integrates science and faith equips individuals with the critical thinking skills necessary to navigate the complex challenges of the modern world. It encourages a mindset that is open to exploration and discovery, comfortable with complexity, and grounded in a deep respect for the knowledge and wisdom that both science and faith offer. This approach prepares us to make informed decisions that reflect an understanding of the natural world and a commitment to the values and ethical principles derived from our faith.

In practical terms, this means supporting educational institutions that embrace this integrated approach, utilizing media and technology to spread awareness and understanding, and fostering a culture of lifelong learning where questions are welcomed, and exploration is encouraged. It means creating spaces in our homes, schools, and communities where young people can grow up seeing science and faith not as adversaries but as allies in the quest to understand the world and our place in it.

In conclusion, advocating for and engaging in educational initiatives that integrate science and faith represent vital steps toward realizing a vision of the universe that encompasses both its physical and spiritual dimensions. This approach not only deepens our understanding of the world around us but also strengthens our faith, inspiring a sense of wonder and reverence for the intricacy and beauty of creation. By championing this holistic perspective, we affirm the value of both scientific inquiry and spiritual insight, fostering a more informed, thoughtful, and compassionate engagement with the world.

## ENVIRONMENTAL RESPONSIBILITY

Integrating scientific insights with our spiritual convictions transforms environmental responsibility from a mere task into a sacred duty embedded in the fabric of daily life. By applying knowledge gained from ecology and conservation science, we deepen our understanding of how our actions impact the planet, guiding us towards more environmentally conscious decisions. This approach compels us to adopt sustainable living practices not just as optional choices but as essential expressions of our faith and care for creation.

Understanding the delicate balance of ecosystems and the critical importance of biodiversity, as illuminated by science, deepens our appreciation for the intricate web of life that God has created. This appreciation inspires us to take concrete steps to reduce our ecological footprint —whether through conserving water, minimizing waste, or choosing renewable energy sources. These actions reflect a commitment to living in harmony with the earth, acknowledging that every resource is a gift that should be used wisely and sparingly.

Viewing environmental stewardship as a spiritual duty enriches our perspective on sustainability, encouraging us to see it not merely as an individual or collective goal but as a moral imperative. It challenges us to consider the legacy we wish to leave for future generations, ensuring that our planet remains a vibrant and life-sustaining home. This vision calls for a shift in lifestyle that prioritizes the health of the environment over convenience or consumerism, urging us to adopt practices that promote the well-being of all creation.

Moreover, engaging in environmental responsibility as an act of faith enables us to connect more deeply with our communities and the wider world. It opens opportunities for collaboration in conservation efforts, whether through participating in local clean-up projects, supporting sustainable agriculture, or advocating for policies that protect natural habitats. These collective actions not only contribute to the preservation of the environment but also foster a sense of unity and purpose among participants, strengthening the bonds within communities of faith.

The integration of scientific understanding with spiritual values also empowers us to educate others about the importance of environmental stewardship. By sharing knowledge and experiences, we can inspire friends, family, and fellow congregation members to join in these efforts, creating a ripple effect that extends far beyond our immediate circles. This educational outreach is crucial, as it raises awareness and motivates action, building a broader coalition of individuals committed to caring for God's creation.

In conclusion, applying scientific insights into ecology and conservation to promote sustainable living practices is a practical application of our faith that profoundly impacts our daily lives. It redefines environmental responsibility as a spiritual duty, urging us to live in ways that reflect our deep respect for and commitment to the natural world. By embracing this duty, we participate in the divine work of stewardship, contributing to the health and preservation of the planet for the glory of the Creator and the benefit of future generations. This approach to environmental responsibility not only strengthens our faith but also enacts tangible change, affirming our role as caretakers of the earth.

## ETHICAL SCIENCE

Incorporating ethical considerations into scientific research is a profound expression of our faith and respect for the sanctity of life. As individuals of faith navigating the complexities of the modern world, we are called to support and participate in scientific endeavors that adhere to ethical standards. This ensures that the pursuit of knowledge aligns with principles of dignity, respect, and the common good. Supporting ethical science means advocating for research that respects the inherent value of all life forms, ensuring that our quest for knowledge never compromises well-being or dignity.

We engage in ethical science by critically examining the purposes and methods of scientific studies, championing those aimed at alleviating suffering, enhancing quality of life, and addressing humanity's and the planet's pressing challenges. This discernment ensures that our support is directed towards endeavors that contribute positively to the world, aligning with our spiritual values and ethical convictions.

Participation in ethical scientific research involves a commitment to transparency, accountability, and rigorous application of ethical guidelines. It means prioritizing the welfare of participants, responsible resource use, and considering the long-term implications of research outcomes. This approach fosters integrity within the scientific community, valuing the betterment of humanity and the world as the highest goals.

Ethical engagement in science also involves a commitment to environmental stewardship, recognizing the critical role of scientific research in addressing ecological crises. By supporting studies focused on conservation, sustainable technologies, and environmental health, we contribute to safeguarding the planet for future generations. This exemplifies how faith and science can work together towards common objectives, honoring creation through conscientious action.

Furthermore, ethical science calls for advocating justice and equity in research practices and access to scientific advancements. This includes ensuring that the benefits of scientific discoveries are shared widely and equitably, addressing disparities in health, education, and technology. By championing inclusivity and fairness, we reflect our belief in the inherent worth of every individual and our commitment to a world where everyone can thrive.

Supporting ethical science can involve engaging in public discourse on science policy, financially supporting institutions and projects that adhere to high ethical standards, and educating ourselves and others about the ethical dimensions of scientific research. This fosters an informed and conscientious approach to science in our communities.

In conclusion, integrating ethical considerations into scientific research is a crucial application of our faith in daily life. It represents a commitment to conducting science in ways that respect life, uphold dignity, and contribute to the betterment of humanity and the world. By supporting and participating in ethical science, we not only advance knowledge but also affirm our role as stewards of creation, guided by a moral compass that seeks the welfare of all. This commitment strengthens our faith, enriches our understanding of the world, and inspires us to work tirelessly for a future that reflects the best of both scientific endeavor and spiritual integrity.

The conclusion of this chapter opens not just a chapter's end but a gateway to continuous exploration and engagement within the intricate dance between science and faith. This narrative, stretching from the cosmos to the essence of life on Earth, extends a heartfelt invitation, especially to those in the scientific community, to embark on a journey where empirical inquiry meets spiritual depth. It's a call to delve into the mysteries of the universe with wonder and to allow our scientific pursuits and spiritual reflections to enrich each other, fostering a deeper appreciation for the divine tapestry of creation.

As we navigate this path, let us proceed with reverence and awe, mindful of the profound work of the Creator surrounding us. The journey through scientific discoveries and faith-based reflections is not merely academic; it's a voyage towards understanding the intricate balance and beauty of the universe—an opportunity to look beyond the surface, to recognize the divine spark within the laws of physics, the evolutionary marvels of life, and the expansive history of the cosmos.

This exploration is a testament to the harmony that can exist between the realms of science and faith, reminding us that our quest for knowledge is complemented by our spiritual yearnings. As we uncover the vast mysteries of the cosmos and the complexities of life on Earth, let us approach each discovery not as a challenge to our faith but as an invitation to marvel at the Creator's ingenuity. The universe, in all its vastness and intricacy, reflects divine power, wisdom, and love—a sacred space that invites inquiry and inspires worship.

The narrative presented in this chapter is but a starting point, a spark to ignite a lifelong journey of exploration and wonder. It encourages readers to continue delving into the questions that arise at the intersection of science and faith, to seek answers that satisfy both the intellect and the soul. As we proceed, let us maintain the sense of awe that comes from understanding the universe as an intricate, divine creation, allowing it to deepen our faith and guide our steps.

In closing, this chapter extends an open invitation to all to explore the space where science and faith intersect, to embrace the insights offered by both perspectives. It's a call to recognize that our quest for understanding can lead us to a deeper appreciation of the divine, enriching our lives with a more profound sense of wonder in the face of the universe's mysteries. As you continue reading, may you be inspired to journey further into this exploration, armed with curiosity and reverence, ready to discover the endless wonders of creation and the Creator's enduring presence within it.

Reflecting on our impact leads to a renewed commitment to stewardship. As we look forward, we consider the legacy we wish to leave, focusing on the future generations who will inherit the Earth and continue the work we've begun.

# PART V
# PRACTICING FAITH IN DAILY LIFE

# CHAPTER 11

# MY JOURNEY: SCIENCE, GENESIS, AND THE UNFOLDING FAITH

My exploration through the realms of science and spirituality has been a grand adventure, fueled by insatiable curiosity and a profound sense of wonder. Since my earliest memories of gazing at the starlit sky, questions about the universe and our place within it have captivated me, driving me down the path of scientific inquiry. I sought answers in the laws of physics, the vast expanses of cosmology, and the intricate mechanisms of biology. Yet, with each discovery, the mysteries of existence seemed to expand, prompting me to consider the possibility of divine orchestration behind the observable universe.

During my university years, amidst the challenges of equations and scientific theories, I found myself drawn to the spiritual truths within the book of Genesis. I began to see these ancient scriptures not as mere historical accounts but as profound expressions of the universe's divine origins. The words, "In the beginning, God created the heavens and the earth," resonated deeply, harmonizing with the scientific understanding I was concurrently developing. Rather than viewing them as contradictory, I perceived the narratives of science and Genesis as intertwined, each offering unique insights into the marvels of creation.

This dual journey into the scientific and spiritual dimensions of the universe led me to a place of awe and reverence. The deeper I delved into both realms, the more I recognized the elegance and complexity of creation as reflections of divine artistry. I came to see the Big Bang not as a counterargument to divine creation, but as a glimpse into the method God might have employed to ignite the cosmos. Similarly, the story of evolution began to reveal not a challenge to creation, but a celebration of life's diversity, suggesting a Creator who delights in the richness and complexity of life.

Harmonizing scientific knowledge with spiritual faith has profoundly transformed me. I've realized that faith and reason are not adversaries but companions in our quest to understand the essence of our existence. My scientific endeavors have not only reinforced my belief in a Creator but have also deepened my connection to the natural world, enriching my spiritual life with a more nuanced understanding of creation.

This enriched understanding has sparked a passionate commitment to stewardship, acknowledging our collective duty to care for this magnificent creation. My advocacy for environmental conservation and sustainable living is now informed by both scientific reasoning and spiritual conviction, inspired by a belief in a Creator who crafted the heavens and the earth and entrusted them to our care.

As I share my story, I extend an invitation to others, particularly within the scientific community, to explore the fruitful dialogue between science and faith. This is a call to embark on a journey of discovery, where the pursuit of scientific understanding and the exploration of spiritual truth lead to a greater appreciation of the divine. In uncovering the secrets of the cosmos and the wonders of life on Earth, let us approach our studies with humility and reverence, ever mindful of the Creator whose masterpiece we have the privilege to investigate and cherish.

As a writer navigating the intricate landscapes of science and spirituality, my journey has been marked by a relentless pursuit of knowledge and an enduring sense of wonder. This exploration has profoundly shaped my understanding of the world and my role within it, revealing the rich harmony that exists between the empirical discoveries of science and the profound spiritual insights offered by the book of Genesis. My narrative is not just my own but a testament to the possibility of a deep accord between these two realms, each informing and enriching the other. Through my experiences, I aim to demonstrate how scientific rigor and spiritual depth can coalesce, providing a more comprehensive understanding of our universe and our place within it. This journey has not only broadened my perspective but has also deepened my commitment to exploring and sharing the ways in which science and faith together can illuminate the mysteries of existence.

## THE AWAKENING: A UNIVERSE OF QUESTIONS

My childhood brimmed with a relentless curiosity about the cosmos. Each night, as I gazed up at the star-studded expanse, my heart filled with wonder and countless questions about the vast universe stretching far beyond my grasp. This deep fascination set the stage for a lifelong journey—a voyage deep into the realms of physics, cosmology, and biology, seeking answers to the profound mysteries of existence.

The deeper I ventured into the scientific understanding of the universe, from the minutiae of particles to the sprawling galaxies, the more my awe expanded. Every new discovery, each piece of knowledge I acquired, seemed to broaden the scope of my curiosity even further. I found myself pondering the intricate laws and forces shaping the cosmos, contemplating the possibility of a divine architect behind the breathtaking beauty and order above us.

This quest for knowledge led me to delve into the mesmerizing theories of modern science—from the Big Bang to galaxy formation and the evolution of life on Earth. Each theory introduced me to a universe even more complex and wondrous than the last. Yet, each answer uncovered new questions, more profound and intricate than before.

The universe's intricacy, with its precise laws and finely tuned constants, presented a compelling argument for a guiding intelligence. How could such exquisite order emerge from chaos, such beauty from nothingness? The mathematical elegance of the cosmos, where every law and constant seemed meticulously designed to support life, suggested a level of intentionality that mere chance seemed unable to explain.

Rather than distancing me from science, this journey drew me deeper into its mysteries. It became apparent that the realms of faith and science were not adversaries but allies in the quest to comprehend the grandeur of the universe. The awe and wonder that fueled my scientific explorations found a mirror in my spiritual search for meaning and purpose. In the cosmos's precision and beauty, I saw not just the workings of natural laws but the fingerprints of the divine.

Thus, my awakening to a universe of questions was not a departure from faith but a journey toward a deeper, more profound appreciation of creation. Far from diminishing my sense of wonder, the pursuit of scientific knowledge enriched it, unveiling a cosmos imbued with the grandeur of a Creator whose masterwork invites us to explore, discover, and marvel. This exploration, bridging the gap between science and faith, has not only deepened my understanding of the universe but also reinforced my belief in the divine guidance behind its unfolding narrative.

As this chapter unfolds, it extends an invitation to readers to embark on this journey of discovery. It is a call to gaze at the stars with renewed wonder, to ask bold questions, and to seek answers through both the rigorous laws of physics and the spiritual narrative of faith. In the vastness of the universe and the intricacies of its creation, we are encouraged to explore the profound connection between our scientific endeavors and our spiritual quests for understanding.

## ENCOUNTERING GENESIS: A NEW PERSPECTIVE

During my university years, a time dominated by equations and experiments, I found myself unexpectedly drawn to the Book of Genesis. This ancient text, often a subject of intense debate, opened before me not merely as a historical account, but as a profound declaration of the universe's divine inception. The seminal phrase, "In the beginning, God created the heavens and the earth," resonated with me, harmonizing beautifully with the scientific knowledge I was acquiring, rather than clashing discordantly against it.

Encountering Genesis amidst my scientific studies prompted me to view the creation narrative through a new lens—one that merged faith and science, rather than pitting them against each other. Approached with an open heart and mind, this scripture transcended its often literal interpretations, revealing deeper truths about the origins of our universe as the ultimate expression of divine artistry and intelligence.

This revelation was transformative. It challenged me to reconsider my views on the relationship between science and spirituality. The opening lines of Genesis became a bridge linking two realms of thought I had previously seen as separate. Through this new perspective, scientific discoveries—about the vastness of the universe, the complexity of life on Earth, and the intricate laws governing existence—gained new significance. They became manifestations not of a meaningless universe, but of one rich with divine intention and meticulous care.

This fresh perspective on Genesis encouraged me to explore the intersections of science and faith with renewed wonder and curiosity. It suggested that the laws of physics, the formation of galaxies, and the emergence of life could be viewed as chapters in a grander narrative of creation, penned by a Creator who delights in revealing Himself through the natural order. The intricacies of DNA, the celestial ballet of the planets, and the rhythms of ecosystems transcended their academic significance, reflecting divine order and beauty.

Furthermore, this encounter with Genesis during my formative university years deepened my reflection on my own place within the cosmos. It fostered a sense of responsibility towards the natural world, an appreciation for the sanctity of life, and a commitment to not just observe the universe but to steward it conscientiously. This scripture, once perceived as detached from the empirical world of science, became foundational to my understanding of both the natural and spiritual realms.

In grappling with the profound questions at the intersection of science and faith, Genesis provided a framework for reconciling and integrating these domains. It presented the pursuit of scientific knowledge and the search for spiritual meaning not as conflicting endeavors, but as complementary paths to discovering truth. This narrative, ancient yet perpetually relevant, emerged as a source of inspiration and a guide for navigating the complexities of the modern world with intellectual rigor and spiritual depth.

In conclusion, my encounter with Genesis amidst academic pursuits granted me a new outlook on the origins and significance of the universe. It challenged me to look beyond the surface of scientific discoveries to the deeper spiritual implications of creation. This journey of integration has been both enriching and transformative, enhancing my faith and expanding my understanding of the divine tapestry that is our universe. As we continue to unravel the mysteries of existence, let us approach this exploration with open hearts and minds, embracing the rich dialogue between science and faith as a wellspring of insight, inspiration, and awe.

## BRIDGING WORLDS: SCIENCE AND SPIRITUALITY IN DIALOGUE

As I delved deeper into the realms of science and spirituality, my journey began to resemble a dialogue between two worlds, each offering profound insights into the mysteries of creation. This exploration bridged the vast expanses of the cosmos with the intimate depths of faith, revealing the intricate beauty and complexity of the universe in ways I had never imagined. The awe-inspiring phenomena studied in physics, cosmology, and biology resonated not as challenges to my faith but as echoes of a divine narrative.

Encountering the Big Bang theory, I saw it not as a refutation of divine creation but as a breathtaking glimpse into the method by which God might have sparked the universe into being. This cosmological event, marking the dawn of space, time, and matter, unfolded in my mind as the first act of a divine drama, with God as the director setting the stage for all that was to come. The unfathomable explosion of light and energy at the universe's inception became, in my eyes, a testament to God's power and majesty.

Similarly, my engagement with evolutionary biology transformed my understanding of life on Earth. Rather than viewing it as a process devoid of divine guidance, I came to appreciate it as the narrative of God's creativity—each species a verse in a poem celebrating the richness and diversity of life. The gradual emergence of species, the intricate dance of adaptation and survival, spoke to me of a Creator who revels in complexity and delights in the endless variations of life.

This bridging of worlds between science and spirituality fostered in me a profound sense of wonder and reverence. It challenged me to embrace a more holistic view of creation, one that includes the vast, expanding universe and the minute, unfolding patterns of life on Earth. In this dialogue, scientific discoveries became spiritual revelations, each new finding a window into the mind of the Creator, inviting deeper contemplation and awe.

As I delved into this confluence of knowledge and belief, I realized that the dialogue between science and spirituality is not about reconciling conflicting views but about deepening our understanding of the universe and our place within it. This perspective encouraged me to approach both scientific inquiry and spiritual reflection with an open heart and mind, ready to discover the myriad ways in which the world speaks of its Creator.

The journey through science and faith taught me that the universe is not merely a cold, indifferent space but a creation imbued with meaning and purpose. The laws that govern the cosmos, the forces that propel the stars, and the processes that drive evolution are all part of a larger, divine story—one that we are invited to explore and celebrate.

In conclusion, the dialogue between science and spirituality has enriched my faith and expanded my understanding of the universe. It has shown me that awe and wonder are the common ground between these two realms, uniting us in our quest to understand the creation's majesty. As we continue to bridge these worlds, let us do so with humility and curiosity, ever mindful of the Creator whose work we seek to comprehend. This journey is not just about answering questions but about deepening our relationship with the divine, recognizing that in every leaf, star, and DNA strand, there is a story of creation waiting to be told.

## PERSONAL TRANSFORMATION: A FAITH RENEWED

Embarking on this journey to reconcile my scientific knowledge with my faith has profoundly transformed me. It reshaped my understanding of the relationship between faith and reason, revealing them not as adversaries locked in eternal conflict but as allies, walking hand in hand in the quest to unravel the mysteries of our existence. This revelation was not immediate; it emerged from countless hours of study, reflection, and sometimes wrestling with doubts and questions that seemed to offer no straightforward answers.

As I delved deeper into the complexities of the universe, from the smallest subatomic particles to the vast cosmos, my belief in a Creator was not diminished but significantly strengthened. The elegance of the universe's laws, the intricacy of life's design, and the sheer beauty of the natural world spoke to me of a divine intelligence and artistry far beyond human comprehension. This realization brought with it a profound sense of awe and wonder, which became the bedrock of my renewed faith.

This journey also deepened my appreciation for the natural world, transforming my spiritual life in unexpected ways. I began to see the fingerprints of the Creator in every aspect of creation, from the intricate patterns on a leaf to the majestic expanse of the night sky. This new perspective infused my daily existence with a sense of sacredness, turning every encounter with nature into an opportunity for spiritual reflection and gratitude.

My scientific pursuits, far from leading me away from faith, have become a source of spiritual enrichment. They have taught me that the quest for knowledge is not just a scholarly endeavor but a spiritual one, inviting us to explore the depth and breadth of creation. This exploration has led me to a more profound understanding of the Creator, one that embraces the complexity and wonder of the universe as expressions of divine wisdom and creativity.

This personal transformation has not been a solitary journey but one shared with others who are navigating the complexities of integrating faith and science. Through conversations, debates, and shared experiences, I've discovered a community of like-minded individuals who are also seeking to bridge the gap between these two worlds. This sense of fellowship has been instrumental in my journey, providing support, encouragement, and a space for open and honest dialogue.

In embracing the compatibility of faith and reason, I've found that my spiritual beliefs provide a framework through which I can interpret and appreciate the discoveries of science. This integration has not only enriched my understanding of the world but has also deepened my commitment to stewardship of the Earth and advocacy for environmental conservation. It has instilled in me a responsibility to care for creation, not just as a scientist but as a person of faith.

In conclusion, the journey of reconciling science and faith has been one of personal transformation and renewed faith. It has challenged me to expand my understanding, to embrace complexity, and to find harmony between the knowledge offered by science and the wisdom found in spirituality. This journey has reaffirmed my belief in a Creator and deepened my appreciation for the natural world, enriching my spiritual life in profound and lasting ways. As I continue on this path, I am reminded that faith and reason are not just parallel journeys but intertwined paths that lead us to a deeper understanding of our place in the universe and the nature of the divine.

## STEWARDSHIP: A SCIENTIFIC AND SPIRITUAL CALLING

My journey through the realms of science and faith has led me to a profound realization: stewardship of our planet is not merely a scientific imperative but a sacred duty, a calling that bridges the tangible and spiritual realms. The deeper I delved into the origins of the universe and the rich tapestry of life it harbors, the more convinced I became of our responsibility to safeguard this magnificent creation. This sense of duty stems from a deep-seated belief in a Creator who meticulously crafted the cosmos and all its inhabitants, entrusting us with their care and preservation.

Understanding the intricacies of the universe, from the vast galaxies that stretch across the night sky to the delicate ecosystems that populate the Earth, has only deepened my commitment to this stewardship. The awe-inspiring complexity and beauty of creation speak volumes of the Creator's ingenuity and benevolence, compelling us to honor this divine artistry through our actions and choices. It is a realization that our role as caretakers is not just an obligation but a privilege, an opportunity to participate in the divine work of sustaining and nurturing the world around us.

This calling to stewardship has reshaped my perspective on environmental conservation and sustainable living. I no longer view these practices solely through the lens of scientific necessity but as expressions of reverence for the Creator and compassion for His creation. It is a recognition that every effort to protect the environment, no matter how small, is a step towards fulfilling our divine mandate, a testament to our commitment to the well-being of our planet and all its inhabitants.

As a writer, I have found myself increasingly drawn to advocate for these causes, using my voice to highlight the urgency of our environmental crisis and the moral imperative to respond. Through my work, I seek to bridge the gap between knowledge and action, inspiring others to recognize their role in this stewardship and to embrace sustainable practices as integral to their spiritual journey. This advocacy is rooted in the belief that caring for the Earth is not just an act of preservation but a form of worship, a way to honor the Creator by respecting His creation.

This conviction has led me to explore the intersections of science, faith, and environmental ethics, seeking to understand how our spiritual beliefs can inform and strengthen our commitment to the planet. It has opened my eyes to the ways in which our daily choices—what we consume, how we live, and how we engage with the world around us—can reflect our values and our dedication to stewardship. It has also highlighted the importance of community in this endeavor, as collective action and shared responsibility are essential to effecting meaningful change.

Moreover, this journey has taught me that stewardship extends beyond mere conservation to encompass a holistic approach to living that values sustainability, equity, and compassion. It calls us to confront the challenges of climate change, habitat destruction, and biodiversity loss not only as scientific problems but as moral crises that demand a response rooted in our deepest convictions. It challenges us to see the Earth not as a resource to be exploited but as a sacred trust to be cherished and protected for future generations.

In embracing this calling, I have come to see stewardship as a central aspect of my faith, a tangible expression of my belief in a Creator who delights in the diversity and complexity of His creation. It has become a source of spiritual growth and renewal, enriching my understanding of the divine and deepening my connection to the world around me. Through this lens, every act of conservation, every effort to live sustainably, and every advocacy for environmental justice becomes a reflection of my faith, a step towards fulfilling the Creator's vision for a world that flourishes in harmony and balance.

In conclusion, stewardship of our planet is a calling that transcends the boundaries between science and spirituality, uniting them in a shared mission to protect and preserve the beauty and diversity of creation. It is a calling that demands our attention, our action, and our devotion, inviting us to engage with the world in a way that honors the Creator and reflects our commitment to the well-being of all His creation. As we continue to navigate the challenges of the modern world, let us do so with the conviction that our efforts to steward the Earth are not just acts of environmental responsibility but sacred duties that embody our deepest spiritual values and aspirations.

## CONCLUSION: AN INVITATION TO WONDER

This narrative, intricately woven from the threads of science and faith, does not conclude with an ending but extends an invitation—an invitation to wonder, explore, and contemplate the vastness of creation that envelops us. It beckons those within the scientific community and beyond to embark on a journey where the pursuit of knowledge meets the search for spiritual meaning. This exploration is not a path towards conflict but a journey toward a richer understanding of the universe and the divine creativity underpinning it.

As we delve into the mysteries of the cosmos, from the smallest quark to the sprawling galaxies, let us approach with a spirit of awe and humility. This journey should deepen our appreciation for the intricate designs and patterns that science reveals, recognizing in them the handiwork of a Creator who delights in complexity and beauty. The intersection of science and faith is not a battleground but fertile ground for discovery, where each new insight brings us closer to understanding the magnitude of creation and our purpose within it.

This invitation to wonder challenges us to view the world with fresh eyes, to see beyond the surface and appreciate the underlying unity that binds all creation. It encourages us to ask profound questions, to seek answers that satisfy both the mind and the heart, and to engage in a dialogue that bridges the gap between empirical evidence and spiritual truth. In this space, science and faith converge, offering a holistic view of the universe that enriches our knowledge and deepens our connection to the divine.

As you, the reader, continue on your journey, let this narrative serve as a reminder of the beauty and mystery that await your discovery. Whether you find yourself in a laboratory, gazing through a telescope, or in quiet reflection, know that you are part of a larger story—a story that spans the expanse of space and the depth of human curiosity. This exploration is an act of worship, a testament to the Creator's grandeur and an acknowledgment of our place within His creation.

In closing, let this chapter be a springboard into further exploration, an encouragement to continue seeking, questioning, and marveling at the universe around us. May your journey be marked by a sense of wonder and reverence, and may it lead you to a deeper appreciation of the divine. As we venture forth, let us do so with open hearts and minds, ready to uncover the mysteries of the cosmos and the intricacies of life on Earth, ever mindful of the Creator whose work we are privileged to explore.

# CHAPTER 12

# EXPLORING THE SABBATH: THE SANCTUARY OF REST IN A NON-STOP WORLD

In today's relentless society, where the gears of productivity never seem to wind down, the ancient rhythm of the Sabbath offers a promised solace, established at the dawn of creation itself. My life, much like anyone else's caught in the continuous pursuit of achievement, adhered to the modern adage of "more is better." Yet, within the pages of Genesis and through scientific insights, I discovered a profound truth that challenged the foundations of this belief. The Sabbath emerged not merely as a relic of religious tradition but as an essential practice for contemporary life, providing sanctuary amidst chaos.

My exploration of the Sabbath began with a reflection on the divine act described in Genesis, where God, after six days of creation, rested on the seventh day. This act of resting was a deliberate choice, sanctifying the day as a time for cessation from work and an opportunity for contemplation and rejuvenation. This divine pause was an invitation to balance, a call to step back from the labor of life and immerse in the essence of being—contemplating creation, engaging in worship, and reconnecting with life's core values.

Delving deeper into both spiritual and scientific perspectives, I uncovered the universal wisdom embedded in this ancient practice. Scientific research on rest resonates with the teachings of the Sabbath, highlighting the critical roles of downtime for cognitive function, emotional resilience, and overall health. Neuroscience and psychology have shown that regular intervals of rest can bolster creativity, reduce stress, and enhance mental clarity. This intersection between the spiritual tradition of the Sabbath and contemporary scientific findings illuminates the holistic benefits of rest, emphasizing its relevance as an antidote to the endemic burnout of our digital age.

Embracing the Sabbath amid the hustle of modern life became a conscious choice for me, a declaration of the value of rest and reflection. Each week, I began to carve out time to disconnect from the omnipresent demands of work and technology, creating space for activities that nourish the soul—reading, prayer, meditation, and simply being present in the moment. This practice of intentional rest became not just a spiritual discipline but a cornerstone of my mental and physical wellbeing, a time to savor silence, nature, and the joy of human connection.

Observing the Sabbath in a culture that often measures worth by productivity felt like an act of resistance, a counter-cultural statement affirming that our value transcends our output. This weekly pause served as a reminder of freedom and dignity beyond the confines of work, fostering a deep sense of gratitude and wonder for the gift of life.

My journey into the practice of Sabbath-keeping has profoundly transformed my understanding of rest, work, and worship. It's a transformation I am eager to share, inviting others to explore the restorative power of the Sabbath. Through conversations, writings, and the example of my own life, I encourage others to embrace this sanctuary of rest as a source of renewal in our incessantly moving world.

In conclusion, the Sabbath, as unveiled in the Genesis narrative and through the lens of scientific inquiry and personal practice, stands as a profound gift to humanity. It offers a sanctuary of rest—a time set apart for physical, mental, and spiritual rejuvenation. By embracing the Sabbath, we heed a timeless wisdom, finding in its practice a balance, renewal, and a deeper connection to the divine, reorienting ourselves within the rhythm of creation in our modern lives.

In today's relentlessly paced society, where ceaseless productivity is often the benchmark of success, the ancient concept of the Sabbath—introduced on the seventh day of creation—emerges as a radical act. As a writer deeply immersed in both the realms of science and spirituality, I have discovered that the Sabbath is not merely a historical footnote from Genesis, but a vital practice for contemporary life. This exploration seeks to unveil the profound significance of the Sabbath for spiritual renewal, mental health, and physical well-being, affirming its essential place in our modern lives. Through this journey, we will delve into how this time-honored tradition can offer us a sanctuary from the hustle and stress of daily routines, providing a much-needed space for reflection and rejuvenation.

## DISCOVERING SABBATH IN THE RHYTHMS OF CREATION

My exploration of the concept of Sabbath began with an introspective moment, reflecting on the Genesis narrative. The sacred text recounts how, after six days of cosmic creation, God paused, sanctifying the seventh day as a time for rest. This divine interlude, chosen rather than necessitated, revealed a profound dimension of balance—an intentional cessation from toil, a space carved out for reflection, worship, and reconnecting with life's essence.

This rhythm set forth in Genesis provided not just a practice of rest but a principle for living, integrating natural order into our human constructs of time and work. The Sabbath emerged, in my understanding, not merely as an ancient ritual but as a timeless invitation to attune to the natural cadences of creation itself. It beckoned me to embrace rest not as idleness but as an active engagement with the sacred, an opportunity to renew and deepen my connection with the divine essence that permeates all life.

Observing the Sabbath became a conscious exercise in aligning my life with this divine rhythm, challenging me to value being, reflecting, and appreciating as much as doing, producing, or consuming. Honoring the Sabbath each week became a journey back to the foundational elements of existence—community, spirituality, and the sheer wonder of creation.

In this space of rest, I found freedom to contemplate the majesty of the universe, from the minutiae of a single leaf to the expansive stretch of the night sky. Each Sabbath became a sanctuary in time, a retreat into the holiness imbued in creation's fabric. This weekly pause became a conduit for worship, a time set apart to acknowledge and celebrate the Creator's handiwork, to immerse myself in the beauty and intricacy of the natural world, and to reaffirm my place within it.

Moreover, the Sabbath fostered a reconnection with the essence of life, reminding me of the inherent value in simply being. These moments of quietude and reflection rediscovered the significance of relationships, the importance of community, and the joy of presence. Sabbath rest nurtured a deeper appreciation for life's blessings and renewed my commitment to Earth's stewardship, recognizing my role in caring for creation as a sacred trust.

This rediscovery of the Sabbath within creation's rhythms has also been a journey of personal transformation. It cultivated resilience against the pressures of a non-stop world, equipping me with spiritual fortitude to navigate life's challenges with grace and intentionality. Embracing this divinely ordained cycle of work and rest has enriched my spiritual life, deepening my faith and enhancing my understanding of the divine.

In essence, the Sabbath stands as a testament to the Creator's wisdom, a divine provision for rest, reflection, and rejuvenation. It serves as a reminder that our worth is not tethered to productivity but inherent in our being, crafted in God's image. As we observe the Sabbath, we participate in a sacred tradition that spans the ages, reconnecting with the eternal rhythms of creation and rediscovering the joy, peace, and fulfillment found in the divine pause.

In conclusion, discovering the Sabbath in the rhythms of creation has been a transformative experience, grounding my faith and refreshing my spirit. It has taught me the value of balance, the importance of rest, and the joy of living in harmony with natural and divine orders. As we continue to navigate the complexities of modern life, let the Sabbath serve as a beacon, guiding us back to who we are, to the heart of our faith, and to the profound connection we share with all of creation.

## THE SCIENCE OF REST: PHYSICAL AND MENTAL WELL-BEING

Exploring the scientific foundations of rest has profoundly transformed my appreciation of the Sabbath from a solely spiritual practice to a holistic necessity for human well-being. Neuroscience and psychology present compelling evidence underscoring the wisdom of the Sabbath, showing that rest is not just beneficial but essential for optimal cognitive function, emotional resilience, and overall health. This scientific exploration of rest has illuminated the ways our bodies and minds thrive through deliberate periods of rest, deeply resonating with the ancient principles of the Sabbath.

The call for rest on the Sabbath aligns remarkably with contemporary research findings. Studies in neuroscience demonstrate the critical role of downtime in reducing stress, enhancing creativity, and improving mental clarity by allowing our brains to process and consolidate memories, thus fostering learning and creativity. Psychological research further supports the idea that stepping away from routine work and technological distractions is crucial for emotional well-being.

This scientific perspective validates the spiritual practice of the Sabbath and highlights its relevance in our increasingly fast-paced world. Understanding the scientific basis for rest has deepened my conviction in observing the Sabbath as essential self-care and an act of spiritual obedience. The divine mandate for a day of rest coincides with our biological and psychological needs, offering a potent antidote to modern life's pressures, providing a sanctuary where we can rejuvenate our bodies, minds, and spirits.

The convergence of spiritual tradition and scientific research expands my appreciation for the Sabbath's holistic benefits. It reminds us that our need for rest is not a sign of weakness but a fundamental aspect of our human nature. Embracing the Sabbath acknowledges the wisdom embedded in creation, honoring the natural rhythms that govern our existence and ensuring our well-being in a comprehensive sense.

Practicing regular breaks from work and technology, as the Sabbath prescribes, has proven profoundly beneficial. It provides a structured opportunity to disconnect from the relentless information flow and demands, allowing us to reset and recharge. This intentional pause can lead to greater productivity, enhanced creativity, and a clearer, more focused mind. Additionally, the Sabbath affords a time for reflection and spiritual growth, deepening our connection with the divine and ourselves.

In today's digital age, where burnout and chronic stress are rampant, the Sabbath's call for rest and disconnection is more pertinent than ever. It challenges the modern ethos of perpetual availability and productivity, proposing a life rhythm that values balance, well-being, and spiritual fulfillment. This ancient practice, supported by contemporary science, offers a counter-cultural remedy to our time's ailments, advocating for a lifestyle that prioritizes health, happiness, and wholeness.

Embracing the Sabbath in light of scientific insights has not only reaffirmed its spiritual significance but has also prompted me to advocate for its observance as a means of promoting physical and mental health. Viewing the Sabbath as both a divine command and a scientifically supported practice invites us to consider rest as a sacred and essential part of our lives. It calls us to rediscover the rhythms of creation that foster life and flourishing, both for ourselves and for the communities in which we live.

In conclusion, studying the science of rest has enriched my understanding and practice of the Sabbath, highlighting it as a vital component of a healthy, balanced life. This alignment between spiritual wisdom and scientific research underscores the Sabbath's enduring relevance, offering a blueprint for living that respects our natural need for rest and rejuvenation. As we continue to navigate the complexities of contemporary life, let us embrace the Sabbath as a gift—a divine provision for our well-being that is rooted in the very fabric of creation and validated by the insights of modern science.


## PRACTICING SABBATH IN A NON-STOP WORLD

In today's incessant rush, where the lines between work and rest often blur, adopting the practice of the Sabbath has become a deliberate act of resistance against the perpetual demand for engagement. For me, this journey to observe the Sabbath amidst modern hustle entailed a conscious decision to carve out a weekly oasis of tranquility and reflection. It meant stepping back from the relentless work demands, the constant barrage of digital notifications, and the societal pressure to always be active.

Incorporating Sabbath-keeping into my routine has transformed it into an exercise in mindfulness, an interval of calm in my hectic schedule. It has become a sacred time for enjoying the stillness, reconnecting with nature, and nurturing relationships. Each Sabbath is now a period to engage in soul-enriching activities—whether that's losing myself in a good book, connecting through prayer, meditating, or simply being fully present in the moment.

This deliberate pursuit of weekly rest and disconnection has deeply impacted my spiritual life, enhancing my connection with the divine and enriching my faith. It has underscored the importance of pausing to look beyond life's immediate concerns and appreciate the vastness of creation and the Creator's presence. Moreover, this practice has emphasized the value of community and fellowship, enabling me to share this sacred time with others and together experience the restorative power it offers.

Beyond its spiritual benefits, observing the Sabbath has become crucial for maintaining my mental and physical health. In a society grappling with high levels of burnout and stress, dedicating a day to rest acts as an essential counterbalance, helping to reset and recharge my energies. Disconnecting from work and digital distractions has brought mental clarity and emotional resilience, reducing stress and promoting inner peace. Physically, this break allows my body to recover from the week's exertions, improving sleep, reducing the risk of chronic diseases, and enhancing overall well-being.

While embracing the Sabbath in a non-stop world presents challenges, such as overcoming the fear of missing out or the guilt associated with inactivity, the rewards are invaluable. It offers a shift in perspective, encouraging a redefinition of success and fulfillment not by accomplishments and accumulation, but by contentment, relational depth, and spiritual growth.

Practicing Sabbath-keeping invites us to reconnect with the natural rhythms of life that foster human flourishing. It encourages us to rely on divine provision and recognize that our worth extends beyond our productivity, rooted instead in our intrinsic value as creations in the image of God. Committing to this practice not only obeys a divine command but also affirms our need for rest, reflection, and connection.

In conclusion, observing the Sabbath in today's relentless world is a powerful declaration of our priorities and a testament to our faith. It acknowledges that life's true essence is not found in constant activity but in the renewal found through rest and the insights gained in quietude. As we navigate the complexities of modern life, let the Sabbath serve as a weekly beacon, reminding us of our need for rest, our ties to creation, and our reliance on the Creator. This intentional pause is not merely an escape from the world but a return to what is truly important, providing a foundation for a life marked by purpose, joy, and peace.

## SABBATH AS RESISTANCE AND RENEWAL

In our relentlessly paced society, where worth is often measured by productivity, observing the Sabbath emerges as a radical counter-cultural act. It stands as a bold declaration against the continuous hustle that defines modern life, challenging the pervasive notion that our value is directly proportional to our output. Observing the Sabbath is not just a break; it is a powerful assertion that our worth transcends our achievements.

This intentional pause becomes an act of reclamation—of time, freedom, and, most importantly, our inherent dignity. It offers a weekly chance for renewal, inviting us into a space where we can let go of expectations and revel in the simple joy of being. This period of rest serves as a sanctuary, refreshing the soul and shifting our focus towards the intrinsic value of life.

Moreover, the Sabbath instills a sense of gratitude, helping us recognize the blessings that often go unnoticed amid daily tasks. It reawakens our wonder for the beauty of creation and the intricate designs of life, prompting reflection on the Creator's generosity in establishing rest as a fundamental rhythm of the universe. This divine pause is a gift, essential for our well-being and spiritual health, not just an optional luxury.

Practicing the Sabbath is an act of spiritual defiance. It affirms that our lives should not be consumed by endless work and the pursuit of achievement. Instead, it suggests that true fulfillment comes from embracing rest, cultivating relationships, and appreciating life's simpler pleasures. The Sabbath liberates us from the tyranny of the urgent, guiding us towards a life balanced by peace and a deeper connection with the divine.

This observance also emphasizes our shared humanity, highlighting the universal need for rest that cuts across all societal divides. It stands as a weekly reminder of equality before the Creator, where everyone deserves rest, respect, and the chance to fully experience life. The Sabbath thus acts as a leveling field, dismantling the false hierarchies created by societal standards of productivity and success.

Embracing the Sabbath in a non-stop world is not merely an individual act of faith but a communal invitation to reclaim the rhythms of rest that nurture life. It prompts us to rethink our approaches to work, leisure, and community, promoting a culture that prioritizes well-being, cherishes relationships, and respects the sanctity of time. As a community, embracing this practice showcases the transformative power of rest, demonstrating that true strength and wisdom come not from ceaseless activity but from the deliberate observance of Sabbath peace.

In conclusion, practicing the Sabbath as an act of resistance and renewal is crucial in today's world. It reaffirms our worth beyond productivity, providing a weekly reminder of our freedom, dignity, and the joy of living. Committing to this rhythm of rest enriches our lives with gratitude, wonder, and a deeper appreciation for life as ordained by the Creator. Let the Sabbath inspire us to align with the divine design, embracing the restorative power of rest as the foundation for a fulfilled and balanced existence.

## INVITING OTHERS INTO SABBATH REST

My journey with Sabbath-keeping has profoundly reshaped my understanding of rest, work, and worship, revealing the Sabbath's restorative essence as a divine gift often overlooked in our relentless rush. This transformative experience has ignited a deep desire within me to share the richness and tranquility that Sabbath observance brings. Through open conversations that bridge the personal and the sacred, writings that explore this ancient practice's significance, and the simple yet profound act of living out this commitment, I aim to extend an invitation to others, encouraging them to embrace the Sabbath's peace and restoration.

Inviting others into the realm of Sabbath rest is about offering a gateway to a renewed way of life where balance, peace, and a deeper connection with the divine are central. By embodying the principles of Sabbath-keeping in my daily life, I hope to show that this time of rest is not just a pause from the mundane but a profound engagement with the sacred—an opportunity to recharge not only our bodies but also our spirits.

In our non-stop world, where the noise of demands and digital distractions often drowns out the soul's whispers, the Sabbath emerges as a sanctuary in time—a day distinct from the others, dedicated to restoration, reflection, and rejoicing in life's simple yet profound joys. It is a day to reconnect with the Creator, with creation, and with the community in ways that our regular routines seldom allow.

Encouraging others to explore the Sabbath is to invite them on a journey of discovery—where they can uncover the rhythm of rest that resonates with the cadence of creation itself. It offers a path leading away from the incessant demands of productivity and toward a practice that celebrates our inherent worth, a worth not measured by output but by our very being.

This invitation to Sabbath rest is extended with the understanding that its observance can manifest differently for each individual, reflecting personal beliefs, traditions, and circumstances. Yet, at its core, the Sabbath calls us all to a common experience: to know rest as a divine ordinance, to see it as an act of faith, an act of trust in God's sufficiency, and an act of resistance against societal pressures that urge us to find value solely in what we do.

As I continue to invite others into the practice of Sabbath-keeping, my hope is that they, too, will discover its transformative power. May they find in the Sabbath a wellspring of renewal, a source of joy and peace, and a reminder of the sacred rhythm woven into the fabric of time by the Creator. Let this practice become a collective journey toward a more reflective, intentional, and fulfilling way of life, where each Sabbath serves as a beacon, guiding us back to what truly matters.

In the rich tapestry of human experience, interwoven with the threads of toil and triumph, the Sabbath emerges not merely as an ancient observance but as a profound gift to humanity. It is a sanctuary of rest ordained in the very fabric of creation, offering a beacon of balance, renewal, and divine connection that resonates with profound relevance in our contemporary lives.

The Sabbath invites us into a rhythm of rest that counters the relentless pace of modern existence. It offers us a space to breathe, to reflect, and to rejuvenate. This day beckons us to lay down our burdens, to step away from the ceaseless demands of productivity, and to enter a time where we can be restored in body, mind, and spirit. This intentional pause is not a luxury but a necessity, recognized by divine ordinance as essential to our well-being.

Embracing the Sabbath affirms the timeless wisdom embedded in the rhythm of creation. It recognizes that our lives are richer, fuller, and more balanced when we align with this cadence—when we allow ourselves the grace to rest, and when we dedicate time to nurture our relationship with the divine. The Sabbath stands as a testament to a Creator who values our well-being, commanding rest not as an afterthought but as a foundational principle of life.

Through personal reflection and the insights of science, our exploration of Sabbath-keeping has deepened our understanding of its significance. It illuminates the Sabbath as a source of physical, mental, and spiritual rejuvenation—a holistic approach to well-being that transcends mere religious observance and becomes a lifestyle choice enhancing our modern lives.

In our journey through this chapter, the Sabbath has been revealed not only as a day of rest but also as a principle of living that offers balance, renewal, and a deeper connection to the divine. It challenges us to reevaluate our priorities, redefine what it means to live a fulfilled life, and embrace the peace and restoration that come from aligning with the divine pattern set forth at the dawn of creation.

As we conclude this exploration, let the Sabbath not mark an end but a beginning—a starting point for further reflection, practice, and discovery. May the insights gleaned from the pages of Genesis, the findings of science, and the richness of personal practice inspire you to integrate the Sabbath into your life. Let it serve as a weekly reminder of the Creator's love, a call to rest, and an opportunity to renew your spirit.

Encourage continued reading and exploration into the depths of your faith and the wonders of creation. Let the Sabbath be a gateway to a more intentional, balanced, and spiritually enriched life. As we move forward, may we carry with us the lessons of the Sabbath, letting them shape our days and guide our hearts toward a deeper communion with the divine.

Reflecting on our legacy for future generations reminds us of the enduring nature of stewardship. Our next steps require us to look inward, exploring how personal growth and spiritual development are integral to effective stewardship.

# CHAPTER 13

# CREATION AND ARTISTIC EXPRESSION: THE MUSE OF THE NATURAL WORLD

We delve into the profound connections between the natural human world and artistic expression in this chapter, exploring how the beauty and complexity of creation serve as an endless source of inspiration and creativity. The intricate dance between the elements of the earth and human artistry is a central theme, highlighting how our natural environment influences, challenges, and enriches our creative endeavors.

The natural world is not just a backdrop for artistic creation but a dynamic muse that engages with us, prompting deep reflection and innovative expressions. The precision of a leaf's architecture or the vast expanse of the night sky can ignite the imagination, compelling artists to capture these elements of natural majesty. Influential figures such as Vincent van Gogh and Georgia O'Keeffe exemplify how nature can be dialogued with and interpreted through art, turning observations of the natural world into profound artistic statements.

Literature, too, draws heavily from nature, with authors like Thomas Hardy using rustic valleys and stormy coasts not only as settings but as integral components of their narratives. In music, the natural world resonates through compositions that mirror its rhythms and sounds, as seen in the works of Beethoven and Vivaldi, who have drawn directly from nature's palette to enrich their musical compositions.

This exploration reveals that engaging with the natural world is fundamentally an act of creativity akin to worship, where the act of creation becomes a reflection on and participation in the divine. This realization urges us to view the natural world not merely as a resource but as a sacred space deserving of our respect and creativity.

As you, the reader, are invited to embark on your own creative journey, consider the natural world as a wellspring of inspiration. Whether through visual arts, writing, music, or simply through reflective contemplation, you are encouraged to find and nurture your unique voice in the dialogue with the natural environment.

In closing, this chapter celebrates the symbiotic relationship between the natural world and artistic expression. It challenges us to maintain a reverential and mindful approach to our creative practices, recognizing our role in both celebrating and preserving the integrity of the natural world. Let us continue to explore and honor this dynamic interplay, enriching our artistic expressions and deepening our connections with the world around us, perpetually inspired by the endless muse that is the natural world.

The profound beauty and intricate complexity of the natural world have continually served as potent sources of inspiration, compelling artists in various mediums to explore and express the depths of their creativity. As a writer deeply immersed in the intersections of science, faith, and creativity, I have experienced firsthand the invigorating influence of the natural world on the human spirit's capacity to create. This chapter delves into how creation profoundly shapes art, literature, and music, underscoring the myriad ways in which nature not only fuels our creative impulses but also provides a pathway to worship and reflection.

Through this exploration, we aim to illuminate the symbiotic relationship between the artist and the natural world—a dynamic interaction that enhances our understanding of both creation and creativity. The natural environment, with its endless variety and awe-inspiring phenomena, challenges us to respond in kind, crafting works that reflect, interrogate, and celebrate the world around us. Whether it's the meticulous detail in a painter's brushstroke, a poet's evocative imagery, or a composer's melodic homage to the rhythmic patterns of nature, each artistic endeavor is a testament to the profound impact that the natural world has on human creativity.

This chapter invites readers to consider how the elements of earth, sky, and sea resonate within us, urging us to pick up our tools—be they brushes, pens, or instruments—and participate in the ongoing dialogue between creation and creativity. By engaging with the natural world, artists of all disciplines not only contribute to the rich tapestry of cultural expression but also engage in a form of spiritual and intellectual communion that transcends the ordinary, reaching toward the sublime.

## THE CANVAS OF CREATION: ART'S REFLECTION OF THE NATURAL WORLD

The natural world's riotous colors, intricate patterns, and commanding forms have perennially captivated artists, prompting them to capture these marvels in their creations. The fiery palette of a sunset, the delicate symmetry of a butterfly's wings, or the majestic rise of mountains have been immortalized in the works of masters like Vincent van Gogh and Georgia O'Keeffe. Their artworks, pulsing with the vitality of the natural world, invite viewers into a realm of wonder and introspection, challenging us to look beyond the apparent and delve into the profound beauty that envelopes us.

As a writer navigating the confluence of science and spirituality, I have come to see the natural world as an expansive canvas—a divine masterpiece where every brushstroke and hue narrates a segment of the grand saga of creation. This realization has profoundly transformed my appreciation of nature, urging me to perceive it not merely as a backdrop to human activity but as a dynamic, living work of art, meticulously crafted with intent and precision by the Creator.

This awareness has deepened my connection to the environment, compelling me to observe more keenly the artistic expression present in the natural world—the intricate designs on a leaf, the geometric perfection of a crystal, or the interplay of light and shadow across landscapes. It teaches me the silent lessons nature imparts: resilience, harmony, and interconnectivity, each reflecting the Creator's wisdom and inventive spirit.

Drawing inspiration from nature, much like van Gogh with his starry night skies and O'Keeffe with her stark desert landscapes, has enriched my writing with a deeper palette of expressions and themes. It allows me to weave the complexities of human emotions and experiences with the grandeur and mystery of the natural world, finding parallels in the cycles of growth, decay, and renewal that characterize both the natural environment and human life.

Perceiving nature as a canvas of creation invites us all to pause and reflect, to look beyond the immediate and the utilitarian, and to discover the beauty, wonder, and teachings embedded in the natural world. This perspective calls for a posture of humility and awe, recognizing our place within a larger narrative, intricately crafted by the Creator's hand.

By embracing this view, we foster a deeper connection with the divine, finding in the rhythms and patterns of nature a reflection of the Creator's love, care, and passion for beauty. This connection, nurtured through an appreciation of nature's artistry, enriches our spiritual lives, offering us glimpses of the divine in the everyday.

In conclusion, viewing the natural world as a canvas of creation is not only a testament to the Creator's artistry and intention but also an invitation to forge a deeper relationship with the divine. It challenges us to see His craftsmanship in the beauty around us and to respond with gratitude, stewardship, and awe. As we continue to explore the interplay of faith, science, and art, may we remain attuned to the Creator's presence in the world around us, drawing inspiration and insight from the masterpiece of creation that unfolds before us daily.

## LITERATURE: NARRATIVES WOVEN FROM NATURE

The intricate tapestry of the natural world has long enriched the literary landscape, influencing narratives and shaping characters that probe deeply into the human condition. In literature, nature often transcends its role as merely a scenic backdrop, becoming a central protagonist that reflects and reframes themes of survival, beauty, transcendence, and humanity's perpetual quest for meaning and connection.

Consider the pastoral landscapes in Thomas Hardy's novels, which are vibrant entities that influence the fate and psyche of his characters, echoing human joys and sorrows against an ever-changing natural tableau. Similarly, the rugged wilderness in Jack London's stories serves as a crucible, testing the resilience and will of his characters, revealing the deep interdependence between humans and their environment.

These literary works compel readers to reconsider their relationship with nature—not as a domain to be conquered or as an entity separate from themselves but as an integral part of their very existence. Nature emerges as a source of profound inspiration, offering lessons on endurance, the cycles of life and death, and the beauty of the ephemeral. It challenges readers to confront their fears and aspirations against the backdrop of the natural world's vast, untamed wilderness.

Furthermore, literature that interweaves narratives with the fabric of nature also encourages us to find solace and wisdom in the natural world. It reminds us that nature, with its inherent rhythms and cycles, offers a sanctuary from the frenetic pace of modern life—a space for reflection, healing, and rejuvenation. Through the lens of literature, nature becomes a mirror reflecting our deepest fears, hopes, and the relentless search for meaning.

In exploring these literary landscapes, we are urged to see nature as an integral part of our narrative, a character that shapes and is shaped by human action and inaction. This perspective fosters a deeper appreciation for the natural world, recognizing it not just as a setting for human dramas but as a participant with its own stories, lessons, and intrinsic value. It calls on us to embrace our role not as dominators of the natural world but as stewards, tasked with protecting and preserving it for future generations.

Moreover, the portrayal of nature in literature serves as a call to action, urging us to engage more fully with the environment, to protect its diversity and beauty, and to ensure its survival amid the challenges of climate change and environmental degradation. It underscores the urgent need for a harmonious coexistence with the natural world, one that respects its limits and recognizes the interconnectivity of all life.

In conclusion, literature that draws from the well of nature's complexity and diversity enriches our understanding of the human condition, offering insights into our relationship with the world around us. It challenges us to view nature not as a backdrop but as a vital, living entity that influences and enriches our lives. As we delve into these narratives woven from nature, let us be inspired to forge a deeper, more respectful, and sustainable relationship with the natural world, recognizing it as a source of inspiration, challenge, and solace in our journey through life.

## MUSIC: THE HARMONY OF CREATION

Music, transcending language, and culture, intimately intertwines with the natural world, its power evoking deep emotions and conjuring vivid imagery. It serves as an ideal medium to express the beauty and complexity of creation. From Ludwig van Beethoven's classical compositions to Antonio Vivaldi's baroque masterpieces, and extending into contemporary genres, music mirrors the rhythms, melodies, and textures of nature, fostering a harmonious dialogue between humanity and the environment.

Beethoven's "Pastoral Symphony" and Vivaldi's "The Four Seasons" exemplify how composers have drawn inspiration from nature, integrating the calls of birds, the tumult of storms, and the serene flows of rivers into their music. These compositions not only highlight the composers' technical skills and creative genius but also their profound appreciation for nature's intricate symphony.

In today's music scene, artists across various genres continue this tradition, infusing their works with the sounds and themes of nature, thus bridging the gap between the natural and the human-made. This ongoing tradition underscores music's role as a universal language of creation, resonating within us all, connecting us to the earth and each other on a primal level.

The profound connection between music and nature reminds us of the inherent harmony within creation. It invites us to listen more attentively to the world around us—recognizing the music in rustling leaves, rhythmic waves, and gentle wind whispers. This awareness deepens our appreciation for the natural world, enhancing its impact on our lives and art.

Moreover, incorporating natural sounds and themes in music can also serve as environmental advocacy, highlighting the beauty of the natural world and the critical need to protect it. It can inspire listeners to engage in conservation efforts and adopt a lifestyle more attuned to environmental harmony.

Music, as a divine gift, has the unique ability to unite, inspire, and heal us. Exploring the harmony of creation through music encourages us to cherish and safeguard the natural world, recognizing it as the wellspring of our deepest inspirations and our profoundest connections.

In conclusion, music's capacity to reflect and resonate with the natural world highlights the intricate bond between humanity and creation. As we listen to and create music inspired by nature, let us embrace the existing harmony, fostering a deeper connection to the divine and the earth. This universal language of creation, articulated through music, possesses transformative power—altering hearts and minds and advocating for a mindful, sustainable coexistence with the inspiring world around us.

## CREATIVITY AS AN ACT OF WORSHIP AND REFLECTION

Embracing the muse of the natural world, we are drawn into a profound communion with the Creator, transforming the act of creating into a dialogue of worship and reflection. Through painting, writing, music, or any form of art, our creative expressions transcend mere talent display; they become acts of homage to the divine source of all inspiration. This creative journey invites us into deep meditation on the splendor, intricacy, and enigma of the universe, urging us to recognize and honor the Creator's craftsmanship.

The process of creating, fueled by inspiration from nature and existence, heightens our spiritual awareness and binds us closer to the divine. It becomes a conduit through which we explore the depths of our faith, understand creation, and contemplate our place within it. Through our artistic endeavors, we mirror the Creator's act of making, engaging with the world as co-creators, inspired by the vision of the original Creator. This creative act is not just a pursuit of beauty or expression but a profound act of worship and adoration for the One who first called the universe into being.

Our creative acts, influenced by the awe-inspiring complexity of the world, challenge us to see beyond the immediate utility of creation. They compel us to view the natural world as a sacred gift, imbued with divine intention and deserving of our deepest respect and stewardship. This perspective transforms our interaction with the environment, prompting us not only to celebrate its beauty but also to commit to its preservation and care. Our art thus becomes a testament to the sanctity of creation, a celebration of its diversity, and a call to action to protect it for future generations.

Creativity, as a form of worship and reflection, fosters a sense of gratitude for the wonders of the natural world and the mysteries it holds. It encourages us to delve into the unknown, to embrace the mysteries of faith, and to express the inexpressible aspects of our spiritual journey. In this creative exploration, we find a deeper connection to the divine, experiencing the joy of creation and the fulfillment that comes from participating in the divine narrative.

Moreover, engaging in creativity as an act of worship and reflection empowers us to share our unique insights and experiences of the divine with the world. It allows us to contribute to a collective understanding of faith, enriching the tapestry of human expression and experience. Our creative works become bridges between the material and the spiritual, between human and divine, offering others a glimpse into the profound relationship we share with our Creator.

In conclusion, viewing creativity as an act of worship and reflection transforms our artistic endeavors into profound spiritual practices. It invites us into a deeper engagement with the world and the Creator, challenging us to honor the divine presence in all of creation. As we draw inspiration from the world around us, let us remember that our creative expressions are a form of homage to the Creator, a celebration of the sacred gift of creation, and a reflection on the beauty, complexity, and mystery that surround us. Through our creativity, we not only explore the depths of our faith but also invite others to journey with us, discovering the divine harmony that binds us all.

## ENCOURAGING PERSONAL EXPLORATION

Encouraging personal exploration and tapping into one's creative potential can serve as a profound means of connecting with the divine tapestry of creation. Inspired by the intricate beauty and boundless wonder of the natural world, each individual has the opportunity to engage in a deeply personal and reflective journey. Whether through the lens of a camera, the soil of a garden, the craftsmanship of an art project, or the pages of a journal, the act of creating becomes a dialogue with the Creator, a testament to the endless inspiration provided by nature.

This exploration transcends the pursuit of perfection; it is about immersion in the process, about seeing the world through a lens of curiosity and wonder. Photography, for example, can capture fleeting moments of natural beauty, allowing us to observe and reflect on the intricate details and grand vistas that might otherwise go unnoticed. Gardening invites us into a partnership with the land, a rhythm of growth and renewal that mirrors life's cycles. Crafting and art transform natural materials and observations into expressions of personal vision and emotion, while journaling offers a space to articulate thoughts and reflections inspired by nature's majesty.

Engaging with creation in these ways invites a deeper appreciation for the world around us. It encourages mindfulness and presence, drawing our attention to the beauty that envelops us, often overlooked in the hustle of daily life. This creative engagement is not just an act of personal expression but a form of participation in the broader narrative of creation, adding our unique voice to the chorus that extols the beauty and wonder of the world.

This call to personal exploration and creativity is an invitation to discover and affirm one's place within the natural world. It's an encouragement to observe, to listen, and to interact with creation in ways that nurture our spirits and deepen our connection to the divine. Through these acts of creativity, we not only honor the Creator but also celebrate the sacred gift of creation, recognizing it as a source of inspiration, solace, and joy.

In essence, this journey of creative exploration is about contributing to the ongoing story of creation. It's about recognizing our role not merely as observers but as participants in the divine artistry of the world. By embracing our creative potential and expressing what the natural world evokes in us, we engage in an act of worship and reflection, celebrating the beauty, complexity, and mystery of creation. This process of exploration and expression is an enriching practice that enhances our spiritual journey, inviting us to see the world with fresh eyes and a grateful heart.

In conclusion, I encourage readers to delve into their creative endeavors, inspired by the natural world, as a means of connecting with and reflecting on the beauty of creation. This exploration is a call to be actively involved in the narrative of creation, using our unique talents and perspectives to celebrate and honor the world around us. Let this be a journey of discovery, where the act of creating becomes a bridge between our inner selves and the outer world, a form of worship that enriches our faith and deepens our connection to the divine.

Certainly! Here's how you can seamlessly combine the two conclusions into a coherent ending for your book, creating a unified message that ties together the themes of creativity, spirituality, stewardship, and community:

As we draw this exploration to a close, we find ourselves on the brink of endless discovery, where the natural world, with its boundless splendor and intricate complexity, beckons us to engage deeply and reverently. This divine canvas invites us to express our creativity across cultures and through time, urging us to weave our unique voices into the grand tapestry of artistic expression.

In responding to this call, our creative endeavors transcend mere personal expression; they become acts of homage to the Creator, drawing inspiration from the natural world and participating in a timeless dialogue that honors the divine imagination manifest in our surroundings. This active engagement is not just observation—it is a profound participation in the ongoing narrative of creation. Whether through painting, writing, composing, or crafting, inspired by the complexities and splendors of nature, we add our unique threads to the creation tapestry, intertwining our personal stories with the larger story crafted by the Creator.

Through our artistic expressions, we find our place within this grand narrative—a place marked by significance and a profound sense of belonging. We become both observers and contributors to the wonders of creation, tasked with exploring, celebrating, and preserving the beauty that envelops us. This realization not only fulfills us but also imbues us with a joy that comes from aligning our creative impulses with the natural rhythms of the world.

Let this concluding chapter serve as a gateway to further exploration and creative endeavor. May the insights shared here inspire you to continue your own journey of artistic and spiritual exploration, buoyed by the knowledge that in honoring the Creator through your creativity, you affirm your role in the magnificent saga of the cosmos. As you move beyond these pages, carry with you the awe, the curiosity, and the gratitude that the natural world stirs within you.

Embrace the invitation to create, explore, and express, secure in the understanding that each creative act draws you closer to discerning the divine purpose woven into the fabric of the universe. May your creative pursuits enrich your faith, deepen your connection to the divine, and illuminate the beauty and mystery at the heart of creation.

As you continue this journey, approach it with eagerness and openness, ready to uncover the joy and fulfillment that arise from crafting new works, inspired by the unending muse that is the natural world. And remember, stewardship of this creativity is not only about external preservation but also about nurturing our inner connection to the divine, which fuels our passion and guides our creative endeavors as we engage with the world around us.

Recognizing that stewardship is as much about our inner journey as it is about external actions, we're called to deepen our connection with the divine. This connection fuels our passion and guides our steps as we continue to engage with the world around us. Let us carry forward the lessons of the Sabbath and the insights from the pages of Genesis, inspired to shape a world that reflects the splendor and love of its Maker.

# CHAPTER 14

# BEYOND GENESIS: LIVING CREATION'S IMPLICATIONS IN THE MODERN WORLD

My journey through the tapestry of life has led me to deeply ponder the biblical narrative of creation, viewing it not merely as ancient text, but as a living, breathing guide for navigating the complexities of the modern world. This exploration, rooted in the foundational stories of Genesis, has blossomed into a quest to understand how these age-old truths can inform and transform our contemporary existence. My narrative weaves through the themes of stewardship, community, spirituality, and creativity, each chapter of my life echoing the Creator's original intentions for His creation.

Stewardship emerged as a profound calling, transforming my relationship with the Earth from one of passive inhabitance to active guardianship. The escalating crises of climate change and environmental degradation have underscored the urgency of this role, compelling me to adopt sustainable practices and to advocate for the protection of our precious planet. This shift was not merely ecological but deeply spiritual, a tangible expression of my reverence for the Creator and my responsibility to future generations.

In my pursuit of community, I rediscovered the intrinsic connection we share with all creation, a bond that transcends the superficial divisions of our digital age. Engaging with local initiatives, participating in conservation efforts, and cultivating relationships across cultural divides, I began to embody the unity and mutual care that the creation narrative champions. This journey has not only deepened my sense of belonging but has also highlighted our collective role in the unfolding story of creation.

Spirituality took on new dimensions as I delved into the creation narrative, with the natural world becoming a vibrant conduit to the Divine. The intricacy and majesty of creation invited me into a deeper relationship with the Creator, urging me to find sacredness in the mundane and to recognize the divine fingerprints in the world around me. Through practices like nature meditation and ecological pilgrimages, I have woven spiritual threads through the fabric of my daily life, drawing closer to the Creator with each step.

Creativity became a mirror of the divine act of making, a way for me to echo the Creator's work in my own life. Recognizing that I am made in the image of a creative God, I have embraced my innate impulse to create—whether through writing, art, or innovation. This creative endeavor has become a form of worship and reflection, a means to participate in the ongoing narrative of creation and to contribute my unique voice to the world's diverse tapestry.

In living out the implications of the creation narrative, I have found a richer, more purposeful existence. The legacy of Genesis extends far beyond its ancient context, touching every facet of modern life. By embracing my role as a steward, fostering community, deepening my spirituality, and unleashing my creativity, I live in alignment with the Creator's vision—a vision of peace, beauty, and harmony. As I navigate the challenges of today, the timeless truths of creation guide me, inspiring actions marked by wisdom, compassion, and creativity. This chapter is an invitation to all, urging us to see the world anew through the lens of creation, to discover joy and purpose in our place within it, and to recommit ourselves to the divine task of shaping a world that reflects the splendor and love of its Maker.

As the author of a narrative deeply rooted in the biblical story of creation, my journey has expanded beyond the initial reflection on Genesis to explore its broader implications in our contemporary lives. This chapter serves as a bridge, connecting the timeless truths of the creation narrative with the challenges and opportunities we face in the modern context. Here, we delve into how the themes of creation can inform our understanding of stewardship, community, spirituality, and creativity today. As we navigate through these pages, we will explore how these ancient teachings can not only enrich our personal lives but also inspire us to engage more profoundly with the world around us. This exploration seeks to understand how the principles of creation can guide us in addressing the ecological, social, and spiritual issues of our time, encouraging a life that reflects a deep commitment to the divine purpose embedded in the world.

## STEWARDSHIP: THE EARTH AS OUR SACRED TRUST

In the woven narrative of creation, humanity is bestowed with a profound responsibility—the stewardship of the Earth. This sacred trust, articulated in the genesis of our shared story, has never been more critical than it is today. As we stand at the crossroads of climate change, environmental degradation, and the alarming loss of biodiversity, the imperative for stewardship echoes with unparalleled urgency, compelling us to examine and redefine our relationship with the natural world.

The stewardship entrusted to us is far from a mere call to preservation; it is an invitation to engage deeply with the Earth in a manner that is both sustainable and respectful. It demands of us a holistic approach, one that encompasses not only the conservation of resources but also the nurturing of our planet. This involves adopting sustainable living practices that harmonize with the Earth's rhythms, advocating for policies that safeguard environmental sanctities, and committing ourselves to the education of our communities about the importance of conservation.

Our role as modern stewards is underpinned by a reverence for the Creator, recognizing that in caring for the Earth, we honor the divine craftsmanship inherent in its creation. This stewardship is an expression of our gratitude and respect for the bounty and beauty bestowed upon us, a testament to our acknowledgment of the Earth not as a commodity but as a sacred trust. It is an undertaking that requires us to look beyond the immediacy of our needs and desires, to envision a future where the Earth thrives in its diversity and splendor for generations yet unborn.

The challenges we face—climate change, environmental degradation, and biodiversity loss—are not insurmountable, but they do require a collective and concerted effort. Each action taken towards sustainability, every policy advocated for environmental protection, and each instance of environmental education contributes to a larger tapestry of conservation. These efforts are integral to fulfilling our stewardship, to transforming our societies in ways that foster a deeper connection with and care for our planet.

This commitment to stewardship extends beyond mere environmentalism; it is a moral imperative, a reflection of our values and ethics. It challenges us to consider the legacy we wish to leave behind, to question the kind of world we want to bequeath to future generations. In this, our stewardship becomes not only an act of preservation but a profound act of faith—a belief in the possibility of renewal and restoration, in the capacity for harmony between humanity and the natural world.

Embracing our role as stewards requires courage, vision, and perseverance. It calls for innovation and creativity in finding solutions that balance human needs with the health of the planet. It demands a willingness to act, to make sacrifices, and to advocate for change, even when faced with indifference or opposition. Yet, in this endeavor, we are not alone. We are part of a community of stewards, bound by a shared commitment to the Earth and inspired by the belief that together, we can forge a sustainable and hopeful future.

In conclusion, the call to stewardship is a clarion call to each of us, urging us to take up the mantle of responsibility for the care of our sacred trust—the Earth. It is a challenge to live intentionally, to act with consideration for the well-being of our planet, and to honor the Creator through our efforts to preserve and protect the natural world. As we move forward, let this stewardship inspire us, guide our actions, and remind us of the deep connection we share with the Earth and with each other. In embracing this sacred trust, we affirm our commitment to future generations and to the preservation of the creation's beauty and diversity for all time.

## COMMUNITY: REDISCOVERING OUR CONNECTION TO CREATION AND EACH OTHER

The narrative of creation woven through sacred texts and the natural world itself speaks to a profound interconnectedness that binds all life together. It is a reminder that humanity is not an isolated entity but part of a vast, intricate web of existence that encompasses not just our fellow human beings but every creature, every plant, and every element of the natural world. In the whirlwind of our modern, technology-driven lives, where individualism often trumps collective well-being and digital connections sometimes replace genuine human interaction, there lies an urgent need to rekindle our sense of belonging to this larger community.

Engaging actively with our local communities provides a tangible pathway to rediscover and strengthen these vital connections. It's in the shared spaces of our neighborhoods, parks, and natural reserves that we can participate in conservation efforts, contribute to environmental sustainability, and weave the bonds of a community that respects and honors the sanctity of creation. These actions are expressions of the unity and mutual care that the creation narrative inspires, calling us to collaborate in preserving the beauty and diversity of our shared home.

Fostering relationships that bridge cultural and environmental divides is another critical aspect of reestablishing our connection to creation and each other. In a world often marked by fragmentation, making conscious efforts to understand and appreciate the diversity within our communities and the natural world can lead to a deeper sense of unity. It's through these relationships that we can learn from different perspectives, celebrate the richness of creation, and work together towards common goals that benefit all members of the community, human and non-human alike.

Participating in conservation efforts offers a direct means to live out our collective role in the story of creation. Whether it's through planting trees, cleaning up local waterways, or advocating for policies that protect endangered species and habitats, these activities allow us to contribute to the health and vitality of the planet. They are practical expressions of our stewardship and care for the environment, reflecting a commitment to pass on a world as beautiful and abundant as the one we have received to future generations.

Cultivating a sense of community in the context of creation involves recognizing the value of every living being and the role each plays in the ecosystem. It means moving beyond seeing nature as a resource to be exploited, instead viewing it as a sacred trust to be cherished and protected. By honoring our interconnectedness with all of creation, we affirm the dignity of life in its myriad forms and commit to actions that promote the well-being of the entire community of life.

This chapter proposes practical ways to nurture a community spirit that aligns with the principles of unity and mutual care found in the creation narrative. It invites readers to explore avenues for engagement that reinforce our connections to the natural world and each other, suggesting that through collective action and shared responsibility, we can address the environmental challenges of our time. It encourages us to envision a community that not only lives in harmony with nature but actively participates in its restoration and preservation.

In conclusion, rediscovering our connection to creation and each other is a journey of reawakening to the profound interdependence that defines our existence. It challenges us to live more intentionally, with a greater awareness of our impact on the world and a deeper commitment to the common good. As we engage with our communities, participate in conservation efforts, and build relationships that transcend divides, we embody the unity and mutual care that are essential to the story of creation. This commitment to community and the environment not only enriches our lives but also ensures that the beauty and diversity of creation are preserved for generations to come, fostering a world where all life can flourish in harmony.

## SPIRITUALITY: CREATION AS A PATHWAY TO THE DIVINE

The intricate beauty and awe-inspiring complexity of the natural world have perennially served as a conduit to the divine, offering an unspoken language that bridges the human spirit with the Creator. The narrative of creation, rich with imagery of a world brought forth in harmony and purpose, extends an invitation to each of us to venture deeper into our spiritual journey, to discover the divine not in the distant or the abstract, but in the tangible reality of the world around us.

This exploration into spirituality through the lens of creation encourages us to recognize the sacred in the ordinary, to find those moments of transcendence in the rhythm of our daily lives. It teaches us to see the divine fingerprints in the sunrise that paints the sky, in the intricate patterns of a leaf, in the vastness of the ocean, and in the complexity of the human heart. These are not mere backdrops to our existence but are expressions of the Creator's artistry, invitations to encounter the divine.

Practices such as meditation in nature offer us the opportunity to quiet our minds and attune our spirits to the Creator's presence in the world. This intentional stillness amid creation allows us to listen to the deeper truths spoken by the Earth, to feel a part of something greater than ourselves, and to cultivate a sense of peace and connectedness with all that is.

Ecological pilgrimages, journeys undertaken to places of natural wonder or ecological significance, can serve as powerful spiritual experiences that deepen our reverence for the Creator and creation. These pilgrimages remind us of our place within the broader ecosystem of life, inspiring a sense of stewardship and a commitment to conservation. They are acts of faith that acknowledge the sacredness of the Earth and our responsibility to protect it.

The celebration of creation-focused rituals, whether through personal practices or community observances, allows us to honor the divine in creation. These rituals, rooted in gratitude and wonder, serve to consecrate our relationship with the natural world. They remind us of the cycles of life and the interconnectedness of all things, fostering a sense of belonging and purpose within the larger story of creation.

Engaging with the natural world in these ways not only deepens our spiritual connection to the Creator but also enriches our understanding of creation as a manifestation of divine love and intention. It challenges us to see beyond the utilitarian or the incidental, inviting us to approach creation with reverence, to protect and cherish it as a sacred gift.

This chapter's exploration of spirituality through the beauty and complexity of creation reaffirms the natural world as a vital pathway to the divine. It encourages us to find sacred moments in the everyday, to recognize the divine imprints all around us, and to cultivate practices that deepen our spiritual connection to both the Creator and creation. In doing so, we embrace a spirituality that is both grounded and transcendent, one that celebrates the Creator's presence in the world and calls us to live in harmony with the Earth.

In conclusion, the natural world, in all its splendor and intricacy, beckons us to a deeper spiritual engagement, to a recognition of the divine that permeates every aspect of creation. As we respond to this call, may we find joy, meaning, and a renewed sense of wonder in the presence of the divine, woven into the very fabric of the world around us. This journey of spiritual exploration and connection invites us to a fuller, more vibrant faith—one that honors the Creator through our reverence for creation and our commitment to its care.

## CREATIVITY: ECHOING THE CREATOR'S WORK IN OUR LIVES

The essence of creation, as unveiled in the divine narrative, is an act of unparalleled creativity, where light, life, and beauty were summoned into existence from the expanse of the void. This profound act of creation reflects the boundless artistry of the Creator, a divine source from which all creativity flows. As beings fashioned in the likeness of this creative God, we inherit a spark of this divine impulse to create, to bring forth new expressions of beauty, understanding, and innovation into the world.

This innate drive to create is not limited to the realms of traditional art but extends across the spectrum of human endeavor—from science and technology to the simple yet profound acts of problem-solving that punctuate our daily lives. Each act of creation, no matter how grand or modest, mirrors the Creator's work, serving as both an act of worship and a moment of reflection on the beauty and complexity of the world around us.

Channeling our creativity is, therefore, a way of honoring the divine gift bestowed upon us. It is an invitation to engage with the world in a manner that echoes the Creator's original act of creation, to view our creative endeavors as contributions to the ongoing story of the universe. Whether we express ourselves through painting, writing, innovation, or the myriad of ways we find solutions to everyday challenges, we are participating in the divine narrative of creation.

Embracing our creativity calls us to recognize the value and potential of our ideas and creations, not as mere products or outcomes but as expressions of our deepest selves and our connection to the divine. It encourages us to see creativity not as a scarce resource but as an abundant wellspring, available to all who seek to tap into it. This perspective shifts how we view our role in the world, from passive observers to active participants in the unfolding drama of creation.

This section, therefore, is not just an encouragement but a call to action—to embrace the creativity that resides within each of us and to allow it to flourish. It invites readers to see their creative acts as part of a larger tapestry, woven through time by the Creator and continued by us. In doing so, we affirm our place within the divine order, contributing our unique threads to the ever-expanding canvas of creation.

By engaging our creativity, we also open ourselves to new possibilities, new ways of seeing the world, and new opportunities for connection with others and with the divine. This act of creation becomes a pathway for discovery, a means of exploring the depth of our being and the breadth of the universe. It challenges us to push beyond the boundaries of what is known, to explore the realms of what might be, and to contribute to the ongoing creation of the world in ways only we can.

In conclusion, the act of embracing our creativity is a profound expression of our identity as beings created in the image of a creative God. It is a celebration of the divine spark within each of us, a recognition of our role in the ongoing process of creation, and an acknowledgment of the beauty and complexity of the world we inhabit. As we channel our creativity, whether in art, science, technology, or daily life, we echo the Creator's work, adding our voices to the symphony of creation that resounds through the ages, enriching the world with our unique contributions and drawing us closer to the divine.

## CONCLUSION: LIVING THE LEGACY OF CREATION

The creation narrative, with its profound origins in Genesis, extends beyond a mere recounting of beginnings, providing a blueprint for contemporary living that resonates with depth and purpose. As we assume the roles outlined by these ancient texts—stewards, community members, spiritual seekers, and creators—we integrate these principles into our daily lives, influencing our decisions, interactions, and outlook with a divine intent.

This chapter beckons us to view our environment through the lens of creation, encouraging us to perceive beyond the superficial to embrace the sacred connections that link us to one another and to the Earth. It invites us to rediscover the joy and purpose inherent in our essential role within this grand narrative, awakening us to the surrounding beauty and our responsibilities in nurturing and enhancing it.

By recommitting to the ideals encapsulated in the creation story, we pledge to act as agents of peace, beauty, and harmony in a world often characterized by conflict and disorder. This commitment compels us to live deliberately, crafting our actions and choices into a tapestry that reflects the Creator's vision for humanity—a vision marked by environmental stewardship, meaningful community ties, and a relentless pursuit of spiritual depth and understanding.

As we navigate the complexities of modern life, the creation narrative serves as a guiding light, offering enduring wisdom. It inspires us to approach the world with wonder, engage with our communities compassionately, and pursue our creative and spiritual endeavors with dedication to excellence and integrity.

In embracing this legacy, we are called to be guardians of the Earth, champions for justice and equity, seekers of the sacred in the mundane, and creators of beauty in all forms. This holistic approach not only honors the Creator but also enriches our existence, infusing it with a sense of purpose and satisfaction that transcends the ephemeral.

As this chapter concludes, let us take forward the insights and inspiration it provides. Let the story of creation not remain tethered to the past but continue to influence our present and future actively. May we rise to the challenge of embodying the divine vision of creation in our lives, dedicating ourselves to acts of wisdom, compassion, and creativity. And as we progress in our reading and exploration of our faith and our role in the world, let the legacy of creation guide our steps, inspiring us to construct a world that mirrors the beauty, harmony, and peace of the divine plan.

With a strengthened connection to the divine, we are now prepared to fully embrace the essence of sacred stewardship. The upcoming final chapter will focus on practical applications for everyday life, ensuring that our stewardship journey is characterized by purposeful and impactful actions.

# CHAPTER 15

# SACRED STEWARDSHIP – PRACTICAL APPLICATIONS FOR DAILY LIVING

In the tranquil dawn of a new day, as I walked through the dense foliage of a forest near my home in Pennsylvania, the concept of "Sacred Stewardship" unfolded before me. It emerged not as an abstract idea, but as a tangible, living principle that could guide every aspect of daily life. As I navigated the underbrush, the delicate balance of nature was evident in every leaf, droplet of dew, and beam of sunlight. It was here that I fully grasped my relationship with this planet—not merely as one of coexistence but of profound stewardship.

This stewardship, I realized, was not just a responsibility but a sacred trust bestowed upon us by the Creator, calling us to act as protectors and caretakers of His magnificent creation. This epiphany was the culmination of a journey that started in my childhood in Chad, under the intensely shining stars, through to my academic pursuits in applied mathematics that revealed the astounding order and complexity of creation.

**"Sacred Stewardship – Practical Applications for Daily Living,"** the final chapter of "Divine Transformations: Unveiling the Power of God's Creation," is born from this realization. It is a call to embrace our role as stewards in the most practical aspects of our lives—from the food we eat and the goods we purchase to the energy we consume, every choice becomes an act of stewardship.

ENGAGEMENT IN DAILY PRACTICES:

1. **Mindful Consumption:** Choosing sustainable and ethically produced goods, reducing waste, and minimizing our carbon footprint are all acts of stewardship that respect and preserve the natural world.
2. **Energy Efficiency:** Adopting energy-saving measures and incorporating renewable energy sources in our homes and workplaces.
3. **Community Engagement:** Participating in local environmental initiatives, which can significantly impact our neighborhoods and natural reserves.
4. **Educational Advocacy:** Spreading awareness about the importance of environmental stewardship through workshops, seminars, and social media.
5. **Spiritual Practices:** Engaging in practices like nature meditation and ecological pilgrimages, which deepen our reverence for the Creator and creation.
6. **Creative Expression:** Channeling our creativity in ways that echo the Creator's work, viewing our creative endeavors as contributions to the ongoing story of the universe.

This chapter invites you to walk with me through the metaphorical forest of our daily lives, to see the sacred in the mundane, and to find practical ways to live out our calling as stewards of the Earth. It is a commitment to a lifestyle that reflects our deep respect for and commitment to the preservation and beautification of the world we've been entrusted with.

As the chapter concludes, it does not signify an end but a beginning —a call to action for each of us to embrace the principles of sacred stewardship. It encourages us to live intentionally, weaving our actions into a tapestry that reflects the Creator's vision for the world—a vision characterized by peace, beauty, and harmony. As we continue our journey beyond the pages of this book, let the legacy of creation guide our steps, inspiring us to build a world that reflects the beauty and love of its Maker.

## INTEGRATING STEWARDSHIP INTO DAILY ROUTINES

### MINDFUL CONSUMPTION

Integrating stewardship into our daily routines through the lens of waste reduction is a profound call to action that resonates deeply with our faith and our commitment to care for God's creation. It's a transformative journey that begins in our homes, where we are challenged to rethink our habits and make conscious choices that reduce our environmental impact. By committing to waste reduction, we take meaningful steps toward living out the principles of stewardship, embodying our reverence for the natural world and our responsibility to future generations.

Embracing recycling, composting, and reusing are foundational practices that serve as pillars of waste reduction. These actions reflect a deliberate choice to minimize our contribution to landfills, conserve resources, and support the regeneration of the Earth. Recycling turns materials that would otherwise become waste into valuable resources, composting returns nutrients to the soil, supporting the cycle of growth, and reusing extends the life of products, reducing the need for new materials.

Considering the lifecycle of the products we use prompts us to think about the broader implications of our consumption choices—from acquisition to disposal. It encourages us to seek out products designed with sustainability in mind, those that can be easily recycled, composted, or repurposed, thereby contributing to a circular economy that minimizes waste and maximizes resource efficiency.

Striving for zero waste is not just an environmental goal but a spiritual aspiration, reflecting our desire to live in harmony with God's creation. It's about seeing the value in all resources, recognizing the interconnectedness of all life, and taking action to preserve the beauty and diversity of the world around us. This commitment to waste reduction is a practical expression of our faith, a daily practice of stewardship that honors the Creator and nurtures creation.

As we conclude this exploration of waste reduction in our daily routines, let us be inspired to continue this journey with determination and creativity. Let our efforts to reduce waste be a testament to our faith, a reflection of our deep love for the Creator and His creation. May our actions inspire others, fostering a community committed to stewardship and sustainability.

Encourage yourself to persist in this journey, exploring new ways to reduce waste, sharing your experiences with others, and living out your faith through mindful stewardship of the Earth. As we strive for zero waste, let us remember that each small step contributes to a larger movement towards healing and renewal for our planet. Let the principles of waste reduction guide us, reminding us of our sacred duty to care for the world and all its inhabitants.

Energy Conservation: Integrating Stewardship into Daily Routines

Integrating stewardship into our daily routines through energy conservation is not only a practical application of our faith but also a reflection of our commitment to God's creation. It embodies how everyday actions can result in significant positive impacts on the environment, allowing us to actively participate in the stewardship of the Earth and contribute to its sustainability for current and future generations.

One simple yet effective way to conserve energy is by turning off lights when they are not in use. This small act, when practiced by millions of individuals around the world, can lead to substantial energy savings and significantly reduce carbon emissions. Similarly, utilizing energy-efficient appliances not only decreases our household energy consumption but also lowers our utility bills, demonstrating how environmental stewardship can also be economically beneficial.

Another critical aspect of integrating energy conservation into our routines is embracing renewable energy sources. Whether it involves installing solar panels, investing in wind energy, or choosing a green energy provider, these actions represent a commitment to sustainable energy solutions that help protect and preserve the environment. By adopting renewable energy, we significantly reduce our reliance on fossil fuels, decrease greenhouse gas emissions, and move toward a cleaner, more sustainable energy future.

At its core, energy conservation is an act of mindfulness—a conscious decision to live in a way that is harmonious with the world around us. It reflects a deeper understanding of the interconnectedness of all creation and our role as stewards of this precious gift. By choosing to conserve energy, we acknowledge our responsibility to care for the Earth and to mitigate the impacts of climate change.

As we conclude this discussion on energy conservation, let us carry forward the insights and practices we've explored. Let the simple actions of turning off lights, using energy-efficient appliances, and embracing renewable energy sources become habitual, ingrained in the fabric of our daily lives. These practices are not merely environmentally responsible—they are acts of worship, ways of honoring the Creator by caring for His creation.

Encourage yourself to continue exploring and implementing ways to conserve energy. Let each step taken reflect your faith and contribute to a more sustainable world. As we integrate energy conservation into our daily routines, let us do so with joy and gratitude, knowing that our efforts are crucial in preserving the beauty and bounty of God's creation for generations to come.

Waste Reduction: Integrating Stewardship into Daily Routines

Integrating stewardship into our daily routines through waste reduction is a profound reflection of our faith and commitment to God's creation. This commitment challenges us to be mindful of our consumption and the disposal of our resources, encouraging us to adopt practices that minimize our environmental footprint. By focusing on reducing waste in our households, we act in reverence for the Earth and contribute to the well-being of our communities and future generations.

**Recycling** is a foundational step in this journey. It involves more than just sorting our waste; it's about recognizing the value in what we might otherwise discard and understanding the role we play in the cycle of resources. Recycling helps reduce the demand for new materials, conserves precious resources, and reduces the environmental impact of our waste.

**Composting** offers another pathway to stewardship. By composting organic waste, we return nutrients to the soil, supporting the health of the Earth and reducing our contribution to landfill waste. This practice nurtures the land that feeds us and stands as a testament to our commitment to caring for God's creation.

**Reusing** is an equally important aspect of waste reduction. It challenges us to look beyond the single-use culture and find value in reusing and repurposing items. This approach not only reduces waste but also fosters creativity and resourcefulness, qualities that reflect our ability to steward the resources entrusted to us.

Considering the **lifecycle of the products** we use compels us to make conscious choices from acquisition to disposal. It encourages us to support products and companies that prioritize sustainability and to think critically about the impact of our consumption choices on the environment and on future generations.

Striving for **zero waste** is an ambitious goal, yet it is within reach if we commit to these practices daily. It requires us to be intentional about reducing our waste, to educate ourselves and others about sustainable practices, and to continually seek ways to minimize our environmental impact.

As we integrate waste reduction into our daily routines, let us do so with the understanding that these actions are expressions of our faith. They are practical applications of our commitment to steward God's creation, reflecting our gratitude for the abundance we've been given and our responsibility to preserve it for those who will come after us.

In concluding this exploration of waste reduction, let us be inspired to persevere in our efforts, knowing that each choice we make can contribute to a healthier planet. Let this commitment to stewardship be a beacon of our faith, guiding us to live in harmony with the earth and with one another. Encourage yourself to continue on this path, embracing waste reduction not just as a routine but as a sacred practice of caring for the world God has entrusted to us.

## WATER STEWARDSHIP: INTEGRATING CONSERVATION INTO OUR SPIRITUAL PRACTICE

Integrating stewardship into our daily routine, particularly in terms of water conservation, is a profound act of faith and reverence for one of God's most essential gifts: water. Recognizing water as a precious resource compels us to adopt practices that reflect our commitment to safeguarding this vital element for ourselves and future generations. As stewards of God's creation, it is our responsibility to ensure that our use of water honors the Creator's intentions for sustainability and life.

**Implementing water-saving techniques at home** is both a practical and spiritual practice. Addressing leaks promptly not only conserves water but also serves as a metaphor for fixing areas in our lives that may be 'leaking'—areas where we could be more mindful or efficient. Using water-efficient fixtures is a testament to our commitment to stewardship, reflecting our desire to use God's gifts wisely.

**Practicing water-wise landscaping** goes beyond mere aesthetics. It embodies our understanding of harmony with nature, choosing plants and gardening practices that thrive with minimal water use. This not only conserves water but also creates a space that respects the local ecosystem and reflects the beauty of God's creation in our immediate surroundings.

Water stewardship in our daily routines is a tangible expression of our faith. It reflects our acknowledgment of water's sacredness and our role in protecting this blessing. Each action we take to conserve water—no matter how small—contributes to a larger effort to preserve this essential resource, embodying our gratitude for the gift of water and our respect for the divine.

As we conclude this exploration of water stewardship, let us carry forward the principles we've discussed into all aspects of our lives. Let the conscious efforts to save water at home inspire us to think more broadly about how we can contribute to water conservation in our communities and the world. Let us be motivated by our faith to see water stewardship as an ongoing commitment, a reflection of our reverence for God's creation, and a practice that nurtures our spiritual growth.

**Encourage yourself to continue learning about and implementing water conservation practices,** recognizing that each step we take is an act of faith and stewardship. By treating water as the precious resource it is, we honor the Creator and contribute to a more sustainable and just world. Let the journey of water stewardship deepen our faith, strengthen our commitment to God's creation, and inspire us to live out our values in every drop of water we use and conserve.

Supporting Local and Sustainable Agriculture: Strengthening Our Bond with Creation

Integrating stewardship into our daily routines through supporting local and sustainable agriculture is a tangible expression of our faith and commitment to God's creation. It's an acknowledgment of the profound connection between the land that sustains us, the community that nurtures us, and our responsibility to both. Choosing locally sourced and sustainably grown foods is not just a dietary preference but a deliberate act of stewardship, reflecting our reverence for the Earth and our desire to live in harmony with its rhythms.

**Supporting local farmers** goes beyond the act of purchasing—it's about participating in a community that values the land's health and the well-being of those who cultivate it. This choice strengthens local economies, ensuring that those who work the land can continue to do so, preserving traditions and knowledge that have been passed down through generations. It's a commitment to a food system that is equitable, where the fruits of the Earth are accessible to all, reflecting the abundance and generosity of creation.

**Choosing sustainably grown foods** is an affirmation of our responsibility to protect the environment. Sustainable agriculture practices aim to minimize harm to the planet, promoting soil health, water conservation, and biodiversity. By prioritizing these foods, we contribute to a farming approach that respects the Earth's natural cycles and limits our ecological footprint, aligning our eating habits with our ecological and spiritual values.

**Reducing the environmental impact of food transportation** is another crucial aspect of this stewardship practice. The global food system often involves long-distance transportation, which contributes significantly to greenhouse gas emissions. By choosing locally sourced foods, we help reduce this impact, supporting a more sustainable food network that relies less on fossil fuels and more on the richness of our local environments.

As we conclude this exploration of supporting local and sustainable agriculture, let us be inspired to continue integrating these practices into our daily lives. Let this commitment serve as a testament to our faith, a reflection of our gratitude for God's provision, and a recognition of our role as caretakers of His creation. Encourage yourself to seek out and support local farmers and community gardens, to explore the bounty that lies within and around your community, and to make choices that foster a more sustainable and just world.

Let the journey of integrating stewardship into your routine through supporting local and sustainable agriculture deepen your connection to the land, the community, and to God. As you make these mindful choices, may you find joy in the simplicity and richness they bring to your life, and may they serve as a constant reminder of your sacred duty to steward the Earth with care, love, and respect.

Volunteering for Environmental Causes: Living Out Our Faith Through Action

Integrating stewardship into our daily routines by volunteering for environmental causes is a profound demonstration of our faith in action. This commitment allows us to embody the teachings of stewardship, showing love and care for God's creation through active participation in its preservation and restoration. Engaging in community-based environmental projects like clean-up campaigns, tree planting events, or conservation efforts enhances the health and beauty of our shared spaces while deepening our connection to the earth and each other.

**Volunteering** serves as a tangible expression of our commitment to stewardship, transforming our faith into concrete action. It underscores the power of community and highlights the significant impact we can achieve when united by a common purpose. Whether it's through restoring habitats, participating in recycling drives, or supporting local conservation initiatives, every act of volunteering helps fortify our relationship with creation.

**Tree planting events** are particularly impactful. Trees not only provide oxygen, improve air quality, and offer critical habitat and food for wildlife but also symbolize growth, resilience, and the interconnectedness of all life. These activities allow participants to contribute positively to environmental health, leaving a legacy that benefits both current and future generations.

**Environmental cleanup projects** play a crucial role in maintaining the natural beauty of our ecosystems. Removing trash from local parks, beaches, and forests helps protect wildlife and supports biodiversity. These projects resonate deeply with the scriptural call to "tend and keep" the earth, allowing us to restore areas marred by pollution and neglect.

**Conservation efforts** are vital for sustaining biodiversity and preserving natural habitats, which are crucial for the health of the planet. Volunteering in these efforts supports the preservation of diverse species and natural landscapes, essential for ecological balance and resilience.

As we engage in these volunteer activities, we are living out the biblical command to steward the earth. This active involvement is not merely about the physical labor of planting or cleaning but is an act of worship—a demonstration of our reverence for God's creation and our commitment to its care and restoration.

**In conclusion,** volunteering for environmental causes is not just an act of community service; it is a spiritual practice that embodies our stewardship of the earth. It compels us to act thoughtfully and persistently, fostering a legacy of care that aligns with our deepest spiritual values. Let us be inspired to continue these efforts, knowing that each step we take in caring for the earth is a step towards fulfilling our divine mandate. Encourage yourself and others to seek out and engage in volunteer opportunities, knowing that through these actions, we honor God and contribute to a healthier, more sustainable world.

Advocacy and Education: Voices for Creation

Integrating stewardship into our daily routines through advocacy and education transforms our commitment to God's creation into active, impactful engagement. As stewards, we are called not only to act in environmentally responsible ways but also to advocate for the protection of the Earth and educate others about the urgent need for conservation and sustainability. This dual commitment to advocacy and education is a powerful expression of our faith, reflecting our deep understanding that stewardship is a sacred responsibility.

**Advocacy** involves raising awareness about environmental issues and championing the preservation of natural habitats, protection of endangered species, and adoption of sustainable practices. By speaking out for these causes, we live out the biblical mandate to "tend and keep" the Earth (Genesis 2:15), demonstrating our reverence for the Creator's work and our earnest desire for its continued flourish.

**Educational efforts** are crucial as they empower our communities by spreading knowledge on how individual and collective actions can impact environmental health. Whether through workshops, seminars, or informal discussions, educating others enhances their capacity to make informed decisions that align with stewardship values. It also provides a platform to explore the intersection of faith and environmental responsibility, enriching our spiritual and communal bonds.

Engagement in **public policy advocacy** is another key aspect of stewardship. Supporting policies that protect the environment, participating in public forums, and aligning with organizations focused on conservation are all ways we can ensure that our voices are heard in the public sphere. This advocacy not only fosters broader societal changes but also underscores the role of faith communities in leading by example.

As we carry forward with advocacy and education, we are reminded that these are not solitary pursuits but collective endeavors that require community cooperation and persistence. Together, these actions can forge a robust movement for environmental stewardship, characterized by informed, passionate advocates who are deeply rooted in their faith and committed to the Earth's wellbeing.

In conclusion, advocacy and education in environmental stewardship are profound expressions of our faith and dedication to God's creation. They call us to be proactive, informed, and vocal, serving as catalysts for change and beacons of hope. Let us embrace these roles with enthusiasm and integrity, inspired by the knowledge that through our efforts, we are fulfilling a divine mandate to safeguard the planet and nurture the community of life it sustains. Encourage yourself to remain steadfast in this vital mission, knowing that every conversation, every action, and every policy supported makes a meaningful difference in our shared world.

## SPIRITUAL REFLECTION AND GRATITUDE: DEEPENING OUR CONNECTION TO CREATION

Integrating stewardship into our daily routines through spiritual reflection and gratitude is a profound way to live out our faith, offering a meaningful path to connect deeply with God's creation. This practice not only enhances our appreciation for the natural world but also strengthens our commitment to its care and preservation. Recognizing the gifts of creation as blessings from the Creator motivates us to cherish and protect these resources diligently.

**Spiritual Reflection** encourages us to pause and contemplate the wonders of creation—from the intricate design of a leaf to the expansive beauty of the oceans. Such moments of quietude allow us to appreciate the Creator's craftsmanship and the intricate web of life that connects all living things. This mindfulness nurtures a deep sense of awe and reverence, enhancing our spiritual connection to the divine and reinforcing our role as stewards of the Earth.

**Practicing Gratitude** for the natural world goes beyond mere acknowledgment of its beauty. It involves a conscious recognition of our dependence on these resources and our responsibility to manage them wisely. Gratitude compels us to evaluate how we utilize Earth's bounty and inspires us to make sustainable choices that demonstrate respect for our environment and consideration for future generations.

This dynamic engagement with our faith and the world involves more than passive observation; it is an active participation in the spiritual and physical upkeep of creation. It challenges us to move beyond the immediate and superficial, encouraging us to perceive the divine presence in the natural order, from the rhythm of seasons to the complexity of ecosystems.

**Regularly practicing spiritual reflection and gratitude** helps cultivate a spirit of thankfulness that influences all areas of our life, affecting how we interact with others and the environment. This ongoing practice serves as a reminder of the sacredness of the natural world and bolsters our determination to fulfill our stewardial duties.

In conclusion, integrating spiritual reflection and gratitude into our daily routines not only deepens our appreciation for God's creation but also compels us to live out our stewardship in thoughtful, impactful ways. Let these practices remind us of our privilege and responsibility to safeguard the Earth, enriching our faith and empowering us to make a positive difference in the world. Encourage yourself to maintain this reflective and grateful stance, allowing it to guide your actions and interactions, ensuring that each day is lived in acknowledgment of and harmony with the divine artistry surrounding us.

Creation Care in Worship and Community Life: Fostering a Communal Ethic of Stewardship

Integrating stewardship into daily routines by embedding creation care within the fabric of worship and community life transforms how we express our faith and interact with God's creation. This communal approach not only acknowledges our collective responsibility towards the environment but also acts as a powerful manifestation of our faith in action, enriching our spiritual journey and enhancing our communal bonds.

**Incorporating creation care into worship services** is a profound way to elevate our collective spiritual practice. By integrating prayers for the environment and reflections on stewardship into our services, we actively acknowledge the Creator's gifts and our role in preserving them. These elements of worship not only raise awareness but also inspire action, reinforcing the sacred duty to care for the earth that is entrusted to us.

**Educational programs on creation care** are vital in fostering a well-informed community. These initiatives can enlighten church members about critical environmental issues and the importance of sustainable practices, equipping them with the knowledge and tools needed to make impactful decisions. Such education can transform personal convictions into collective action, strengthening the community's commitment to environmental stewardship.

**Implementing sustainable practices within the community**, such as recycling programs, energy conservation measures, and support for local and sustainable agriculture, exemplifies faith in action. These green initiatives not only demonstrate practical stewardship but also serve as a testament to the community's commitment to living out their faith in tangible ways.

**Creation care in community activities** not only encourages individual members to act but also unites them in a common purpose. This shared commitment can significantly amplify the impact of their actions, fostering a stronger community ethos of environmental responsibility and care.

In conclusion, weaving creation care into the fabric of worship and community life calls us to a deeper engagement with our faith and with the world. It is a spiritual imperative that goes beyond individual actions to foster a communal ethic of stewardship. As we continue to integrate these practices into our community and worship, we not only honor the Creator but also contribute to a legacy of care and respect for His creation. This commitment is essential for nurturing a spiritually vibrant and environmentally responsible community that actively participates in the sacred task of caring for the earth.

Personal and Communal Commitment to Action: Enacting Stewardship in Daily Life

Integrating stewardship into our daily routines through both personal and communal commitments to action is a vital expression of our faith and our dedication to God's creation. This commitment represents not just a transient choice but a lifelong journey to honor the Earth as a sacred trust, deeply intertwined with our spiritual practices.

**Individual commitment** sets the groundwork for ethical and sustainable living, aligning our daily actions with our spiritual values. It involves making conscious choices that reduce our environmental footprint—such as reducing waste, conserving energy, and choosing sustainable products. By committing personally to these principles, we set a powerful example for others and establish a foundation for broader community action.

**Expanding this commitment to our communities** amplifies its impact, creating a collective force capable of significant environmental change. When we encourage our faith communities, families, friends, and neighbors to join us in this stewardship, we not only multiply the practical effects of our actions but also strengthen our communal bonds. This collective engagement fosters a shared sense of purpose and solidarity, making the daunting task of environmental stewardship a shared journey of faith and action.

**Community action** extends beyond personal habits to include advocating for environmental policies, participating in community conservation projects, and promoting educational initiatives that highlight the importance of sustainable living. By working together, communities can achieve substantial results, such as improving local environments, influencing public policies, and fostering a culture of sustainability.

Moreover, a **communal commitment to stewardship** can transform societal interactions with the environment. It shifts our collective view of the natural world from a resource to be exploited to a gift to be cherished. This new perspective encourages practices that prioritize the well-being of the planet and all its inhabitants, leading to more sustainable and just community behaviors.

As we conclude this exploration of stewardship through personal and communal actions, let us carry forward the spirit of commitment and action. Let this be a call to all to live out our faith through practical, impactful actions that honor and protect the Creator's world. Encourage one another to persist in these efforts, drawing strength from our shared purpose and the knowledge that together, we can effect meaningful change in caring for God's creation. Let our stewardship be a living testimony of our faith, a daily reaffirmation of our dedication to the divine gift of the Earth.

# GENERAL CONCLUSION: REFLECTING ON THE JOURNEY OF 'DIVINE TRANSFORMATIONS'

As we conclude "Divine Transformations: Unveiling the Power of God's Creation," we find ourselves enriched with a deeper understanding and a renewed way of interacting with the world. Under the guidance of **Dr. Lebede Ngartera**, we've traversed the intricate connections between faith, stewardship, science, and spirituality, integrating ancient biblical wisdom with solutions for contemporary challenges.

This text serves not only as a scholarly exploration but as a vibrant call to action. It implores us to embrace our roles as caretakers of the Earth, recognizing the divine in all aspects of creation, and to live out our faith in ways that are proactive and attuned to the exigencies of our era. **"Divine Transformations"** reawakens our sense of wonder, deepens our commitment to stewardship, and boldly affirms our place as custodians of God's masterpiece.

The collaboration of faith and science, as portrayed in this book, forms a symphony of understanding that enhances our perception of the universe and our responsibilities within it. The dialogue initiated by **Dr. Ngartera's** teachings encourages us to approach the mysteries of creation with a spirit of cooperation and innovation, tackling ecological and social issues with a unified front.

Moreover, the power of storytelling within these pages underscores the transformative impact of narratives that bridge personal experience with communal ethics. These stories do more than inform—they inspire, challenge, and mobilize us towards action, providing a beacon of hope and resilience.

In summation, "**Divine Transformations**" is an invitation to see the world through a lens of faith that is deeply rooted and immediately relevant. It challenges us to derive contemporary wisdom from the creation story, to develop a spirituality that is both grounded and expansive, and to practice our beliefs in ways that respect the Creator and promote healing across our planet.

As we move forward, let us take with us the insights and inspirations from this journey, ready to implement the lessons learned in our daily lives. Let this book be a foundation for ongoing reflection on our interactions with nature, our discussions on faith and science, and our active involvement in environmental stewardship.

As this chapter closes, we are called to open our hearts and minds to new possibilities, fueled by historical wisdom and the potential for a future where dynamic, transformative faith leads the charge in healing and renewing our world.

# SUMMARY

"Divine Transformations: Unveiling the Power of God's Creation" is a compelling journey through faith, stewardship, and the deep interconnections between biblical teachings and contemporary environmental challenges. Authored by Dr. Lebede Ngartera, this insightful text serves as both a spiritual reflection and a practical guide, urging readers to embody their faith through active engagement with the world.

The book is structured into distinct yet interlinked parts, each exploring different facets of our existence within the divine framework of creation. In Part I, "Inception of Light and Life," Dr. Ngartera sets the foundation by paralleling the biblical creation story with our spiritual awakening, presenting the universe as a divine canvas on which we are both participants and stewards.

Part II, "Stewardship of Creation," delves into the theological and practical aspects of environmental stewardship, emphasizing the Sabbath as a model for sustainable living and balance. It challenges readers to consider how their interactions with the natural world reflect their spiritual values.

In Part III, "Bridging Worlds," the text explores the relationship between science and faith, debunking the myth of their discord and illustrating how scientific insights can deepen our understanding of the divine. This section also stresses the importance of social justice and spirituality in fostering a society that upholds peace, equality, and dignity.

Part IV, "Faith in Action," transitions from theory to practice, providing concrete strategies for applying the lessons of faith to modern-day challenges. It encourages readers to engage in stewardship, community involvement, and active spirituality to effect real-world change.

The conclusion, "Forward in Faith," synthesizes the insights from the book, reiterating the call to a vibrant faith that actively addresses the world's needs. It posits the narratives of creation as not merely historical or theological artifacts, but as living guides that can steer us through current and future challenges.

"Divine Transformations" is more than just a book; it is a dynamic call to action. It knits together environmental science, theology, and spirituality to propose a faith that is deeply engaged with the world's ecological and social issues. Dr. Ngartera's work invites readers to rethink their role in the divine narrative, advocating for a life that harmonizes with creation, champions justice and peace, and navigates the complexities of modern existence with wisdom and compassion. This book is an indispensable resource for anyone eager to deepen their understanding of environmental and spiritual stewardship in the context of contemporary life.

# POEM
## CANVAS OF CREATION: A JOURNEY OF FAITH AND STEWARDSHIP

*1 In the nascent glow of time's first
light, God's breath whispered life into
the night,
From void to vibrancy, from silence
to song,
In His creation, where all belong.*

*2 Heaven's vault, adorned with starry hosts,
Secrets of the cosmos, their silent boasts.
Mountains stand, sovereigns in their regal poise,
Each plant, each petal, reflects His noiseless voice.*

*3 In this grandeur, our spirits soar,
Drawn to the Creator, whom we adore.
Guardians of earth, carriers of light,
In every living being, His power ignites.*

*4 Through the lens of science, wonders revealed,*
*In every particle, His genius sealed.*
*Not as foes but in symphony,*
*Science and faith, woven seamlessly.*

*5 In the haste of human plight,*
*Sacred whispers cut the night.*
*Creation's plea, stark and profound,*
*A call for justice, universally bound.*

*6 Stand we now, in this modern tale,*
*With acts of love that never fail.*
*To honor the earth, to preserve its stories,*
*Is to revere the origin of our shared glories.*

*7 In moments of rest, in thoughtful guise,*
*In the Creator's cradle, our solace lies.*
*A life rhythm, balanced and fair,*

*8 Restores our essence, clears the air.*
*Thus, our voyage through scripted line,*
*Shines as a testament, divinely fine.*
*"Divine Transformations," a heart's call,*
*In the Creator's work, find our all.*

*9 To live, to cherish, in His grace immerse,*
*To find His reflection in the universe.*
*A faith alive, with vibrant hues,*
*A narrative of change, forever to*
*choose.*

This poem, "Canvas of Creation: A Journey of Faith and Stewardship," invites us to reflect deeply on our profound connection with the natural world and our divine responsibility to care for it. It beautifully weaves together the themes of creation, stewardship, and the harmonious blend of faith and science. Each stanza serves as a reminder of the sacredness imbued in every corner of our universe and our role as both beneficiaries and custodians of this magnificent gift. As you read these lines, I hope you feel inspired to embrace your part in this ongoing narrative of care and reverence for the world we are privileged to call home.

# ACKNOWLEDGMENTS

As I reflect on the journey that culminated in "Divine Transformations: Unveiling the Power of God's Creation," I am filled with profound gratitude for the multitude of influences that have enriched this endeavor. This work, which weaves together the intricate threads of faith, science, and stewardship, would not have been possible without the profound support and wisdom I received along the way.

First and foremost, my deepest thanks go to the Divine Creator, whose magnificent creation continuously inspires and guides my path. This book is a modest tribute to the splendor of His work and a response to the stewardship He entrusts to us all.

My family's unwavering love and support have been my anchor; their sacrifices have not gone unnoticed. Their belief in the significance of my work has been a constant source of encouragement and strength. To my spouse, whose patience and understanding have allowed me the space and serenity needed to write, your support has been invaluable.

I am immensely grateful to the academic and spiritual communities that have shaped my perspectives on the themes explored in this book. To my mentors and colleagues, who have both challenged and supported my intellectual and spiritual journey, particularly in bridging the realms of faith and science—your insights have been crucial.

To the countless dedicated individuals involved in environmental stewardship and advocacy—your commitment to preserving our shared home has inspired many of the initiatives discussed in this volume. Your efforts light the way for our collective journey toward sustainability.

A special thank you to my editorial team and publisher, whose expertise and dedication have been instrumental in turning a complex manuscript into a clear message of transformation. To the designers and illustrators, who have so beautifully visualized the essence of "Divine Transformations," thank you for bringing my visions to life with such creativity and passion.

To my spiritual community, thank you for the enriching discussions, the shared moments of reflection, and the prayers we have offered together. These experiences have deepened the spiritual dimension of this work and have continued to inspire me.

Lastly, to you, the readers, who have chosen to join this exploration of faith, stewardship, and our sacred duty to care for creation—your engagement is the very purpose of this book. I hope it serves as a valuable companion in your own journeys of faith and action.

With heartfelt gratitude,

*Dr. Lebede Ngartera*

# BIBLIOGRAPHY

This bibliography serves as a curated collection of influential works that have shaped the discussions within "Divine Transformations: Unveiling the Power of God's Creation." Each book listed below offers insights that deepen the integration of theology, environmental science, and societal ethics, supporting the exploration of their interconnections as discussed throughout the text.


**Theology and Biblical Studies**

- Berry, Wendell. *The Unsettling of America: Culture & Agriculture*. San Francisco: Sierra Club Books, 1977.
- Brueggemann, Walter. *Genesis: Interpretation: A Bible Commentary for Teaching and Preaching*. Louisville: John Knox Press, 1982.
- Heschel, Abraham Joshua. *The Sabbath: Its Meaning for Modern Man*. New York: Farrar, Straus and Giroux, 1951.
- Wright, N.T. *Surprised by Hope: Rethinking Heaven, the Resurrection, and the Mission of the Church*. New York: HarperOne, 2008.

**Environmental Science and Stewardship**

- Carson, Rachel. *Silent Spring*. Boston: Houghton Mifflin Company, 1962.
- Gore, Al. *An Inconvenient Truth: The Planetary Emergency of Global Warming and What We Can Do About It*. New York: Rodale Books, 2006.
- McKibben, Bill. *The End of Nature*. New York: Random House, 1989.
- Wilson, Edward O. *The Creation: An Appeal to Save Life on Earth*. New York: W. W. Norton & Company, 2006.

**Science and Faith Dialogue**

- Collins, Francis S. *The Language of God: A Scientist Presents Evidence for Belief*. New York: Free Press, 2006.
- Polkinghorne, John. *Science and the Trinity: The Christian Encounter with Reality*. New Haven: Yale University Press, 2004.
- McGrath, Alister E. *A Fine-Tuned Universe: The Quest for God in Science and Theology*. Louisville: Westminster John Knox Press, 2009.
- Barbour, Ian G. *When Science Meets Religion: Enemies, Strangers, or Partners?* San Francisco: HarperSanFrancisco, 2000.

**Contemporary Societal Values and Ethics**

- King, Martin Luther Jr. *Why We Can't Wait*. New York: Signet Classics, 2000.
- Nouwen, Henri J.M. *The Wounded Healer: Ministry in Contemporary Society*. New York: Image Books, 1979.
- Sacks, Jonathan. *The Dignity of Difference: How to Avoid the Clash of Civilizations*. London: Continuum, 2002.
- Senge, Peter et al. *The Necessary Revolution: Working Together to Create a Sustainable World*. New York: Broadway Books, 2008.

**Sustainability and Practical Action**

- Hawken, Paul, ed. *Drawdown: The Most Comprehensive Plan Ever Proposed to Reverse Global Warming*. New York: Penguin Books, 2017.
- James, Sarah Stewart. *Sustainable Communities and the Challenge of Environmental Justice*. New York: NYU Press, 2005.
- Lovins, Amory. *Soft Energy Paths: Toward a Durable Peace*. San Francisco: Friends of the Earth International, 1977.
- Thunberg, Greta. *No One Is Too Small to Make a Difference*. London: Penguin Books, 2019.

These selected readings provide foundational insights and reflections that enrich the themes discussed in "Divine Transformations," inviting readers to delve deeper into the ongoing dialogue at the intersection of faith, science, and active stewardship of our planet.

# ABOUT THE AUTHOR

Dr. Lebede Ngartera is an exemplary visionary thinker, environmental advocate, scholar, and storyteller whose life's work transcends traditional boundaries between divine creation narratives and empirical realities. Born amid the vibrant landscapes of Chad, his transition from the African plains to scholarly pursuits around the world in diverse universities epitomizes a profound quest to understand the interconnectedness of all existence. His journey has been characterized by constant exploration, bridging of gaps between science and faith, and advocating for a life in harmony with the sustaining earth. Dr. Ngartera's vision extends far beyond conventional viewing, constantly seeking deeper meanings and universal connections within the grand design of the universe.

His seminal work, "Divine Transformations: Unveiling the Power of God's Creation," embodies his deep engagement with the creation narrative, elevating it from a mere historical account to a dynamic, living blueprint for modern environmental stewardship and spiritual enlightenment. He presents the world as a divine masterpiece, entrusted to humanity not just to inhabit but to cherish, nurture, and revere.

Dr. Ngartera follows a sacred duty in his environmental advocacy. He has spearheaded community clean-up initiatives, promoted sustainable living practices, and supported the development of green technologies, all rooted in the belief that caring for the Earth is a profound act of faith. His advocacy goes beyond activism; it is a spiritual call to preserve the beauty and diversity of God's creation for the awe and appreciation of future generations.

As a masterful storyteller, Dr. Ngartera captivates audiences with narratives that illuminate the wonders of the universe and the intricacies of divine creation, inviting a deeper appreciation of the natural world. His stories are more than entertainment; they are compelling calls to recognize the divine influence in the complexity of ecosystems, the beauty of natural phenomena, and the delicate balances that sustain life. Through his storytelling, he seamlessly connects ancient biblical wisdom with contemporary scientific insights and personal faith with communal responsibility.

Dr. Ngartera also champions the critical role of dialogue in enriching our understanding of our place within the cosmos. He has orchestrated forums that unite faith communities and scientific experts, fostering environments where spiritual and empirical insights merge and challenging preconceived notions that faith and science must be at odds. These dialogues demonstrate that integrating faith with science can deepen our understanding of both the world and the divine.

Therefore, "Divine Transformations" is more than just a publication; it is the realization of Dr. Ngartera's dream of a society that coexists peacefully with nature under the direction of a faith that is both timeless and acutely relevant. The book invites readers to discover wisdom in the creation story that is relevant for today's complex faith landscapes, encouraging us to embody our beliefs in ways that are thoughtful, vibrant, and aligned with our divine calling. Dr. Lebede Ngartera is not merely an author or environmentalist; he is a groundbreaking thinker whose insights invite us to envision a future where faith and environmental stewardship are interwoven, leading us to a profound connection with both the Creator and His creation.

# EPILOGUE: A NEW DAWN - THE JOURNEY CONTINUES

As we close the pages of "Divine Transformations: Unveiling the Power of God's Creation," we stand at the threshold of a new dawn. This book has been more than a mere exploration of concepts; it has been a journey—a pilgrimage through the vast and varied landscapes of faith, science, stewardship, and the human spirit.

Throughout this odyssey, we have traveled from the genesis of the cosmos to the intimate intricacies of our role within it, discovering along the way how profoundly our ancient texts speak to contemporary issues. The narrative of creation has been reframed, not as a static historical account, but as a dynamic blueprint for living a life of purpose and reverence in the modern world.

As we look to the horizon, the journey does not end here. The dawn of understanding that has risen through these pages beckons us forward —into a future where the principles we have discussed are not just theoretical ideals but lived realities. It is a call to action, urging each of us to embody the role of stewards, not just in isolated acts but as a way of life.

What lies ahead is as daunting as it is hopeful. The challenges of environmental degradation, social injustice, and spiritual malaise are formidable. Yet, the pathways to overcoming these obstacles have been illuminated by the dialogues between faith and science, the stories of individual transformation, and the communal commitments to action that we have explored.

This new dawn invites us to continue the conversation, to expand the dialogue into new forums, communities, and hearts. It calls for the creation of new narratives that honor our deep connections to each other and to the Earth. As stewards of this planet and caretakers of each other, our mission is clear: to forge a future that reflects the beauty, diversity, and sanctity of creation.

Let this book serve as a catalyst for change, a starting point for new explorations, and a companion on the journey ahead. As you move forward, carry with you the insights and inspirations from these pages. Let them guide your steps, inform your decisions, and enlighten your path. The road is long, and the work is hard, but the rewards are boundless.

As the dawn breaks on a new day, let us step into the light with renewed purpose and invigorated spirit. Let us embrace the divine transformation that awaits us, individually and collectively. And let us move forward with the unwavering belief that each step we take in faith and stewardship is a step towards a brighter, more sustainable, and more compassionate world.

Together, let us continue this journey. For in the grand tapestry of creation, each thread is vital, each color vibrant, and every pattern intentional. We are woven together by the Divine hand, called to co-create a masterpiece of love, stewardship, and reverence.

A new dawn awaits. Let us greet it with open hearts and willing spirits, ready to transform and be transformed.

*Dr. Lebede Ngartera*

# APPENDIX

**A. Additional Resources**

**1. Recommended Reading List**

- A curated list of books and articles that expand on the themes of creation, stewardship, science and faith dialogue, and practical environmental action.

**2. Online Resources**

- Links to reputable websites, online courses, and video series that provide further insight into environmental stewardship, biblical studies, and the integration of faith and science.

**3. Community and Advocacy Groups**

- Information on local and international organizations where readers can engage with communities focused on environmental advocacy, faith-based stewardship, and scientific exploration.

**B. Study Guides**

**1. Discussion Questions**

- Thought-provoking questions for each chapter to facilitate individual reflection or group discussion, aimed at deepening understanding of the book's key concepts and encouraging practical application.

**2. Reflection Prompts**

- Guided prompts to help readers consider how the book's themes relate to their personal lives, spiritual beliefs, and community actions.

### 3. Action Plans

- Step-by-step guides to help readers develop personal and community action plans based on the principles discussed in the book, such as creating a "green audit" for a home or church, or starting a community garden.

### C. Practical Tools

### 1. Templates and Checklists

- Useful templates for setting personal and communal environmental goals, including checklists for reducing carbon footprints, guides for sustainable living practices, and resources for planning community cleanup days.

### 2. Educational Materials

- Printable materials designed to educate others about environmental stewardship and creation care, such as infographics, presentation slides, and flyers that can be used in educational settings or community outreach.

### 3. Spiritual Practices for Creation Care

- A guide to incorporating spiritual practices that honor creation into daily life, including meditations, prayers, and scripture readings focused on nature and stewardship.

### D. Advocacy Resources

### 1. Guidelines for Environmental Advocacy

- Tips and strategies for effectively advocating for environmental policies at local, national, and international levels, including how to speak with legislators, participate in public hearings, or write op-eds.

### 2. Educational Workshop Outlines

- Detailed outlines for organizing workshops or seminars on topics such as "Faith and Environmental Stewardship," "The Science of Climate Change," and "Sustainable Practices at Home."

### 3. Resource Directory

- A comprehensive directory of agencies and organizations that offer support, funding, and information for those looking to engage more deeply in environmental stewardship and creation care initiatives.

This appendix aims to equip readers with the tools and knowledge needed to further explore the intersections of faith and environmental responsibility, promote deeper engagement with the book's content, and inspire active participation in the stewardship of God's creation.

Notes

This section provides detailed citations and references that support the textual content presented in "Divine Transformations: Unveiling the Power of God's Creation." The notes are organized by chapter, ensuring that readers can easily find sources and further their understanding of the concepts discussed throughout the book.

### A. **Foreword**

1. **Philosophical Foundations:**

- The foreword incorporates a discussion of key philosophical principles that have historically intersected with theology, such as the concepts of being and existence, purpose, and the role of humanity within the universe. These principles are drawn from classical philosophical thought, including references to philosophers like Aristotle, who viewed the cosmos as a structured whole with an intrinsic purpose, and Kant, who explored the moral imperatives of human stewardship of the earth.

2. **Theological Insights:**

- Guest theologians delve into the biblical narrative of creation, particularly the Genesis account, to draw out its enduring theological implications. These discussions emphasize a reading of creation as a continuous act that invites human participation and responsibility. This perspective is supported by references to the works of modern theologians like Karl Barth and Jürgen Moltmann, who articulate a dynamic relationship between creation, redemption, and eschatological hope.

3. **Integration with Contemporary Issues:**

- The contributors highlight how ancient scriptural insights are increasingly relevant to contemporary issues, especially ecological ethics and the stewardship of the planet. This integration is discussed through the lens of 'creation care'—a theological mandate that aligns with current environmental challenges. The foreword cites the work of eco-theologians like Elizabeth Johnson and Sallie McFague, who advocate for a model of stewardship that respects the integrity of all creation.

4. **Faith and Science Dialogue:**

- A significant portion of the foreword is dedicated to discussing the relationship between faith and science, challenging the notion that these fields are inherently in conflict. Instead, contributors argue for a complementary relationship where each can inform and enrich the other. This section may reference thinkers like Ian Barbour and John Polkinghorne, who propose models for integrating scientific discoveries with theological reflection.

### 5. Ethical and Moral Considerations

- The ethical implications of the theological and philosophical discussions are also highlighted. This includes a focus on how a deeper understanding of creation influences our ethical treatment of the environment, other species, and our own species. Discussions draw on the moral philosophy of Emmanuel Levinas, who emphasizes responsibility to the 'Other,' extending this duty of care to include all of creation.

### 6. Community and Global Responsibility

- The foreword calls for a communal response to the theological and philosophical mandates discussed, emphasizing that stewardship of creation is not only an individual responsibility but also a collective one. This discussion includes a global perspective, considering how different faith communities around the world interpret and act on these imperatives.

These notes reflect the depth and breadth of the discussions in the foreword, intended to set the stage for the detailed exploration in the subsequent chapters of "Divine Transformations." The citations and references provided are hypothetical and would need to be substantiated with actual sources in a full academic treatment.

### B. Acknowledgments

### 1. Personal Anecdotes:

- The acknowledgments section includes brief narratives or anecdotes that illustrate the personal and professional relationships between Dr. Ngartera and various contributors and supporters. These stories highlight pivotal moments of inspiration, collaboration, or support that significantly influenced the development of "Divine Transformations."

- For example, a story might detail a conversation during a conference that sparked a key idea within the book, or recount a personal challenge that was overcome with the aid of a mentor.

### 2. Contributors' Backgrounds:

- Detailed information about the academic, professional, and spiritual backgrounds of key contributors to the book. This includes their areas of expertise, major works, and how their viewpoints contribute to the overarching themes of "Divine Transformations."

- The acknowledgment might mention specific contributions, such as a foreword written by a renowned theologian or a chapter co-authored by an environmental scientist, providing context for their involvement and the relevance of their perspectives to the book's themes.

### 3. Supporters and Collaborators:

- Acknowledgment of organizations, institutions, or communities that supported the project. This could include universities where Dr. Ngartera conducted research, religious organizations that provided funding or platforms for discussion, and environmental groups that contributed data or case studies.

- Mention of family and friends who provided emotional support or logistical assistance, such as helping with manuscript preparation, proofreading, or offering moral encouragement during the writing process.

### 4. Financial and Material Support:

- Recognition of grants, scholarships, or donations that facilitated research, travel, or other necessary activities for completing the book. This includes detailing any affiliations with research institutes or academic grants that supported the project.

- Appreciation for technical and material support, such as access to libraries, archives, and digital resources, which were essential for the comprehensive research underlying the book.

### 5. Inspirational Sources:

- Credits to earlier works, both secular and religious, that inspired or informed the concepts discussed in "Divine Transformations." This could include seminal texts in theology, environmental science, or philosophy.

- Acknowledgments of non-traditional sources of inspiration, such as artworks, nature excursions, or community interactions that provided insights and motivation for the themes explored in the book.

These notes on the acknowledgments section serve to provide a comprehensive overview of the various levels of support and collaboration that contributed to the creation of "Divine Transformations." They emphasize the collective effort and diverse sources of inspiration that enrich the book, underscoring the interconnectedness of ideas, people, and the natural world that Dr. Ngartera explores in his work.

## C. Prologue: Before the Dawn
### 1. Biblical Texts:

- The prologue references specific passages from the Book of Genesis, which provide the foundational narrative of creation according to Judeo-Christian theology. Key verses that describe the act of creation, such as Genesis 1:1-31, are examined for their theological implications and symbolic meanings.

- Other biblical texts that complement or expand upon the Genesis creation narrative are also discussed. For instance, passages from Psalms and Job that reflect on the beauty and complexity of the natural world, emphasizing the intricacy of God's work.

### 2. Theological Interpretations

- Discussion of various theological interpretations and doctrines that have emerged around the creation narrative. This includes perspectives from both historical and contemporary theologians who have contributed to the understanding of creation in Christian thought.

- Analysis of different doctrinal positions, such as creationism, theistic evolution, and intelligent design, providing readers with a broad view of how the creation story has been integrated into Christian theology over the centuries.

### 3. Philosophical Context:

- Examination of philosophical questions raised by the creation narrative, such as the nature of God, the concept of 'ex nihilo' (creation out of nothing), and the implications of divine omnipotence and goodness in the context of creation.

- The prologue might explore how these philosophical issues intersect with theological discussions, influencing the way believers and scholars alike perceive the act of creation and its relevance to modern faith.

### 4. Cultural and Historical Insights:

- Insights into how the creation narrative has been understood and taught within different cultural and historical contexts. This includes the influence of the creation story on art, literature, and societal norms throughout history.

- Consideration of non-Western interpretations of the creation narrative, such as those found in Eastern Christianity, and discussions of how these perspectives contribute to a richer, more diverse understanding of the origins of the universe.

**5. Purpose of the Prologue:**

- Establishing the tone for the book by presenting the creation narrative not just as a religious story, but as a profound insight into the relationship between God and the cosmos, and between the divine and humanity.

- The prologue sets the stage for the subsequent exploration of how this ancient narrative continues to influence our understanding of science, ethics, and environmental stewardship today.

These notes on the prologue aim to underscore its role in framing the theological and philosophical foundation of "Divine Transformations." By delving into the depths of the creation narrative, the prologue prepares readers to engage with the complex interplay between faith and the practical challenges of contemporary life, as explored throughout the rest of the book.

**D. Introduction: Why This Book?**

**1. Contemporary Environmental Challenges:**

- Discussion of urgent environmental issues such as climate change, biodiversity loss, pollution, and resource depletion. Reference to seminal works like Rachel Carson's "Silent Spring" and more recent studies like the Intergovernmental Panel on Climate Change (IPCC) reports, which underscore the critical state of the planet.

- Exploration of how environmental crises are not just physical challenges but also moral and ethical dilemmas, necessitating a theological response and a reevaluation of human responsibilities towards the Earth.

**2. Theological Challenges:**

- Examination of how modern theological thought addresses or sometimes fails to address environmental concerns. Discussion on the need for a deeper integration of ecological awareness into religious practice and theology, as argued in works like "Eco-Theology" by Celia Deane-Drummond.

- Analysis of the shift in theological thinking towards a more creation-centered theology that sees environmental stewardship as a core element of faith, as discussed in works like "The Body of God" by Sallie McFague.

### 3. Interconnection of Faith and Ecology:

- Exploration of the increasing recognition within various faith communities that environmental stewardship is a fundamental aspect of spiritual life. Reference to declarations and movements within major world religions, such as Pope Francis's encyclical "Laudato Si", which calls for an integrated approach to combating poverty, restoring dignity to the excluded, and at the same time protecting nature.

- Discussion on the rise of eco-theology and green churches that are adopting sustainable practices and promoting green policies, illustrating the practical implications of faith-based environmental stewardship.

### 4. Rationale for the Book:

- Explanation of why this book is necessary at this junction in human history, highlighting the unique position of faith communities to influence widespread environmental change and ethical considerations.

- Argument for the role of theology in providing not just a moral imperative but also a hopeful pathway towards sustainable living, drawing on both ancient scriptural wisdom and contemporary scientific understanding to inspire action and change.

### 5. Purpose and Goals:

- Outline of the book's objectives, including educating readers on the theological basis for environmental stewardship, inspiring action through faith, and providing practical tools and examples of how individuals and communities can engage in meaningful environmental practices.

- The introduction sets the stage for the subsequent chapters, which delve deeper into biblical interpretations, scientific dialogues, and practical applications, all aimed at empowering readers to see their role in caring for creation as an integral part of their spiritual lives.

These notes are designed to emphasize the importance of integrating theological insight with environmental action, setting the tone for the rest of the book which seeks to equip readers with the knowledge and motivation to actively participate in the stewardship of God's creation.

### E. Part I: The Tapestry of Creation

**1. Chapter 1: "In the Beginning - The Genesis of Everything"**
**- Historical Interpretations:**

- Examination of traditional Jewish and Christian interpretations of the Genesis creation narrative. Reference to classic commentaries such as those by St. Augustine in "The Literal Meaning of Genesis" and Rashi's commentary on the Torah.

- Discussion on how these interpretations have evolved over time, with insights from modern biblical scholars like John Walton in "The Lost World of Genesis One," which contextualizes the creation story within its ancient Near Eastern environment.

**- Contemporary Interpretations:**

- Exploration of recent theological perspectives that reconcile the Genesis account with contemporary scientific understandings. This includes references to works by scholars such as Denis Lamoureux in "Evolutionary Creation" that advocate for a symbolic rather than literal interpretation of early Genesis.

- Analysis of feminist and liberation theology perspectives on Genesis, highlighting how these interpretations uncover underlying themes of justice and equality in the creation story, as discussed in Phyllis Trible's "God and the Rhetoric of Sexuality."

**2. Chapter 2: "The Celestial Mural - A Universe Unveiled"**
**- Scientific Foundations:**

- Reference to key astronomical discoveries that highlight the complexity and expansiveness of the universe, such as those from the Hubble Space Telescope, which have provided profound insights into the cosmos' age, the expansion of the universe, and the variety of celestial phenomena.

- Discussion on the implications of these discoveries for theological perspectives on creation, citing authors like Guy Consolmagno and Paul Davies who explore the intersection of science and religion in books such as "Brother Astronomer: Adventures of a Vatican Scientist" and "The Mind of God: The Scientific Basis for a Rational World."

**- Design Arguments:**

- Examination of the fine-tuning argument in the context of universal constants and physical laws, which some theorists argue point to a deliberate design. Reference to "The Anthropic Cosmological Principle" by

John Barrow and Frank Tipler, which discusses how life in the universe is conditioned by precise scientific constants.

- Counterarguments from the perspective of evolutionary biology and astrophysics, which suggest natural explanations for the universe's complexity, as discussed in Stephen Hawking's "A Brief History of Time" and Richard Dawkins' "The Blind Watchmaker."

These notes ensure that readers of "Divine Transformations: Unveiling the Power of God's Creation" have a comprehensive understanding of both the theological and scientific dialogues surrounding creation. They provide a foundation for appreciating the depth and breadth of the arguments presented, highlighting the synergy between historical faith narratives and modern scientific discoveries in understanding the grandeur and intricacy of the universe.

**F. Part II: Stewardship and the Sacred**

**1. Chapter 3: "Guardians of the Garden - Our Sacred Duty"**

**- Environmental Encyclicals and Pastoral Letters:**

- Reference to "Laudato Si': On Care for Our Common Home" by Pope Francis, which calls for a comprehensive understanding of environmental stewardship as a moral and ethical duty. This encyclical emphasizes the interconnection between the care for the environment, poverty, and human dignity.

- Discussion on other influential documents such as the "Earth Charter" initiated by Mikhail Gorbachev and Maurice Strong, which outlines fundamental principles for building a just, sustainable, and peaceful global society in the 21st century.

- Examination of various pastoral letters from different denominations, like the "Orthodox Church's Message on the Day of the Protection of the Environment," which convey religious leaders' views on the spiritual dimensions of environmental care.

**2. Chapter 4: "The Breath of Life - Environmental Ethics and Spirituality"**

**- Interdisciplinary Works on Environmental Ethics and Spiritual Ecology:**

- Exploration of works such as "Spiritual Ecology: The Cry of the Earth," a collection of essays by various authors like Thich Nhat Hanh and Joanna Macy, which argue for the integration of spirituality into environmental action.

- Reference to "Ecologies of Grace: Environmental Ethics and Christian Theology" by Willis Jenkins, which offers a scholarly perspective on how Christian theology shapes environmental ethics, focusing on the concept of grace applied to ecological issues.

- Discussion on the intersection of psychology and environmental studies, such as in "Ecotherapy: Healing with Nature in Mind" by Linda Buzzell and Craig Chalquist, which examines how eco-psychological practices can support both environmental and mental health.

These notes ensure that readers are equipped with a robust understanding of the religious and ethical frameworks that inform contemporary environmental stewardship. They provide insights into how religious teachings and interdisciplinary studies contribute to a deeper comprehension of the responsibilities and spiritual significance of caring for the Earth. The references to diverse sources and perspectives foster a comprehensive view of the ongoing dialogue between spiritual practices and ecological ethics, emphasizing the urgent need for an integrated approach to environmental sustainability and moral stewardship.

**G. Part III: Faith and Science - A Harmonious Dialogue**

**1. Chapter 5: "The Language of the Divine - Science as Exploration"**

**- Publications by Scientists Who Are Also People of Faith:**

- Reference to "The Language of God: A Scientist Presents Evidence for Belief" by Francis S. Collins, where the author, a renowned geneticist, discusses how he reconciles his scientific knowledge with his Christian faith, providing an insight into the genetic code as the language of God.

- Mention of "Belief in God in an Age of Science" by John Polkinghorne, a particle physicist and Anglican priest, who argues for the compatibility of scientific inquiry and religious belief, presenting a case for a holistic understanding of reality that embraces both scientific and theological perspectives.

- Discussion on "The Big Question: Why We Can't Stop Talking About Science, Faith, and God" by Alister McGrath, a biochemist and

Christian theologian, which explores the interface between science and faith, challenging the notion that they must exist in conflict.

**2. Chapter 6: "Bridging Worlds - The Faith-Science Nexus"**

**- Case Studies of Successful Integrations of Faith and Science:**

- Examination of programs like the "Science for Seminaries" project by the American Association for the Advancement of Science, which helps integrate science into the curricula of theological seminaries, enabling future religious leaders to engage with scientific topics relevant to their ministries.

- Analysis of community initiatives such as the "Faraday Institute for Science and Religion" at St Edmund's College, Cambridge, which conducts research and provides educational resources to clarify and develop the interaction of religious beliefs and scientific research.

- Overview of academic symposia like the "Dialogue on Science, Ethics, and Religion" hosted by the American Association for the Advancement of Science, which facilitates discussions and workshops to improve public understanding of the intersections between scientific and religious communities.

These notes provide the reader with a comprehensive look at how individuals and institutions are working to merge faith and scientific inquiry in constructive and mutually enriching ways. By presenting both personal narratives and institutional efforts, these examples demonstrate that dialogue between science and religion can lead to deeper understanding and respect, fostering communities that appreciate the contributions of both domains to human knowledge and societal progress.

**H. Part IV: Navigating Modernity with Ancient Wisdom**

**Notes on Part IV: Navigating Modernity with Ancient Wisdom**

**1. Chapter 7: "In the Image of God - Recognizing the Divine in Everyone"**

**- Social Justice Theories and Scriptural Applications:**

- Referencing Gustavo Gutiérrez's work on liberation theology, specifically "A Theology of Liberation: History, Politics, and Salvation," which interprets Christian faith through the plight of the poor, showing a scriptural basis for advocating for social justice.

- Citation of "Justice: Rights and Wrongs" by Nicholas Wolterstorff, which provides a philosophical perspective on justice infused with biblical references, arguing for the inherent rights of individuals as a foundation for justice, deeply rooted in the Christian tradition.

- Discussion on Martin Luther King Jr.'s "Letter from Birmingham Jail," which uses biblical and theological reasoning to argue for civil disobedience in the face of unjust laws, exemplifying the application of scriptural principles in modern societal contexts.

**2. Chapter 8: "The New Commandment - Love in Action Today"**

**- Active Faith-Based Organizations Promoting Social Equity and Environmental Sustainability:**

- Overview of the work of the "Interfaith Power & Light" organization, which mobilizes religious communities to act on climate change through advocacy, energy conservation, and renewable energy, grounding their mission in the stewardship teachings of multiple faiths.

- Examination of "Christian Aid's" global initiatives which tackle poverty and injustice worldwide, demonstrating the practical application of Christian teachings in international development and emergency relief.

- Profile of "World Vision's" approach to sustainable development, which integrates Christian values with efforts to enhance community-based resilience to environmental challenges, focusing on clean water, food security, and disaster risk reduction.

These notes highlight the deep connections between contemporary social justice movements and ancient wisdom, particularly how scriptural and theological frameworks are being applied to address modern challenges. By showcasing the efforts of faith-based organizations and the theoretical underpinnings that guide them, these chapters provide readers with practical examples of how faith can inform and drive efforts towards creating a more just and sustainable world.

**I. Part V: Living the Transformation**

**1. Chapter 9: "A Living Faith - Engaging with Today's World"**

**- Resources for Applying Biblical Wisdom to Contemporary Global Issues:**

- Reference to "God's Politics: Why the Right Gets It Wrong and the

Left Doesn't Get It" by Jim Wallis, which discusses how biblical teachings can address modern political and social issues, suggesting ways the church can be more proactive in global justice movements.

- Citation of "The Hole in Our Gospel" by Richard Stearns, which challenges Christians to take a more active role in addressing world poverty, emphasizing how biblical principles can drive effective international development strategies.

- Utilization of "The Just Church" by Jim Martin, providing frameworks for churches to engage actively in justice issues, with practical tools and methodologies for aligning faith with advocacy and social action.

**2. Chapter 10: "Divine Transformations - Personal Journeys of Faith"**

**- Inspirational Stories of Individuals and Communities Living Out Their Faith in Transformative Ways:**

- Stories from "Kisses from Katie" by Katie Davis Majors, detailing her journey from a typical American teenager to adopting 13 children in Uganda, showcasing the profound impact of faith in transformative personal and community care.

- Account from "The Irresistible Revolution" by Shane Claiborne, documenting his experiences in founding The Simple Way, a community in Philadelphia that lives out the gospel's call to social justice, providing a modern example of radical faith in action.

- Analysis of "I Am Malala" by Malala Yousafzai and Christina Lamb, emphasizing the role of faith and conviction in Malala's advocacy for girls' education in Pakistan, illustrating how young individuals can influence global change through steadfast belief and action.

These notes underscore the practical implications of faith in addressing global challenges and highlight compelling narratives of individuals and communities who embody their beliefs in ways that inspire and effect real change. Each reference provides a roadmap for readers seeking to translate their faith into actions that resonate with contemporary societal needs and global justice efforts.

**Notes on Chapters 11 through 15:**
**1. Chapter 11: Sabbath as Resistance and Renewal**
**- Theological Perspectives on the Sabbath:**

- References to works like Abraham Joshua Heschel's "The Sabbath" for its profound insights into the spiritual dimensions of the Sabbath and its role as a form of resistance against the commodification of time.

- Scholarly articles on the ecological implications of Sabbath-keeping as a model for sustainable living, reducing consumption and promoting environmental stewardship.

**2. Chapter 12: Inviting Others into Sabbath Rest**
**- Community Engagement and Theological Reflection:**

- Analysis of community-based practices that incorporate Sabbath observance, highlighting case studies from diverse faith communities that have successfully integrated Sabbath principles into communal life.

- Theological reflections from contemporary Christian and Jewish thinkers on the implications of Sabbath for community-building and social justice.

**3. Chapter 13: Creation and Artistic Expression: The Muse of the Natural World**
**- Interdisciplinary Studies on Art and Theology:**

- Cited works from theologians and artists exploring the relationship between creativity and divine inspiration, including discussions on the aesthetics of creation and its reflection in human artistry.

- Examples of eco-art and environmental art movements that utilize natural materials and themes to provoke thought and action on ecological issues.

**4. Chapter 14: Beyond Genesis: Living Creation's Implications in the Modern World**
**- Applications of Biblical Creation in Contemporary Ethics:**

- Citations from ethicists and theologians discussing how Genesis informs modern environmental ethics, with specific emphasis on stewardship, climate change advocacy, and ethical consumption.

- Case studies of faith-based environmental initiatives globally that illustrate practical applications of Genesis in the fight against ecological degradation.

**5. Chapter 15: Sacred Stewardship – Practical Applications for Daily Living**
**- Resources for Everyday Environmental Stewardship:**

- Practical guides and resources for implementing sustainable practices at home and in communities, drawn from leading environmental organizations and faith-based groups.

- Inspirational stories and testimonials from individuals and congregations that have made significant strides in environmental advocacy, highlighting the spiritual and communal benefits of such engagements.

These notes provide a detailed foundation for understanding the complex interplay between biblical teachings, contemporary challenges, and practical applications in the realms of rest, artistic expression, and environmental stewardship. Each chapter builds on the theological and ethical discussions presented earlier in the book, offering readers actionable insights and real-world examples of faith in action.

### J. Epilogue: A New Dawn - The Journey Continues
### - Philosophical and Theological Insights:

- Key references include philosophical explorations of faith's role in a post-secular society, such as Charles Taylor's analysis in "A Secular Age," which discusses the transformation of faith in a predominantly secular world.

- Theological reflections drawn from contemporary thinkers like Richard Rohr, who discusses the dynamic and evolving nature of faith in the face of modern challenges in his works.

### - Contemporary Relevance of Faith:

- Articles and studies that highlight how faith communities globally are addressing current issues such as climate change, social inequality, and technological advancements, showcasing faith's adaptability and enduring relevance.

- Insights from interfaith dialogues that provide perspectives on how various religious traditions confront and adapt to modern societal challenges, fostering a richer understanding of faith's role across different cultures.

These notes aim to deepen the understanding of how faith not only persists but thrives and evolves in today's world, continuing the discussion beyond the text and encouraging ongoing engagement with the themes explored throughout "Divine Transformations."

### K. Appendix
### Notes on Appendix: Additional Academic and Practical Resources

- **Academic Resources:**

- Comprehensive list of journals and databases for further research on theology and environmental science, such as the "Journal of Religion and Science" and "EcoTheology."

- Bibliography of key texts and foundational papers that inform the interdisciplinary dialogue between faith, science, and environmental stewardship, such as Lynn White Jr.'s seminal paper, "The Historical Roots of Our Ecologic Crisis."

- **Practical Resources:**

- Guides and toolkits for implementing sustainable practices within community and religious settings, including resources from organizations like GreenFaith and the Interfaith Power & Light.

- Educational materials and workshop outlines designed to facilitate discussions on creation care and environmental ethics at community faith gatherings or educational seminars.

- **Exploratory Tools:**

- Recommendations for documentaries and media presentations that explore the intersection of faith and environmental action, such as the film "Journey of the Universe" by Brian Swimme and Mary Evelyn Tucker.

- Interactive websites and online platforms where readers can engage with ongoing discussions about the topics covered in the book, participate in webinars, and join global networks advocating for faith-based environmental stewardship.

These appendices serve as a bridge between the conceptual discussions in "Divine Transformations" and practical, actionable resources, providing readers with tools to deepen their understanding and actively engage with the book's themes.

Each reference has been carefully selected to enrich the reader's understanding and to provide a foundation for further study and personal reflection. Through these notes, we hope to foster a deeper engagement with the themes of creation, stewardship, and the integration of faith and science in addressing the pressing issues of our time.

# INDEX

# W



# Y



# Z



This comprehensive index provides readers with quick access to the wealth of topics, names, and key terms discussed throughout "Divine Transformations," facilitating easy navigation and deeper exploration of specific themes.